Sustainability
and Luxury Management

Recently, sustainability has become a focal point for companies across all sizes and sector, and the luxury industry is no exception. This shift reflects a growing awareness of the environmental, social, and community impacts of business activities. However, integrating sustainability into the luxury industry poses unique challenges due to the apparent mismatch between luxury and sustainability. While luxury often connotes indulgence and opulence, sustainability emphasizes altruism, ethical practices, and moderation, seemingly conflicting with traditional luxury values. This book, first attempts to resolve the abovementioned divergence between luxury and sustainability. Thanks to an in-depth analysis of the definition of luxury, the authors demonstrate that sustainability is in line with the young consumers' idea of luxury. Moreover, leveraging a structured review, the book organizes the scientific production on sustainable luxury in the research area and explains the reasons for matching luxury and sustainability. Then this book also attempts to explain to what extent luxury brand companies are improving their commitment to sustainable actions. In this endeavor, the authors explore the fundamental issues within sustainable luxury and the integration of sustainability into the corporate business model. The explorations also include the companies' efforts to communicate sustainability both offline and online with a focus on the themes and tools. Finally, this book offers a benchmark by providing the audience with several business cases. The discussion of case studies aims to meet the needs of a wide and varied audience, from university students to CSR managers, who try to steal the best practices and adapt them to their businesses.

Fabrizio Mosca is a Full Professor of Corporate, Business Strategy and Marketing at University of Torino. He took a Ph.D. at Bocconi University. His research interests include Corporate and Business Strategy, Strategic Marketing with a focus on luxury markets. His most recent work focuses on Corporate Social Responsibility applied to different companies and industries. He has published several books, book chapters and papers in International Journals such as the Journal of Business Research, Psychology and Marketing, Symphonia – Emerging Issues in Management and The Italian Journal of Marketing. He has been involved during his career in several MBA Programs such as the ESCP-Europe MIM Master in Turin, the Master of Il Sole24Ore. During his career he was invited as Visiting Professor at University of Córdoba (Argentina), Pompeu Fabra University in Barcellona, University Paris Nanterre, International University of Monaco "Prince Albert I" (IUM) in Monaco.

Valentina Chiaudano holds a Ph.D. in Business and Management from the University of Turin, Italy. She is currently a research fellow and lecturer in Marketing and Sustainability Management at the University of Turin, Italy. Her research interests include Marketing and Sustainability Management applied to various industries with a focus on Luxury Brand Management. She adeptly applies her expertise in Marketing and Business Management by collaborating on consulting projects with a range of national and international organizations.

Fabrizio Mosca - Valentina Chiaudano

Sustainability and Luxury Management

Routledge
Taylor & Francis Group
LONDON AND NEW YORK

G. Giappichelli Editore

First published 2025
by Routledge
4 Park Square, Milton Park, Abingdon, Oxon OX14 4RN

and by Routledge
605 Third Avenue, New York, NY 10158

Routledge is an imprint of the Taylor & Francis Group, an informa business

and by G. Giappichelli Editore
Via Po 21, Torino – Italia

British Library Cataloguing-in-Publication Data
A catalogue record for this book is available from the British Library

Library of Congress Cataloging-in-Publication Data
A catalogue record for this book has been requested

ISBN: 978-1-032-84126-7 (hbk-Routledge)
ISBN: 978-1-003-51133-5 (ebk-Routledge)
ISBN: 978-1-032-84127-4 (pbk-Routledge)
ISBN: 979-12-211-0610-7 (hbk-Giappichelli)

Typeset in Simoncini Garamond
by G. Giappichelli Editore, Turin, Italy

The manuscript has been subjected to a peer review process prior to publication.

CONTENTS

LIST OF FIGURES AND TABLES

Tables

PREFACE

Contemporary corporate social responsibility (CSR) theory emerged in the 1980s in response to Milton Friedman's shareholder value theory, which asserted that a company's sole responsibility was to maximize profits for its shareholders (Friedman, 1970). Friedman's assertion faced criticism as it failed to encompass the broader concept of social responsibility in business. The academic and conceptual origins of social responsibility can be traced back to 1979 when Carroll identified four components of CSR and introduced the idea that businesses have a responsibility to society beyond market-related activities (Carroll, 2021). Then Freeman and Evan published a pivotal contribution that introduced the Stakeholder Theory as an alternative to Friedman's dominant shareholder value perspective. Freeman and Evan's approach replaced minimalism with a broader vision where managers were seen as key actors in a "trust relationship" with a wide range of stakeholders (Evan & Freeman, 1988).

These stakeholders included suppliers, customers, employees, shareholders, and the local community, each with a legitimate interest or claim on the company. Stakeholder theory asserts that the company's goal should be to meet the expectations of all stakeholders, a perspective rooted in Kantian ethics, treating individuals not to an end but as ends in themselves (Freeman et al., 2010). This theory challenged the absolute nature of shareholder rights, considering stakeholders as moral subjects with rights rather than means to corporate ends.

In recent times, the growing emphasis on CSR has captured the attention of businesses across diverse sizes and sectors, encompassing even those operating within the luxury market. Luxury companies have become aware of the implications of their activities on environmental conservation, community welfare, and societal well-being. However, within the luxury industry, incorporating sustainability into the business model presents unique challenges, as the coexistence of luxury and sustainability may appear incongruent. The notion of luxury often evokes images related to hedonism, opulence, and extravagance, while sustainability, rooted in altruism, sobriety, ethics, and moderation, seems to be guided by opposite ideals. Some authors have coined the term "CSR-luxury paradox" to highlight the evident contrast between luxury and sustainability. Given the lack of clarity on the relationship between luxury and sustainability, our book contributes to the literature related to sustainable luxury with theoretical and empirical studies conducted over more than three years of research. Specifically, this book is organized into six chapters that address the dichotomy between luxury and sustainability as follows:

1. Deepening the evolution of the luxury brand concept to understand the match between luxury and sustainability.
2. Systematizing the literature on sustainable luxury to set the stage for theoretical and methodological advancements in the field of sustainable luxury management.
3. Proposing a framework to assess to what extent sustainability is integrated into luxury brands' business models.
4. Offering empirical evidence of the impact of CSR initiatives on luxury brands' financial performance.
5. Analyzing the different tools that luxury companies use to communicate their commitment to sustainability.
6. Exploring the best practices of sustainability integration among the leading luxury companies by using case studies.

In more detail, Chapter 1, entitled "The evolution of luxury: From unnecessary to customer-centric", explores the definition of a luxury brand according to two opposite points of view: the product-centric and the customer-centric perspectives. While the product-centric perspective explains a luxury brand as a concept that is static and pre-determined by certain attributes, the customer-centric point of view sees the meaning of a luxury brand as dynamic and shaped by consumers and how they experience the brand itself. Thus, by adopting the customer-centric perspective, the chapter elucidates why luxury branding can approach emerging trends such as sustainability. At first glance, luxury and sustainability may seem incompatible, but from the customer-centric perspective, linking sustainability with luxury meets the meaning of luxury proposed by the younger generation of consumers. These consumers want luxury brands to prioritize environmental and societal well-being.

In Chapter 2, entitled "Sustainability and luxury: Is there a match?", we perform a structured literature review aimed at conducting a deep exploration of the state of the art of literature on sustainability in the context. Specifically, leveraging academic literature, we attempt to shed light on the link between luxury and sustainability and offer interesting insights for theoretical and methodological advancements in sustainable luxury management.

Chapter 3, entitled "A strategic approach for managing sustainability in the luxury market", clarifies the extent to which luxury brands have integrated sustainability into their business model. This endeavor applies the CSR integrated framework, leveraging stakeholder theory and providing the readers with a framework to identify the sustainable activities performed by luxury brand companies.

Chapter 4, entitled "Social reporting and the impact of CSR practices on luxury companies' financial performances", is focused on environmental, social, and governance (ESG) and social reporting within the luxury brand market. This exploration examines the importance of matching sustainability performances with stakeholders' expectations and investigates the current commitment to social reporting in the high-end market. Moreover, the chapter responds to the need for deeper exploration into the impact of CSR on financial performance.

In Chapter 5, entitled "Communicating CSR in the luxury market", we contribute to the literature on sustainable communication in the luxury market by exploring the extent to which luxury brand companies communicate their sustainable goals in the online context. The online context considers luxury companies' presence on corporate websites and their profiles on various social media platforms. The results show that most luxury brands have created a section dedicated to sustainability on their websites where they communicate not only their promises but also their performances. Considering social media, the results show that luxury brands' content mainly focuses on world preservation, inclusion, materials, and production processes. Furthermore, the circular economy is a hotly debated topic online, indicating that it is no longer perceived as an alternative business standard but a real effort for all luxury brands.

We conclude the book with Chapter 6, entitled "The best practices in the sustainability approach: case studies from different luxury segments", analyzing best practices in the luxury market in terms of sustainable performance. This offers a more comprehensive understanding of the sustainable strategies employed by luxury brand companies, presenting the audience with a model for the proper implementation of sustainable practices that can contribute positively to overall well-being. The analysis facilitates the recognition of top corporate strategies across five luxury sectors to shed light on the primary initiatives undertaken within the integrated CSR framework, encompassing standards, strategic philanthropy, and integrated output.

Given its focus on exploring challenges and opportunities for managing sustainability in the luxury market, which is a global market, our book has a global appeal. It serves as a valuable resource for researchers and academics who are interested in current developments related to sustainability within the luxury brand market. It is particularly well-suited for university courses, both at the undergraduate and postgraduate levels, as well as specialized programs offered by non-governmental business schools. The specific modules that this book addresses include luxury brand management, international luxury management, luxury business, luxury marketing, corporate social responsibility, sustainability, and sustainable marketing. Moreover, the balance between theory and practice makes our book appealing to professionals in luxury management and anyone eager to learn more about how to manage sustainability in the luxury brand market.

Turin, May 2024

Fabrizio Mosca
fabrizio.mosca@unito.it
University of Turin, Italy,
Department of Management

Valentina Chiaudano
valentina.chiaudano@unito.it
University of Turin, Italy,
Department of Management

Chapter 1

THE EVOLUTION OF LUXURY: FROM UNNECESSARY TO CUSTOMER-CENTRIC

Fabrizio Mosca

ABSTRACT: *This opening chapter illustrates why luxury branding can address emerging trends such as sustainability. At first glance, luxury and sustainability may seem incompatible, but from the customer-centric perspective, linking sustainability with luxury aligns with the meaning of luxury proposed by the young generation of consumers. These consumers request luxury brands to prioritize environmental and societal well-being.*

1.1. Introduction

> *"Luxury is about pleasing yourself, not dressing for other people".*
>
> Mark Jacobs, American fashion designer.

Two years after the Covid-19 pandemic, the revenues of luxury companies are quickly returning to their pre-crisis level. After experiencing a collapse in profitability by 22% in 2020, the luxury market [1] value reached the threshold of €1.14 billion in 2021, showing a 15% growth compared to 2020. While in 2022 the global luxury market grew by 21% to achieve the milestone of €1.400 billion (D'Arpizio et al., 2022). In 2023 the luxury market has experienced a growth of 8-10% compared to 2022, reaching a total value of €1.500 billion. The scenario is forecasted to be favourable for 2024 when the revenues of high-end companies are expected to grow by +4%. Although the pandemic did not hurt the long-term profitability of luxury companies, it acted as an accelerator for some key trends that were struggling to take off. The boom in influencers has changed ways of advertising, the integration between digital and physical platforms has led to the growth of omnichannel strategies, the aptly named "sharing economy" has produced second-hand luxury and more and more luxury players are taking care of sustainability.

Most of these trends started years ago and are driven by younger generations of luxury brand consumers, Millennials and Generation Z. Millennials refer to people born from 1981 to 1996, while Generation Z includes young consumers born from 1997 to 2009 (Kotler et al., 2021). According to many studies, the new generations of consumers are profoundly different from the previous ones (Batat, 2019a; Kapferer & Michaut-Denizeau, 2020; Rolling et al., 2021). Such younger generations do not interpret luxury brands according to the product-centric viewpoint, which uses static and predetermined series of attributes. On the contrary, they consider luxury as a customer-centric and dynamic concept that changes over time to meet customers' individuality and personality (Seo & Buchanan-Oliver, 2019).

Particularly, the younger generations of consumers look for luxury brands that are more inclusive and inclined to protect both the environment and the social community (D'Arpizio et al., 2022).

Therefore, luxury companies must learn how to integrate sustainability into their traditional brand image and practices.

Thus, starting from the explanation of the temporal-spatial dependence of luxury and how it changes through the epochs, the chapter explores the definition of the luxury brand, comparing the product-centric perspective with the customer-centric one. Finally, by leveraging the customer-centric perspective, the chapter introduces an approach for luxury companies toward emerging trends including sustainability.

1.2. The timeline of the luxury concept

An ultimate and complete consensus on the definition of "luxury" does not exist (Dubois & Duquesne, 1993; Kapferer, 1997; Roberts, 2019; Kim & Lee, 2019; Rathi et al., 2022).

The etymology of luxury itself reveals that the luxury concept has contradictory meanings. It derives from "luxus", a Latin word that embodies contrasting connotations. On the one hand, luxus is related to negative terms such as "excess", "intemperance", and "debauchery". On the other hand, it means "pomp" and "magnificence", resulting in a positive connotation (Cristini et al., 2017).

According to Kapferer (1997) the word luxury contains the Latin root "lux", which means light. In this case, the author connects the word luxury to "glitter", an attribute of materials like gold and gems that increase visibility due to their brightness. Another author suggests luxury derives from the Greek word λοξός (loxos), which means "to grow in a non-straight way" and highlights how luxury is "askew" concerning the ordinary. Thus, the etymology of luxury confirms its dual nature, ranging from a negative value of excessive sumptuousness, dissipation superfluous, moral decay, and a positive character of dream (Kapferer, 2016). Moreover, the luxury's etymology, together with a deep analysis of the literature, reveals that luxury is not a modern age phenomenon as many people think. On the contrary, the concept of luxury is ancient, and it has changed throughout historical epochs.

Going back to the Magna Grecia, condemnation of luxury frequently recurs, as it was related to spending to fill a need refined that exceeds the necessary and socially accepted consumption. Thus, spending on luxury implied purchasing unnecessary things, and it was considered a symbol of corruption. Plato, a Greek philosopher, living during the classical period, is well known for condemning luxury in *The Republic* (380-370 B.C). The author considered luxury as all the pleasures originating from those things that are not strictly necessary and move men away from virtues. Therefore, in his work, it emerged that luxury was a source of laziness and political instability that led to a bloated and unhealthy state.

Even during the Roman Empire, luxury was considered a matter of political morality that favored incitement to individual desires, and potentially threatened public order. Romans extended their influence throughout the world and brought to their homeland all kinds of new pleasures and delights. These included, for instance, gold, olive oil and honey from Spain, fresh figs and scented cedar wood from Africa, wines made from herbal infusions and woolen tunics from northern Gaul, dogs, and bathtubs from Britain. The abandonment of sensual pleasures was a debilitating regression that led to a general weakening and deprived Roman soldiers of their legendary prowess. The Romans were so concerned about the effects of excessive enjoyment in their society that passed "sanctuary laws", such as Lex Oppia 215 B.C., Lex Orchia 181 B.C., and Lex Iulia 90 B.C, to reduce the unnecessary expenses of the aristocracy. Seneca, Cicero, Juvenal, and Horace publicly condemned customs corruption and supported the favors of a frugal, simple, natural life. We can understand the idea of luxury supported in the Roman empire epoch from Trimalchio, the main character of "Satyricon" (I sec A.C), the famous novel of Petronio. He describes the concept of luxury with the following sentence: "Credite mihi: assem habeas, assem valeas; habes, habeberis" (English translation: "Believe me: who has any money, worth a penny; what you have, so you will be considered.").

Then, in the Middle Ages, the Church influenced the meaning of luxury. On the one hand, the ecclesiastics condemned the use of luxury goods such as apparel or spices because they were considered guilty pleasures. On the other hand, the Church became the leading consumer of luxury. The opulence of gold inside the place of worship, like in the Vatican State, represented God's magnificence.

Starting from the Renaissance, the increasing trade across Europe and Asia let luxury be seen as an economic advantage. Thus, luxury lost its negative connotations and returned to its profane sphere, synonymous with beauty, pomp, and immense wealth. From the Renaissance and in the following centuries enjoying pleasures was not perceived as guilt. On the contrary, the emerging lifestyles were characterized by hedonism, the search for pleasure and the joy of living. The court of King Louis XIV, best known as Sun King (le Roi Soleil), is a tangible example of luxury at that time. For its court, the French King transformed Versailles – a dilapidated royal hunting building 12 miles from Paris – into a showroom of the best in the French luxury industry. Luxury became the absolutist policy of the French king that weakened the aristocracy's political role.

During the 17th and 19th centuries, luxury enforced its role as an element of distinction among social classes. In these eras, the upper bourgeoisie aspired to possess luxury goods to manifest its social affirmation and emulate the aristocracy's lifestyle. As tensions between the classes increased, many philosophers, economists and sociologists entered the debate about the meaning of luxury with a different view. John Locke (1632-1704) expressed a negative view of luxury because it caused the "discomfort of the mind, due to the desire for an absent good", while David Hume (1711-1776) asserted that "luxury is only pernicious when it ceases to benefit society". Then Adam Smith (1723-1790), considered the father of modern economics, intervened in the luxury debate. He agreed that opulence and freedom were two of the most important achievements and that happiness had to do with "comfort of body and peace of mind". Moreover, he highlighted that luxury aspiration is not harmful to society because "the growth and improvement" experienced by everyone led to a good collective economic state, creating employment for many and a state of wealth. In his exploration of late-nineteenth-century American culture, Thorstein Veblen (1857-1929) discovered that money had become the foundation of social regard and self-respect. As a result, it was no longer enough for the leisure class to have wealth, but people belonging to the upper class must have demonstrated their wealthier conditions through consumption and waste of goods. In other words, the purchase of luxury goods became a symbol of ostentation that permitted the upper classes to be identified. In his book *The Theory of the Leisure Class*, Veblen first talked about the conspicuous consumption of purchasing goods or services to display one's wealth and social status (Veblen, 1912).

The debate about the luxury concept has not been over in the 21st Century. Jean Baudrillard (1929-2007), in his book titled *Pour Une critique de l'èconomie politique du signe*, published in 1979, explained that the driving force of capitalist society is consumption. The French sociologist revealed that when people buy goods, they look for one of the following types of values: functional, economic, symbolic, and sign value. Among these values, the sign one describes the luxury purchase, as it indicates the importance accorded to goods due to the social status awarded by the owner, rather than functional value and utility derived from their primary use (Baudrillard, 1995). Even Pierre Bourdieu (1930-2002), a French philosopher and sociologist who focused on power dynamics in society, also offered his vision of luxury. His work titled *La Distinction: Critique sociale du jugement* (1979) theorized that luxury consumption is driven by the need to show social status. Moreover, he agreed that people couldn't develop a "taste" for luxury, because it is innate in those who belong to a higher class.

In the Twenty-first Century, starting from mature markets like Europe and the US, the meaning of luxury has taken on a new connotation. In a world where everyone could buy everything, luxury was more than the materialistic possession of goods that showed off people's wealthy condition. On the contrary, luxury became a means of self-expression (Lipovetsky & Roux, 2003). In recent times, most authors agree that the meaning of luxury depends on customers' individual and personalized perceptions (Armitage & Roberts., 2016; Banister et al., 2020 and Wang et al., 2021). For example, Banister et al. (2020) developed a framework to illustrate the practices for everyday luxury moving from the product-centric perspective to consumers' interpretation of luxury. Holmqvist et al. (2020) describe luxury as an individual, or group's need to escape or caretake in rare, exciting moments that contrast with mundane life. Wang et al. (2021) introduce an alternative framework of luxury consumption focused on the relevance of customer experience. The author explains that consumers who consume luxury in addition to status-seeking "are also intrinsically motivated to spend resources and time learning and enjoying the unique features of luxury products (e.g., their exquisite design and workmanship, sensory appeal and distinct socio-cultural narratives)". Moreover, in recent years Armitage & Roberts (2016) have introduced a new stream of research called Critical Luxury Studies. They suggest that researchers draw on anthropological consumer-focused approaches to provide a more comprehensive conceptualization of luxury perceptions and vicissitudes. According to Armitage & Roberts (2016), luxury avoids an objective definition, since it depends on cultural, social and individual contexts and meanings. Hence, the concept of luxury varies through time and space and across economic, social, and cultural contexts.

Key points related to the luxury definition through the historical epochs are summarized in Figure 1.

Figure 1. The timeline of the luxury concept

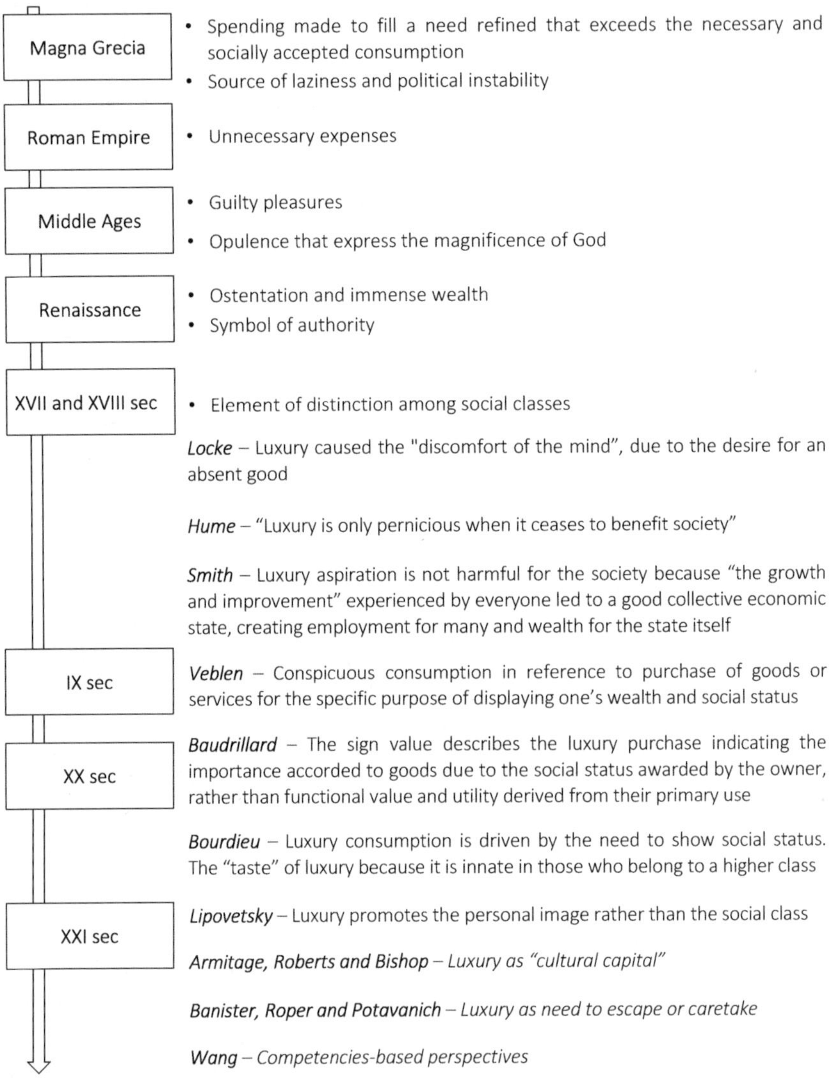

Source: Author's elaboration.

1.3. Defining the luxury brands

Brands are vital resources for every company since, unlike tangible assets, brands cannot be copied, duplicated, or replaced. Thus, for a company to succeed in building strong brands, it needs to be clear how the strategy will be developed to successfully manage the brand in the target market. The role of brand management is even more crucial in the luxury brand markets than in any other industry because it is easier for luxury brands to incur brand dilution, which may compromise their positioning in the market. Therefore, most authors attempt to put boundaries on the luxury brand definition, aiming to support companies in implementing a careful and well-developed luxury strategy, in line with luxury rules. What emerges is that the purpose of a luxury brand is defined according to two opposite points of view: the product-centric perspective of luxury brands and the customer-centric one.

In the following sub-section, the chapter deepens the meaning of the luxury brand according to the above-mentioned opposed perspectives, whose main characteristics are summarised in Table 1.

Table 1. Origin of different approaches

Luxury perspective		Concepts, themes and theoretical sources
Product-centric perspective		Functional value (Berthon et al., 2009); utilitarian value (Tynan et al., 2010); old luxe (Miller & Mills, 2012); brand DNA; craftsmanship; heritage; quality; high price, etc. (Dubois et al., 2001; Fionda & Moore, 2009; Kapferer & Bastien, 2009; Keller, 2009).
Consumer-centric perspective	Social meanings	Symbolic/expressive (Tynan et al., 2010); symbolic luxury (Berthon et al., 2009); social meaning (Miller & Mills, 2012); status symbol (Kapferer & Bastien, 2009); perfectionism effect and conspicuousness (Vigneron & Johnson, 2004); social construction of luxury (Roper et al., 2013).
	Personalized meanings	Experiential/hedonic (Tynan et al., 2010); experiential luxury (Berthon et al.,2009); individual meaning (Miller & Mills, 2012); luxury experiences; personal pleasures, 'my luxury' (Kapferer & Bastien, 2009); consumer-centric and luxury brand value co-creation (Roper et al., 2013; Tynan et al., 2010).

Source: Author's elaboration.

1.3.1. The product-centric perspective: the luxury brand as a pre-determined concept

In the endeavor to deepen the definition of the luxury brand, most authors focused on the product-centric perspective, also called the "old luxury" (Miller & Mills, 2012), as it is the most traditional point of view about luxury branding.

The product-centric perspective explains the luxury brand using a series of attributes that differentiate luxury brands from "ordinary ones" (Seo & Buchanan-Oliver, 2019). These attributes that make the concept of luxury stable and pre-determined can be collected from different studies. According to Chevalier & Mazzalovo (2012), luxury brands have three main characteristics in common: artistic, international, and hand-craft dimensions. While the artistic dimension plays a key role "in the overall impression" of luxury brands, the international dimension refers to the need for luxury brands to be globally recognizable. Finally, the hand-craft dimension is related to the importance of human capacity in realizing a high-end product.

Fionda & Moore (2009) include marketing communications, luxury environment, and culture as essential brand luxury ingredients. Instead, Keller (2009) uses brand symbols, secondary associations, brand architecture, competition, and trademarks to refine the dimensions of luxury brands. Then, Kapferer (1997) states that functional and practical values affect consumers' decision-making when buying luxury brands. Functional values are related to usability, quality, and uniqueness, while utilitarian values regard excellence and craftsmanship. Finally, Dubois & Duquesne (1993) contribute to the literature with a more comprehensive definition of luxury brand attributes by sorting out six main traits of luxury brands, namely high price, excellent quality, aesthetics and polysensuality, scarcity and uniqueness, heritage and superfluousness (Figure 2).

High price

In the case of luxury brands, the price is generally high and not directly proportional to the goods' production cost. The high price, indeed, is justified by the high intangible benefits that a consumer perceives with the purchase of the luxury good. Furthermore, the high price is considered by luxury consumers as the highest quality indicator: several studies have shown that luxury consumers who decide between two perfectly substitutable brands prefer the one with a higher price. This is because luxury consumers assume a positive correlation between high prices and excellent quality (Lichtennstein, 1993).

Excellent quality

Luxury brand refers to valuable and superior quality goods. Thus, this attribute represents a precondition for a brand to be placed in the highest segment of the market. The excellent quality results from: the perceived quality of the product components (good fabrics like cashmere for Brunello Cucinelli or vicuna for Loro Piana), and by the quality granted by high-end workmanship (i.e. diamond cutters for Tiffany & Co.), defined by either very laborious and complex manufacturing process, such as building a Ferrari, or by the experience of the artisans who make the product, like the case of Louis Vuitton bag.

Aesthetics and polysensuality

These are the attributes that are exploited to increase the perceived value of the luxury brand and to enhance the elements of differentiation when compared to other brands whose goods are only able to fulfil the functional benefit.

Looking at Poltrona Frau, its function could be replaced by any other cheaper armchair. However, the quality of the materials and the unique design give Poltrona Frau a higher value than ordinary armchairs.

Scarcity and uniqueness

Rarity can be considered in different ways in the case of luxury products. Notably, it can be configured as natural rarity (use of precious materials such as diamonds, gold, and platinum), technological rarity (use of a technology that is difficult to reproduce as, for instance, Tesla cars), and customization (creation of limited series and made-to-measure goods). Moreover, luxury brands support rarity through exclusive distribution strategies, meaning that luxury products are available to a very small number of outlets, and consequently to a group of privileged consumers.

Heritage

Heritage identifies a set of factors that constitute the history of the brand. For this reason, heritage is a unique and intangible component of the luxury brand, which cannot be replicated or imitated by competitors (Mosca, 2017). According to Corbellini & Saviolo (2009) heritage consists of the link between the luxury brand and the mythical creator, secret formulas, or the mysterious production process. According to Mosca (2017) four factors should be put together to create an effective heritage marketing campaign: the link with the past, the founder and his/her family, the processing techniques and the people who made the brand famous.

In recent years, luxury brand managers have understood heritage's high strategic value, which has become a highly recommended element in managing powerful marketing strategies.

Superfluousness

This attribute refers to the fact that luxury goods are not purchased to satisfy primary needs. On the contrary, consumers buy luxury products to meet other types of needs, such as esteem or self-actualisation needs.

Figure 2. The product-centric perspective[2]

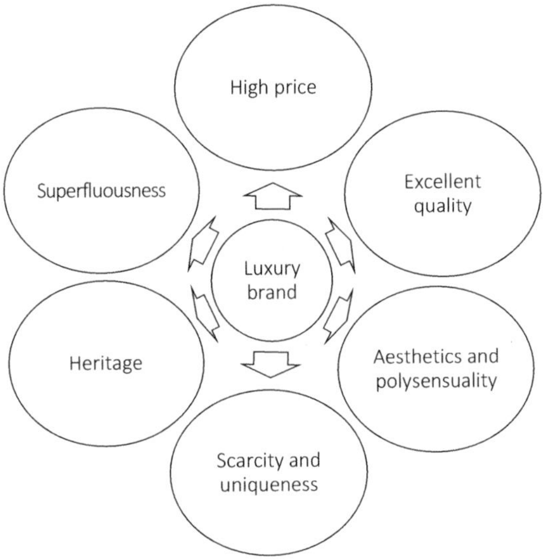

Source: Author's elaboration.

1.3.2. The consumer-centric perspective: the luxury brand defined by the youngest consumers

The product-centric perspective is not the only way to define luxury brands. According to other authors, luxury brands are defined by more than a limited number of attributes (Berthon et al., 2009; Tynan et al., 2010; Roper et al., 2013; Seo &Buchanan-Oliver, 2019). They argue that in addition to a functional and utilitarian component, the definition of a luxury brand includes social and personalized meanings that consumers attach to it (Vigneron & Johnson, 2004).

Based on this emerging approach, luxury is better understood as a need for self-gratification and the pursuit of unique personal experiences, making individuality triumph over belonging (Lipovetsky & Roux 2003; Kapferer & Bastien, 2009). The authors, in line with the conceptualization of the luxury brand, suggest that it is better defined from a customer perspective, by considering the subjective and personal interpretation of luxury, in addition to the product-centric perspective that emphasizes its features (Berthon et al., 2009; Tynan et al., 2010; Roper et al., 2013; Seo & Buchan-an-Oliver, 2019). Specifically, Berthon et al. (2009) argue that defining luxury involves going beyond material content. They state that the definition of luxury focuses on its holistic dimension, adding collective and subjective spheres to the material one, and aiming at capturing connections among individuals, items, and brands. Even Roper et al. (2013), in their examination of luxury brands, do not focus on product characteristics, but on consumers' emotional and cultural dimensions, illustrating how consumers define the meaning of luxury for themselves. Finally, Tynan et al. (2010) demonstrate that luxury increasingly pertains to the consumer experience. Consequently, in line with the spatial-temporal dependence of the luxury concept of Armitage & Roberts (2016), scholars agree that the luxury brand is a dynamic concept that takes on different roles depending on the era and consumer expectations. According to D'Arpizio et al. (2022), from 2025 onwards, Millennials and Generation Z will account for 60% of the entire customer base of luxury brand companies. Therefore, the change process, aimed at meeting the expectations of young customers, can no longer wait.

The following subsection presents Millennials and Generation Z traits, striving to provide managers and scholars with a better understanding of the future consumers of luxury brands.

1.3.2.1. Millennials and Generation Z: the young luxury consumers

Segmentation by age results in five main groups of consumers: the Alpha Generation, Generation Z, Millennials, Generation X and Baby Boomers. In recent times, due to their future potential purchase power and the influence on other generations, consumers belonging to the Millennials and Generation Z groups have attracted the attention of the luxury brand market. Generation Y better known as Net Generation or Millennials, as its members turned eighteen in the early years of the new millennium, refers to consumers born between 1981 and 1996 (Kotler et al., 2021).[3] They participated in some important historical events, such as the introduction of the Euro and European citizenship, but at the same time they experienced the consequences of the economic crisis and social instability. They grew up during the digital age and experimented with new forms of communication by enjoying several advantages, such as the easy retrieval of information from different sources and dual-way communication (Berkup, 2014). The use of technology makes them a multitasking generation, with an attitude to flexibility, and less inclined to sacrifice the right balance between work and private life (Kurz et al., 2018). Thus, influenced by the sociocultural events experienced, Millennials strongly differ from previous generations. While Generation X and Baby Boomers used to look for a profitable job, get married, create a family, and then try to improve their born status by demonstrating with purchases their social condition, Millennials pursue new values. Family, spirituality, religion, patriotism, and well-being are no longer fundamental principles. On the contrary, they are outperformed by new ones such as sustainability, professional success, fun, physical health and travel experiences. They are considered more responsive to environmental changes and inclined to seek innovative challenges to prevent boredom.

There are two main reasons to explain why Millennials have developed such attitudes and principles. First, differently from the previous generations, Millennials approached adulthood in unfavorable economic conditions. Then, they are the first generation very affected by the digital revolution, which has profoundly changed the perception of time and space. These factors imply that Millennials interpret luxury differently from past generations. Specifically, luxury goods are not only a means to create their identity, but also to seek an emotional connection with brands. Thus, they expect luxury brands to not remain anchored to traditional attributes and the celebration of heritage. Instead, brands should be open to external collaborations and creativity, adapting to contemporary trends, and allowing Millennials to identify themselves in the brand and its values.

The main traits of Millennials are summarised in Figure 3.

Figure 3. The main traits of Millennials

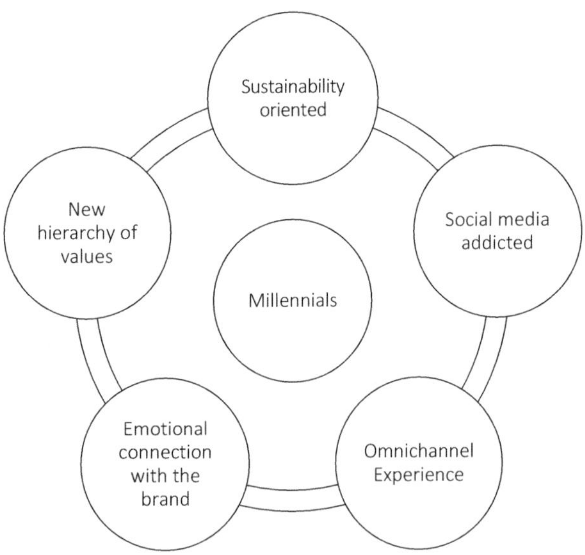

Source: Author's elaboration.

Figure 4. The main traits of Generation Z

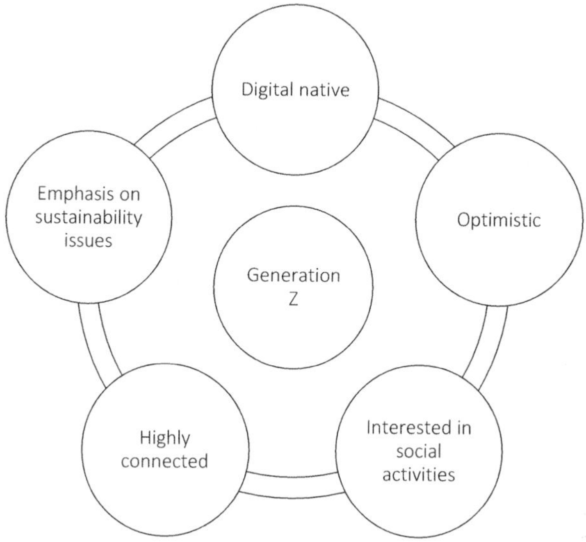

Source: Author's elaboration.

Generation Z refers to people born from 1997 to 2009 (Kotler et al., 2021). As this generational cohort includes digital natives and highly connected people, it is also called iGeneration or Net Generation. Growing up in an epoch characterized by terrorism, recession and climate change, the members of this generation feel able to change the course that history has taken following these events (Kurz et al., 2018). They are hopeful about the future, having at the same time great confidence in their abilities, considered as capable means to achieve greater personal fulfilment. Individuals from this generation are self-confident and very keen on taking part in social activities, compared to members of previous generations (Francis & Hoefel, 2018), and they believe that success in life comes from the choices made in the present (Kurz et al., 2018). Moreover, more than other generations, members of Generation Z demonstrate a greater familiarity with technology, which is not perceived as an innovation, but rather as an integral part of everyday life. Consequently, they are the first generation that cannot perceive any boundaries between digital and physical worlds. While presenting some aspects in common with Millennials, especially when browsing the Internet, unlike them, the members of Generation Z do not post images on social media for personal branding. On the contrary, they are used to portray authentic and truthful personal images and hate brands that spread artifact images to promote products or services. Following this trend, many luxury companies chose people who did not meet the traditional and artifact aesthetic standards, for their promotional campaigns (Kotler et al., 2021). For example, Gucci proposed the "Unconventional Beauty" campaign during the Photo Vogue Festival in November 2019. The project celebrated beauty in all its forms and redefined the fashion world's canons of beauty, which were once stereotyped and far from reality, and now are increasingly inclusive and attentive to enhancing diversity, uniqueness, and authenticity, even with its imperfections. Figure 4 summarises the main characteristics of Generation Z.

1.4. The consumer-centric perspective to explain sustainable luxury

As already anticipated at the beginning of this chapter, the luxury market has recently experienced new trends that seem opposed to the traditional rules of luxury. Streetwear collaborations have become the new exclusivity. Rental and second-hand consumption is growing among luxury consumers by changing how luxury products are consumed. Digitalization offers new methods for communicating and delivering products and services. Sustainability has changed the priorities of luxury brand companies in managing their businesses. Rathi et al. (2022; p.241) underlined that "themes like experiential luxury (Batat, 2019b; Batat & Manika, 2020) hedonic escapism (Holmqvist et al., 2020), liquid luxury (Bardhi et al., 2020) have gained the spotlight" … and that "the attempts to capture new meanings and formulate definitions are ongoing". All these new trends and themes related to luxury branding can be explained by dropping the idea that the luxury brand should be exclusively interpreted through static and pre-determined attributes according to the product-centric perspective. On the contrary, a clear understanding of the luxury brand requests to go beyond the traditional luxury attributes, by considering how consumers reshape the luxury brand conceptualization. Thus, leveraging on the customer-centric perspective, the interpretation of luxury brands as a tool to contribute to the collective well-being or to express customer value through co-branded streetwear products, is in line with the concept of luxury indicated by the new luxury brand consumers, Millennials and Generation Z. These targets of consumers, that will represent 60% of luxury consumers in 2025 (Willersdorf et al., 2020), are profoundly different from traditional generations of buyers, in terms of their needs, tastes and purchase behaviors (Karatzas et al., 2019; Arli et al., 2020). Millennials are more visionary and interested in experiences, rather than in the possession of luxury (Gentina et al., 2016; Mundel et al., 2017). At the same time, Generation Z consumers look for products that fit their personalities. They ask luxury brands to evolve and innovate in terms of their product offerings, communication, distribution and online and offline engagement strategies (Karatzas et al., 2019; D'Arpizio et al., 2022). The singular characteristics of Millennials and Generation Z, with their relevance in number and power of influence, pose a challenge to luxury companies, which must learn how to meet their new expectations by combining their interpretation of luxury with traditional luxury attributes.

Among the emerging challenges given by the younger generation of luxury consumers, the integration of sustainable activities into corporate strategies is at the top of luxury brands' agenda. Sustainability, indeed, has assumed increasing relevance from young consumers' point of view. If consumers first perceived a mismatch between luxury and sustainability (Kunz et al., 2020) in a matter of years they understood that sustainability can no longer be ignored. Younger luxury brand consumers have become more and more aware that luxury brand companies need to offer more sustainable products from recycled materials to sustainable processes.

Recently, the pandemic has accelerated consumers' awareness and concerns about the impact of goods and services on the environment (Retail X, 2021). Notably, after the Covid-19 pandemic, the need for sustainability spread wider into the general population of luxury, including the elderly generations of consumers. In fact, the "Millennials State of Mind" has pervaded the luxury market, involving all consumers. Consequently, efforts of luxury brands toward sustainability increased. Retail X report published in 2021 reveals that in December 2020, 75% of the Top fashion luxury brands adopted sustainable materials, used recyclable packaging, and reduced carbon emissions by growing the use of renewable energy. Moreover, the consumers' attention to pursuing sustainable practices drives the reusing and reselling of luxury items, especially apparel, jewelry, accessories, furniture, cars, and *objet d'art*. Bof, & McKinsey & Company (2022) show 28% of luxury consumers decided to buy pre-owned products instead of new items, to contribute to sustainability. Figure 5 summarises the main differences among old and new luxury consumers.

Figure 5. Old luxury consumers vs new luxury consumers

OLD CONSUMERS	NEW CONSUMERS
Interested in possession of luxury goods	Interested in luxury experiences
Products as a mean for status symbol	Products that express their personalities
Celebrating the old luxury habits	Open to innovations
Social distinction, elitism	Equity and Inclusion

Source: Author's elaboration.

1.5. Some questions about sustainability and luxury brand management

Although the data mentioned above show an increasing commitment to sustainability by luxury companies, sustainability remains a thorny issue in the luxury market (D'Arpizio et al., 2022). In fact, matching the values of sustainability with luxury brand attributes is still a real challenge that requires further investigation.[4] Moreover, companies need guidelines for integrating more deeply sustainability into their business model. Even communication remains a concern, especially when considering the use of websites and social media for communicating sustainable practices.

To summarise, the integration of sustainability into luxury brand strategies calls for further investigation, considering the following topic:

- Identifying the relationship between luxury and sustainability to define the potential touchpoints.
- Defining the practices for managing sustainability in the luxury market and what the impact of sustainability on competition is.
- Identifying to what extent sustainability is integrated into the business model of luxury brand companies.
- Integrated sustainable practices adopted by luxury companies with their brand.
- Exploring the different tools that luxury brand companies use to communicate their efforts to sustainability to the target audience.
- In-depth analysis of sustainable practices, considering the best-in-class

luxury companies in terms of their commitment to sustainable development.

The book contributes to the luxury literature by answering the abovementioned questions.

First, this book attempts to solve the divergence between luxury and sustainability. By leveraging a structured review, we organise the scientific production on sustainable luxury in the research areas and explain the reasons for matching luxury and sustainability. Then the book investigates the fundamental issues within sustainable luxury and the integration of sustainability into the corporate business model, by providing an overview of the extent to which luxury brand companies are improving their commitment to sustainable actions. In this endeavor, we also deal with luxury companies' efforts to communicate their commitment to sustainability, both offline and online, with a focus on themes and tools. Finally, the book presents several business cases that exemplify best practices for implementing sustainability. The discussion of case studies aims to meet the needs of a wide and varied audience, from university students to CSR managers looking to adapt such best practices to their businesses.

Notes

1 Traditionally the luxury market was considered transversal to only four sectors, namely apparel, leather goods, hard luxury, cosmetics, and perfumes. These are products intended for personal care, and for this reason are defined personal luxury goods. However, in more recent times, alongside the traditional luxury sectors, new sectors, defined as emerging luxury segments, increased in importance. Emerging luxury includes those products and services that seek the satisfaction of an experiential need, rather than a material one, and refer to the following sectors: luxury cars, luxury hospitality, fine wines and spirits, gourmet food and fine dining, high quality design furniture and homeware, fine art, luxury cruises, private yacht, and jet.

2 Figure 2 considers the main attributes to identify what a luxury brand is and what is not, according to Dubois et al. (2021) definition. Because the authors define luxury brands according to static and predetermined attributes, their interpretation of luxury is in line with the product-centric perspective.

3 The segmentation by age divides the market in different clusters according to people's age. Marketing demographic age brackets are not always the same. On the contrary, they vary according to different authors. In

this chapter, the segmentation follows the age brackets proposed by Kotler et al. (2021).

4 Recently, the relationship between luxury and sustainability has influenced the spreading of new stream of research. For example, Batat et al. (2020) introduced the "Transformative Luxury Research" (TLR) as an emerging field in marketing that investigates the relationship between luxury, ethics, and well-being.

Chapter 2

SUSTAINABILITY AND LUXURY: IS THERE A MATCH?

Valentina Chiaudano

ABSTRACT: *Given the lack of clarity over the relationship between luxury and sustainability, this chapter organizes the scientific production on sustainable luxury to explain the evolution of sustainability in the luxury brand market. After a brief overview of the definition of sustainability, the chapter sheds light on the connection between luxury and sustainability. Then the authors describe the major milestones of sustainable development in the luxury market and the current evolution of sustainability for managing luxury brands. Finally, the chapter concludes by providing opportunities for theoretical and methodological advancements in sustainable luxury management.*

2.1. Introduction

"Buy less. Choose well. Make it last".

Vivienne Westwood, renowned luxury fashion designer.

Nowadays, sustainability is experiencing a boost in relevance. The call for action to fulfil the Sustainable Development Goals (SDGs) [1] has become a priority for companies across all business sectors (Latapí Agudelo et al., 2019). On the one hand, national and international institutions such as the United Nations, European Commission and Environmental Protection Agency (EPA) [2] require global companies and small and medium competitive enterprises to comply with environmental, ethical, and governance regulations. On the other hand, all stakeholders [3] encourage companies' efforts toward sustainable practices (Freeman et al., 2020; Visser, 2010). Notably, consumers are more aware that their behavior might affect the society they live in.

Considering the luxury market, the approach to sustainability is more complex than in other industries, since "luxury" and "sustainability" seem to have nothing in common (Costa Pinto et al., 2016; Janssen et al., 2017). Some authors have adopted the "CSR-luxury paradox" expression to indicate the apparent mismatch between luxury and sustainability. The idea of luxury has been traditionally linked to excess, hedonism, and ostentation. In contrast, sustainability is focused on opposite principles, such as altruism, sobriety, ethics, and moderation (Achabou & Dekhili, 2013). In addition, people consider luxury companies focused on certain products such as leather goods, apparel, and jewelry, but also luxury cars and yachts as parties in question in the context of climate change. Indeed, these types of companies are generally responsible for water pollution, exploitation of raw materials and CO_2 and harmful emissions.

Given the lack of clarity over the relationship between luxury and sustainability, this chapter organizes the scientific production on sustainable luxury to explain the evolution of sustainability in the luxury brand market. After a brief overview of the definition of sustainability, the chapter sheds light on the connection between luxury and sustainability. Then it describes the major milestones of sustainable development in the luxury market and the current evolution of sustainability for managing luxury brands. Finally, the chapter concludes by providing opportunities for theoretical and methodological advancements in sustainable luxury management.

2.2. General aspects of sustainability

With the growing awareness of global warming and climate change, it has become essential to safeguard the entire ecosystem by adopting a sustainable approach. The concept of sustainable development is first mentioned in the Brundtland Report.[4] The document defines sustainable development as follows: "the development that meets the needs of the present without compromising the ability of future generations to meet their needs" (p. 8). In other words, sustainable development means satisfying the needs of the current population while safeguarding opportunities for the next generations. To do this, it is necessary to quantify the current resources and immediately adopt measures to ensure their availability in the future. Thus, the management of a resource is only sustainable when, once aware of the ability to reproduce, the resource is not exploited beyond a certain threshold, to allow its complete regeneration. However, in addition to being difficult to apply, the definition of sustainability of the Brundtland Report provides little guidance on how to perform sustainable development. On the one hand, the definition gives limited direction on the identification of present and future needs. On the other hand, it does not offer suggestions about the technologies and resources for meeting these needs (Hart, 1995; Starik & Rands, 1995).

Figure 1. The Triple Bottom line

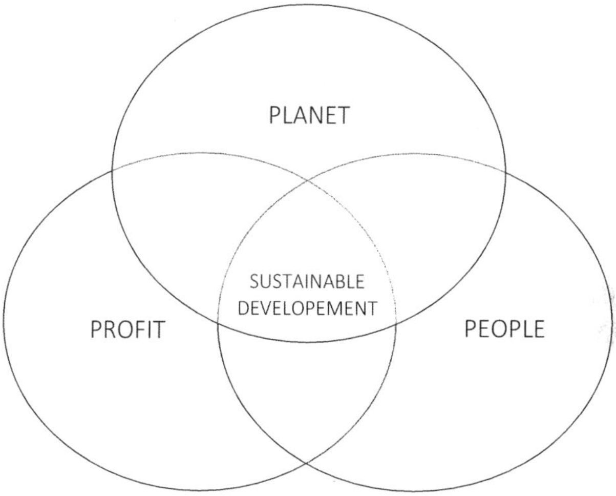

Source: Author's elaboration.

This lack of clarity in guiding toward a more sustainable behavior is covered by Elkington (1998), who effectively operationalized the concept of sustainable development by creating the Triple Bottom Line (Figure 1). It is a framework that defines sustainable development as a reconciliation between three spheres: economic, social, and environmental dimensions. According to the Triple Bottom Line framework, the company should not give priority to any of the three objectives but must achieve them together through the establishment of equal and long-term relationships with its stakeholders. In other words, Elkington suggests that companies do not focus exclusively on economic goals: on the contrary, they survive in the long term by pursuing environmental (planet) and social (people) goals while making a profit. The recent contributions of Serafeim (2022) and Ruper Younger follow the same pattern. In particular, Serafeim (2022) in his publication "Purpose and Profit" shows the best ways to manage the three dimensions of sustainability to make a profit while contributing to the collective well-being. While, Ruper Younger, the founding Director of Oxford University Centre for Corporate Reputation, gives some insights about the power of ESG in a recent participation to Global Conversations with Global Leaders Podcast Series organized by Intesa San Paolo, the European leading bank.

2.3. The relationship between luxury and sustainability

In recent times, the concept of sustainable development has become fundamental for all companies, regardless of the sector where they operate. More and more companies pay increasing attention to the procurement of raw materials, while preserving rare materials, avoiding pollution through production processes, ensuring high standards, respecting workers, and taking care of recycling processes. This also applies to the luxury industry, which is often accused of having reacted late to the progressive awareness of environmental issues (Chevalier & Mazzalovo, 2021). In particular, the main criticisms related to the application of sustainability to the luxury brand market do not concern the ecological impact on the environment, but rather the lack of transparency present in the supply chain – in the case of raw materials such as precious stones or animal skins – the treatment of animals, and working conditions (Kapferer, 2010).

The companies' delay in considering sustainability issues depends on the initial skepticism about the match between luxury and sustainability. For example, at first, scholars were hesitant to extend the sustainability debate to luxury brand management. Citing the luxury-sustainability paradox, they emphasized the divergence between luxury and sustainability (Achabou & Dekhili, 2013; Cervellon & Shammas, 2013; Torelli et al., 2012; Wong & Dhanesh, 2016). Several authors argued that luxury and sustainability are different by nature. Achabou & Delhi (2013) explained that helping the underprivileged versus purchasing expensive luxury goods, is naturally in conflict. Likewise, Wong & Dhanesh (2016) found that luxury and sustainability share inconsistent characteristics. Luxury is associated with excess, social distinction, self-enhancement, and dreams. In contrast, sustainability recalls self-transcendence, rationality, equality, frugality, and reality. Moreover, the common scandals involving greenwashing practices, such as those concealed behind luxury garments or fashion accessories validated the perception of incongruence between luxury and sustainability.

Figure 2. The opposite roots of luxury and sustainability[5]

LUXURY	SUSTAINABILITY
Irrationality	Rationality
Excess	Moderation
Inequality	Equality
Self-enhancement	Self-transcendence
Dream	Reality

Source: Author's elaboration.

However, over time the skepticism surrounding the mismatch between luxury and sustainability has faded. Luxury companies, indeed, understood articulating a strategy that includes sustainable practices behind luxury goods besides accomplishing national and international regulations can provide a competitive advantage. No matter their size and country of origin, most luxury companies have increased their commitment to social and environmental causes by engaging in CSR activities (Amatulli et al., 2021a; Batat, 2020; Batat & Manika, 2020). On the one hand, CSR activities allow luxury brand companies to meet stakeholders' expectations related to environmental and social responsibility behaviors. On the other hand, consumers make purchase decisions by observing the company's CSR and look for companies that can guarantee a joint effort on CSR activities and marketing plans and promptly communicate goals and targets.

Thus, the literature, from investigating the reasons for the incongruence between luxury and sustainability, started to focus on the touchpoints between the luxury and sustainability concepts. First, the literature reveals there is no ontological incompatibility between luxury and sustainability, since both definitions do not show an incongruence (Chevalier & Mazzalovo, 2020). If sustainability means "development that can meet the needs of the present without preventing future generations from doing the same", there are no reasons to believe that luxury companies cannot comply with this concept. In fact, authentic luxury is based on the "rejection of the profit at all cost", typical of the fast fashion market where companies strive to minimize costs as much as possible. Consequently, luxury and sustainability are fully compatible even when environmentally friendly processes generate higher costs. Then, Joy et al. (2012) argued that the durability and quality of luxury goods already demonstrate the connection between luxury and sustainability. Authentic luxury does not accept the "disposable" features typical of fast fashion, where the logic of economies of scale and planned obsolescence prevail. On the contrary, authentic luxury bases its success on the ability of products to last over time. Therefore, luxury is naturally suitable for providing direct benefits to consumers and indirect benefits to environmental resources. When companies meet consumer needs by offering good quality, durable, or recycled products at the same time, they benefit the environment and the collective well-being (Kapferer & Michaut-Denizeau, 2014).

In addition, the use of natural materials is an integral part of the identity of luxury brands: linen, silk, cotton, cashmere, wood, and precious stones are fundamental elements of the identity of some brands. The production of these materials generally involves a lower energy expenditure than producing by using synthetic materials and, above all, they are all recyclable. Producing with natural materials means not relocating the production process, to preserve the so-called country of origin factor. The country of origin represents the influence exerted by the historical, artistic, and cultural background of the country, on the process of choice and purchase of goods and services by consumers (Bertoli & Resciniti, 2013; Usunier, 2006). For example, Italy is closely linked to fashion, design and good food. Thus, when a luxury brand decides to allocate its production in Italy, it guarantees quality and safety to consumers, but is also a sustainable choice, especially considering the reduction of CO_2 emissions, which could be higher in the case of production in Asian countries. Finally, another factor that matches sustainability and luxury is the care towards employees' skills development and the perpetuation of cultural traditions. Hermes, Chanel, Bulgari, and many other brands have always implemented projects combining creativity and craftsmanship excellence (Chevalier & Mazzalovo, 2020).

Thus, all the reasons above-mentioned and represented in Figure 3 support[6] that luxury is the ideal basis for designing and marketing products that are intrinsically linked to social and environmental values, sustainable development, natural beauty, and excellence. In other words, we can confirm the match between luxury and sustainability, considering that luxury is by its nature ecological and, as such, can only be a promoter of sustainable development (Chevalier & Mazzalovo, 2020).

Figure 3. The matching between the concept of luxury and sustainability

Source: Author's elaboration based on Chevalier & Mazzalovo (2021).

2.4. The sustainable journey in the luxury market

Considering the global luxury market, corporate efforts to promote more sustainable businesses date to the first years of the twenty-first century. As stated by Gardetti & Torres (2017), since 2005, the commitment to sustainable practices has mainly affected jewelry companies, which increased their efforts in carrying out a more ethical business. Most luxury companies such as Bulgari, Chopard and Cartier became members of the Responsible Jewellery Council (RJC), an international regulatory body created in 2005 to strengthen consumer confidence in the jewelry sector, promoting respect for human rights and ethical practices, social and environmental responsibility throughout the supply chain.

Furthermore, since 2006 a series of scandals have also involved fashion systems with companies accused of harmful behavior towards employees or the environment, such as animal cruelty or a non-transparent supply chain. As a result, the exploration of sustainability immediately attracted managers' attention, enhancing their efforts to implement more sustainable measures to meet stakeholders' expectations, in addition to laying the foundations for memberships of no-profit associations in favor of conducting business in a more sustainable manner. First, in 2009 Patagonia and Walmart signed the Sustainable Apparel Coalition, a multi-stakeholder non-profit alliance among the leading companies that operate in the apparel industry, aiming to implement an index to measure the environmental impact of their products (Radhakrishnan, 2015). This represents the first significant effort of luxury companies toward a more sustainable way of conducting their business. Then, as shown in Figure 4, another important event that guides the attention of luxury brand companies is the Modern Slavery Act's approval in 2015. Subscribed by the UK Parliament, this law was signed with the aim of the fight against slavery in the UK. It requires all companies to manage a business – or part of their business – in the UK, including England and Wales, to publish an annual slavery and human trafficking statement, which must be approved by their board of directors and posted in a prominent place on their website (Hodkinson et al., 2021). Moreover, in the same period, "The Sustainable Development Goals" (officially known as "Transforming our World: The 2030 Agenda for Sustainable Development") by the United Nations increased the attention on sustainability. This document includes an intergovernmental set of 17 goals with 169 targets covering a broad range of sustainable development issues. Even if these goals do not affect the companies' business immediately, as the Modern Slavery Act did, they should be a guideline for developing future strategies. Indeed, companies should use the SDGs as a source of inspiration to implement a sustainable marketing plan (Hepner et al., 2020).

The attention to implementing more sustainable practices took off in 2019. The growing interest in sustainability is the result of many events. First, in 2018, the European Commission published a "Sustainable Finance Action Plan" to promote a financial system capable of supporting sustainable development from an economic, social, and environmental point of view (Zetzsche & Anker-Sorensen, 2022). Then, in December 2019, the 27 member countries of the European Union signed the Green Deal, an agreement containing a series of proposals to lead the EU policies on climate, energy, transport, and taxation towards reducing greenhouse gas emissions by at least 55% by 2030. Finally, the current interest in sustainability is affected by Covid 19. The advent of the pandemic provoked a systemic crisis that has proven once again the unsustainability of our economic model, which is struggling to restart due to the scarcity of resources. Consequently, the attention on sustainability increased among institutions and companies that made significant efforts to convert the current business model into a more sustainable manner (D'Arpizio & Levato, 2022).

Figure 4. The sustainable journey in the luxury brand market

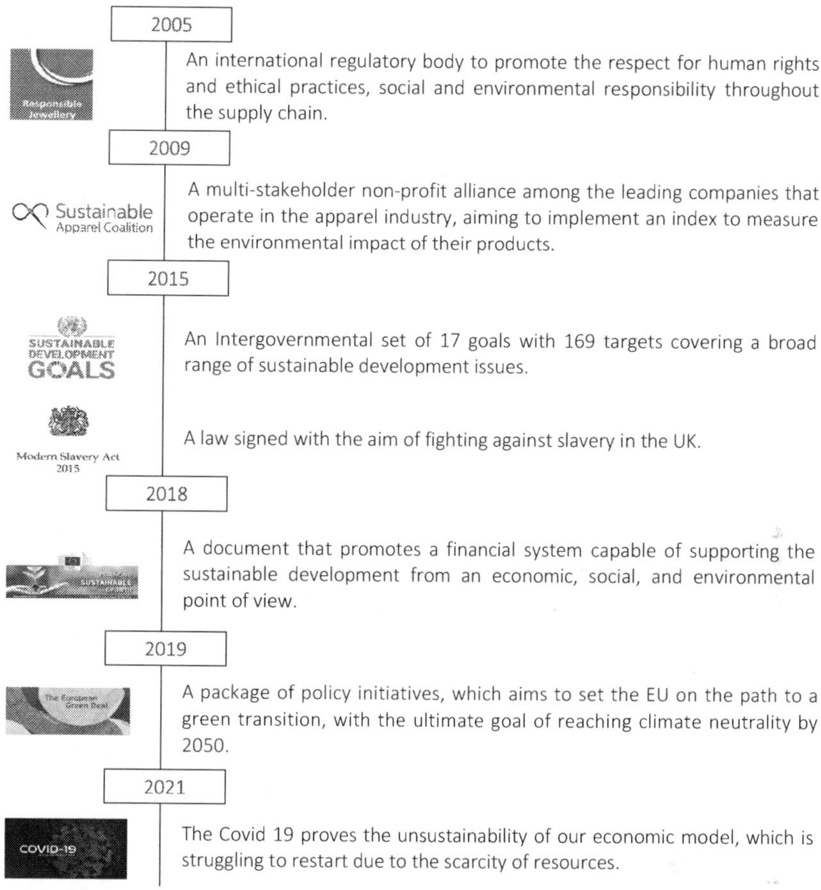

Source: Author's elaboration.

2.5. Sustainability in the luxury market from the perspective of the current literature

After analyzing why there is congruence between luxury and sustainability and explaining the journey of sustainability in the luxury market, in this section, we focus on the following question: "What are the insights provided by the academic literature on sustainability for luxury brand management?".

The articles published by top academic journals help in understanding the current evolution of sustainability in the luxury brand market. Particularly, the analysis of the literature reveals three areas of progress (Figure 5):[7]

1. Sustainable business model innovation.
2. Sustainability for managing employees.
3. Motives for sustainable consumption.

Figure 5. The area of evolution regarding sustainability in the luxury market

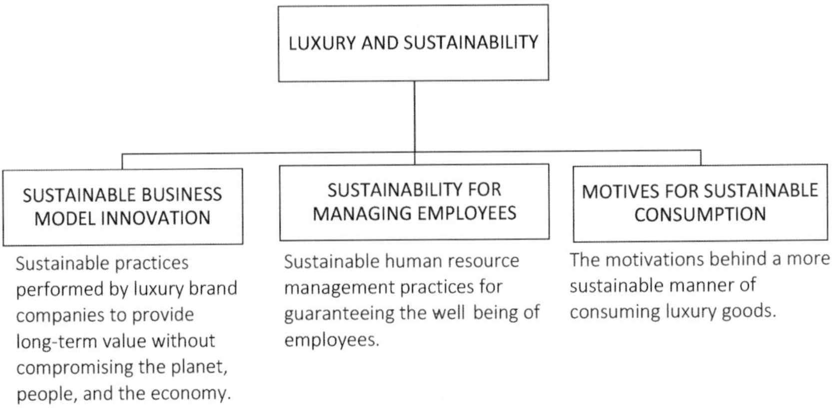

Source: Author's elaboration.

2.5.1. Sustainable business model innovation for luxury brands

The first area to advance knowledge on sustainability regards corporate social responsibility practices to provide long-term value without compromising the planet, people, and the economy. In recent times, more and more luxury brand companies have shown a real commitment to sustainability actions, considering both traditional and emerging luxury sectors. Although manufacturers and retailers initially have been reluctant to increase the production and sales of sustainable products (Campos Franco et al., 2019; Di Benedetto, 2017; Jaegler, 2016), nowadays luxury fashion companies demonstrate sound knowledge and skills in sustainability. The fashion system developed a growing commitment to sustainability, thanks to producers' movements, such as the actions of individual brands, designers, big retailers, and institutions in favor of consumers' well-being (Ertekin & Atik, 2020). Analyzing within CSR reports of luxury cosmetics companies it emerges the implementation of multiple objectives typical of a circular approach (eco-design, reuse, low energy consumption, zero emissions) (Fortunati et al., 2020). During the pandemic, even Michelin star restaurants

have implemented response strategies to contribute to collective well-being. We refer to philanthropic activities targeting the community's well-being, socially responsible business practices to support the food service actors and initiatives centered on consumers (Batat, 2020).
Some studies demonstrated that successfully implementing sustainable practices impacts the market positively. Bhattacharya et al. (2020) show how CSR initiatives during recessions increased the perceptions of brand value, especially actions such as charitable contributions, which signal higher brand quality to customers. Moreover, according to Faust, (2013) and Bernardi et al. (2022), companies can achieve a competitive advantage by being sustainable and innovative, while pursuing corporate solid values, cultural heritage, and stable relationships with the territory. Other academic papers try to shed light on companies' efforts to communicate sustainability. Hepner et al. (2020) demonstrate that information can be an essential selling point for more environmentally friendly consumers, so it is necessary to provide this information efficiently. However, the literature reveals that luxury brand companies still communicate sustainability in an ineffective way (Luo et al., 2021). Most luxury companies neither are used to providing any form of sustainability reports nor do they have sustainability departments. Policies and governance information is prioritized for public release over any supply chain information (Jestratijevic et al., 2020). For example, in the jewelry market, only 3% of print advertisements contain CSR messages (Pankiw et al., 2021). Another interesting theme is related to stakeholders' empowerment. Nayak et al. (2021) demonstrate that by collaborating with local artisans to create unique clothing lines, companies can promote the diversity of ethnic cultures. Regarding the hospitality industry, Sotomayor et al. (2021) suggest that activities such as education, training, health projects, and supporting local fair-trade suppliers and entrepreneurs, positively contribute to local communities' well-being. Zhang et al. (2019) conducting action research on residents' perceptions, reveal that the presence of luxury hotels is not always perceived as an opportunity for local communities. This is because residents may perceive hotel chains as a threat to the survival of ethnic communities, feeling that the empowerment of the population could move local people away from traditions.

2.5.2. Sustainable practices for luxury companies' employees

The second area of research focuses on the impact of sustainability on employees. All papers investigate sustainable human resource management practices, mainly in the hospitality sector. Empirical studies show that positive employees' perception of CSR activities increases employee engagement (Nazir & Islam, 2020a). As stated by Nazir & Islam (2020b) and Sharma et al. (2022), good CSR practices inside companies lead to increased employee motivation and job retention, which in turn positively affect business performance. Addressing employees' psychological needs for autonomy, competence, and relationship through CSR-specific activities motivates them to find their work engaging and carry out their activities innovatively (Farooq et al., 2022). Also, Sourvinou & Filimonau (2018) demonstrate that involving employees in a well-designed and perceived environmental management program can strengthen staff job satisfaction and organizational commitment. According to Peng & Lee (2019) and Raza et al. (2021), CSR practices directly affect voluntary pro-environmental employees' behavior, leading the staff to protective actions toward the environment. In contrast, occupational stress, such as unfair treatment, contributes significantly to turnover intention (Hwang et al., 2014). Finally, in recent years Han et al. (2021) demonstrated that green indoor atmospherics in luxury hotels enhance employees'' behavioral intentions.

2.5.3. Sustainable consumption in the luxury market

Finally, this subsection explores the third area of research that deepens our knowledge about sustainable consumption in the luxury brand market. Sustainable consumption[8] means responsible consumption, where the natural environment is respected, and resources are not used in ways that have destructive impacts on the planet. The less recent articles focused on sustainability in the luxury market revealed that luxury consumers did not value the sustainable practices of luxury brand companies when buying luxury products (Achabou & Dekhili, 2013). On the contrary, consumers' behavior was contradictory. While luxury consumers required luxury companies to act ethically (Arrington, 2019) they were unwilling to buy or pay more for ethical products or services (Baker et al., 2014). Kapferer & Michaut-Denizeau (2014) explained that at first consumers agreed luxury and sustainability were incompatible, especially considering sustainability's economic and social dimensions (Cheah et al., 2016). Moreover, Baker et al. (2014) suggested that products made from recycled materials discouraged consumption.

Nowadays, the situation has changed, and the attention to sustainability has grown thanks to the new generations of consumers, who show a real commitment to sustainable practices. Especially, they are the ones often asking luxury brand companies to increase their attention to managing a sustainable business.

From our analysis, it emerged that scholars opened the debate about sustainable luxury branding by exploring consumers' internal dynamics to understand antecedents, motives, perceptions, attitudes, and values related to luxury brands' consumption. Notably, publications deal with three main topics: motives for sustainable consumption, reasons for rental consumption and motives for second-hand consumption.

Rental consumption[9] and second-hand consumption[10] represent novel approaches to enjoying luxury brands, enabling an extended product lifecycle and fostering more sustainable practices, thus contributing to the development of more sustainable consumption patterns.

2.5.3.1. Motives for sustainable consumption

The literature review reveals several motives that lead to sustainable luxury consumption (Figure 6). First, environmental concerns play a crucial role in affecting luxury consumers' attitudes towards sustainability. Eco-friendly attributes influence positively consumers' evaluations of sustainable products (Perez et al., 2020; Robinot et al., 2021; Rosenbaum & Wong, 2015; Schill & Godefroit-Winkel, 2022) and their willingness to pay a premium price (Chia-Jung & Pei-Chun, 2014). Similarly, more integrated sustainability practices such as sustainable product innovations that include recycling, upcycling, and sustainable alternatives, affect the product and service demand of luxury brand consumers positively (Adıgüzel & Donato, 2021; Hemonnet-Goujot et al., 2022). Moreover, individuals give more importance to animals' welfare, resulting in less reluctance to reduce the proportion of real fur in clothes (Achabou & Dekhili, 2013). Consequently, luxury brands that incorporate sustainability into their business strategy by offering faux fur alternatives, instead of animal fur, significantly impact consumers' cognitive dissonance (Rolling et al., 2021).

According to Amatulli et al. (2021a), companies should not be limited to environmental sustainability, because generating benefits for customers, community, or employees increases consumers' willingness to buy sustainable products. Furthermore, the literature provides guidelines on how to engage consumers and avoid their skepticism or misunderstanding when communicating sustainability practices. A type of communication focused on sustainable practices may lead to a higher willingness to buy a product or book a room because sustainability enhances consumers' perceptions of companies' integrity (Amatulli et al., 2021b; Kang & Sung, 2021). Firms' eco-friendly efforts in advertisements generate favorable consumer attitudes and increase their behavioral intentions towards both hospitality and personal luxury goods companies (Lim et al., 2021). According to Shashi et al. (2021) "green text, green certification logo, green with visual cues, and green combination" affects consumers' attitudes towards luxury hospitality brands. In addition, Vilasanti et al. (2020) highlight that the combination of green messages and luxury brand positioning positively influences brand evaluation in the personal luxury goods market. Even when luxury bases its communication strategies on donations (Sengabira et al., 2020), especially environmental ones, such as planting trees or philanthropic deeds like donating to poverty, it benefits from positive brand evaluations (Karatzas et al., 2019). Considering consumers' skepticism towards sustainability, Sthapita et al. (2017) and Teah et al. (2022) revealed that consumers are less skeptical when values-driven CSR motives emerge, rather than egoistic-driven ones. Companies' CSR activities, guided by binding foundations, indeed, lead to more favorable attitudes than CSR activities conducted by individualizing foundations (Hang et al., 2021). Furthermore, Kapferer & Valette-Florence (2022) suggest that luxury brands need to implement guilt-reducing communication strategies. Notably, guilt plays a crucial role in the case of unsustainable luxury. A purchased luxury fashion product made in an unsustainable manner leads consumers to experience a higher sense of guilt over that product, generating negative word-of-mouth about the producer. Moreover, the risk of negative word-of-mouth spreading is more significant in countries characterized by a collectivistic and feminine orientation, rather than ones where an individualistic and masculine orientation prevails (Amatulli et al., 2021). Thus, as Kong et al. (2021) indicate, luxury brand advertisers should consider cultural settings when providing sustainability information. For example, in China, the need for exclusivity in sustainable luxury items is negatively related to consumers' purchase intentions, while the demand for conformity is positively related. On the contrary, in the UK, the relationship among the variables is reversed (Wang, 2021). Similarly, sustainability information negatively impacts the perceived quality of luxury in Saudi Arabia, while in France, no significant effect was observed (Dekhili et al., 2019). Finally, according to Rolling & Sadachar et al. (2018), Kapferer & Michaut-Denizeau (2020) and Rolling et al. (2021) even age influences consumer perceptions and attitudes toward sustainable luxury products.

Figure 6. Motives for sustainable consumption in the luxury market

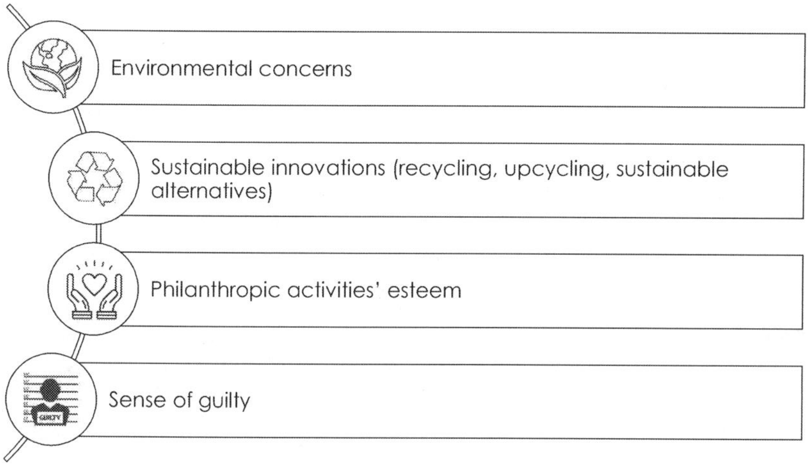

Source: Author's elaboration.

2.5.3.2. Motives for rental consumption

Luxury consumers, especially Millennials, have shown an increasing interest in emerging and more sustainable forms of consumption, including the no-ownership model, favored by rental platforms. We found several studies that deepen the motivations behind this new way of consuming luxury goods. From the analysis conducted by Vincent & Gaur (2021) fashion innovativeness, hedonic experience, economic, utilitarian, social, need for uniqueness, sustainability and no burden of ownership emerged as the eight reasons for using closet sharing. Pantano & Stylos (2020) discovered that consumers increased their attitude to show their social status through renting rather than owning luxurious apparel, based on five main motivations: the need to wear new clothes for a special event, inspirations created by the products/brands, possibility to explore a new way of consuming luxury goods, the need to make more sustainable choices, and to increase the life cycle of each luxury product. Finally, according to Jain (2019), the social projection value is the most significant predictor of intention to consume luxury fashion on a sharing basis. However, as the overall attitude toward luxury fashion rental consumption differs significantly across markets Mishra et al. (2021), motives for rental consumption request a further investigation to identify the specificities of the market under investigation.

2.5.3.3. Motives for second-hand consumption

Another emerging sustainable consumption practice that is rapidly growing is second-hand consumption.

Some authors, aiming to define the motives that lead luxury consumers to favor second-hand products instead of buying new ones, found that sustainability, environmental concerns, and past sustainable behavior affect second-hand consumption (Neerattiparambil & Belli, 2020). However, Ramkumar et al. (2021) discovered that when consumers shop online for second-hand clothing, they need more motivation than just environmental benefits. For example, Medalla et al. (2020) demonstrated that intrinsic characteristics and financial instability are the drivers of the second-hand consumption of Millennials. Moreover, Turunen et al. (2020) highlighted that social status can lead to a second-hand consumption choice. They demonstrated that social selling of second-online products generates an alteration to the symbolic value of the items stripped down to being objects of a transaction, giving consumers empowerment and a change in terms of their social role. Also included in this sub-section is the consumption of vintage items, and products of a particular era that evoke memories of the past and represent the fashion trend of a specific historical period. Vintage products, therefore, are second-hand products that, through their purchase, contribute to environmental well-being. However, these products appeal to consumers for personal reasons like self-confidence, a sense of fulfilment (Amatulli et al., 2018), fashion involvement and nostalgia proneness (Cervellon, 2013) in addition to sustainable motives.

2.6. Future challenges for studying sustainability in the luxury brand market

The debate about sustainability in the luxury market has increased in a few years, especially after the Covid-19 pandemic. The value of this chapter derives from the attempt to organize the knowledge about sustainability management in the luxury market. The analysis provided in this chapter reveals that luxury and sustainability are not perceived as incompatible concepts as in the past. On the one hand, luxury brand companies focused their efforts on managing a more sustainable business model that positively impacts the collective well-being. On the other hand, luxury brand consumers increased their attitude towards more sustainable consumption practices, including rental and second-hand consumption. Academics contributed to the issue with some publications, dealing with a wide range of topics, from papers mainly focused on sustainable consumer behavior, to others that analyze companies' practices.

Regarding consumers, recent papers provide information about motives, perceptions, and values that affect luxury brand consumption, the attitude to rental consumption and the consumption behavior in the second-hand luxury industry. In terms of organizational practices, some papers explore the positive effect of sustainable programs on employees' performance and focus on "deep" sustainability, which means integrating CSR into the business model. Finally, some papers test sustainable practices in different countries to understand how cultural settings affect sustainable behavior.

However, the integration of sustainability in the luxury brand market has just begun and requires further investigation from scholars. Considering the stream about the sustainable business model and innovation, a more in-depth investigation is needed. First, only one paper investigates the impact of sustainability on luxury brand companies' financial and economic performance (Bhattacharya et al., 2020). Thus, a correlation between financial performance and ESG indexes also requires further investigation. Even the topic of communication is not entirely covered. According to several authors, how to communicate sustainability, especially online (social media, websites), is a gap to explore more deeply. Finally, the stream of sustainable development may be improved by considering new technologies like blockchain or artificial intelligence applied to the supply chain. Considering the area of research about employees, all the papers investigate employees' well-being in the hospitality industry. Further research may consider other sectors, like for instance the personal luxury goods sector, where most brands firmly commit.

Finally, the stream of research dealing with luxury brand consumers and motives for sustainable consumption is undoubtedly the most covered during the last few years, as more than half of the papers are focused on it. However, some issues need additional exploration. Some papers analyzed consumers' motives for sustainable consumption, by focusing on environmental sustainability. According to Amatulli et al. (2021a) a sustainability practice that benefits customers, the community, or the employees increases consumers' willingness to buy sustainable products. Thus, new research on consumers' motives for sustainability may deal with other sustainable practices (women's quota, stakeholders' empowerment, employees' well-being, etc.). Another topic to cover deals with customer experience. Han et al. (2021) demonstrated that managers who develop and stage memorable consumer-centered experiences orient consumers towards sustainable fashion consumption. Hence, developing the right customer experience may increase luxury consumers' attention to sustainable consumption, especially in the online context. Moreover, the stream of research about motives for sustainable consumption lacks studies that investigate the existence of a link between high/excellent quality and sustainability. Generally, if the good has a very high quality, its durability is higher. Consequently, it is more sustainable because it will be replaced less frequently. This is the case of luxury brands that, differently from fast fashion goods, have high quality and for this reason, are more durable and therefore more sustainable. In the future, we welcome research that uses experiments to explore if luxury consumers perceive a link between luxury/higher quality and sustainability.

In general, most studies focus on personal luxury goods and hospitality sectors. We encourage future studies exploring sustainability in emerging luxury sectors such as wine and spirit or gourmet food and fine dining. Furthermore, surveys and experiment results are more common research methods when looking at the methodologies used. Considering the topic under investigation, we suggest analyzing the case with emerging methods. For example, ethnography (and netnography) can explore the online community of luxury consumers and their approach to sustainability. At the same time, QCA (qualitative comparative analysis) may analyze the combination of sustainable practices that better impact the financial performance of luxury brands.

Figure 7. The future research agenda for luxury brand management

Source: Author's elaboration.

This chapter collects the body of research on sustainable luxury to illustrate a brief overview of the definition of sustainability and its relationship with the luxury brand market. The chapter clarifies how luxury and sustainability are related and describes the most significant achievements in sustainable development in the luxury market and the current evolution of sustainability for managing luxury brands. However, in the chapter's conclusion some issues remain uncovered (Figure 7). In the following chapters, we aim to deal with the research gap concerning the innovation of sustainable business models by investigating the extent to which luxury brand companies implement sustainable business models and how to communicate sustainability, with a focus on online communication (social media and website).

Notes

1 The Sustainable Development Goals (SDGs) are 17 interconnected goals, defined by the United Nations in the Agenda 2030 to achieve a better and more sustainable future for the world. The official launch of the Sustainable Development Goals coincided with the beginning of 2016 and companies should be able to reach the settled goals by 2030. More information about the SDGs can be found by accessing the following link: https://www.un.org/sustainabledevelopment/sustainable-development-goals/.

2 The Environmental Protection Agency (EPA) is a federal agency established by the Nixon Administration for the protection of public health and the environment. It is the responsibility of the EPA to develop and enforce environmental laws, inspect the environment, and provide technical support to minimize threats and assist with recovery planning. https://www.epa.gov/.

3 A stakeholder is a person or organization that has an interest in a company and can either affect or be affected by the business.

4 The Brundtland Report is a document published in 1987 by the World Commission on Environment and Development (WCED) that defines for the first time what sustainable development is. https://www.are.admin.ch/are/en/home/media/publications/sustainable-development/brundtland-report.html.

5 Figure 2 considers the article of Kapferer (2010) "All that Glitter is Not Green" to show the inconsistency between luxury and sustainability. Particularly, in the article, the author explores the concepts of luxury and sustainability, pointing out that "the challenge for sustainable luxury is the fact that its symbolic nature of irrationality, excess and inequality is not aligned with the symbolic nature of sustainable development,

which represents equalitarian and humanitarian values, and encourage us to be frugal in our consumption".

6 Figure 2 shows the motives of the compatibility between luxury and sustainability according to the literature and the work published by Chevalier & Mazzalovo (2021).

7 Appendix 1 explains the research protocol implemented to identify the three topics of research about luxury and sustainability. We perform a structured review, a research methodology that allows scholars to integrate the literature review with the bibliometric analysis.

8 SDG 12 is titled "Responsible consumption and production". This SDG aims to ensure sustainable consumption and production patterns to protect the environment and resources. More information about the SDG can be found by accessing the following link: https://www.un.org/sustainabledevelopment/sustainable-consumption-production/.

9 Rental consumption is an emerging form of collaborative consumption defined as "a transaction in which one party offers an item to another party for a fixed time in exchange for money and in which there is no change of ownership" (Durgee & O'Connor, 1995, 90). It is an effective sustainable solution because renting clothes increases the life of the garments and reduces fashion waste. By 2023, the online clothing rental market is expected to reach USD1.96 billion with a compound annual growth rate (CAGR) of 10.76%.

10 The second-hand consumption consists of the purchase of items that has been previously owned and used. According to the BCG & Altagamma (2023), the second-hand luxury market continues to accelerate (65% interested in purchasing preowned luxury, +5pp vs 2019).

Chapter 3

A STRATEGIC APPROACH FOR MANAGING SUSTAINABILITY IN THE LUXURY MARKET

Fabrizio Mosca and Valentina Chiaudano

ABSTRACT: *This chapter clarifies to what extent luxury brands have integrated sustainability into the business model. The integrated CSR framework, using the definitions of residual and integrated CSR practices, serves as a valuable tool for categorizing sustainable practices, spanning from basic to highly integrated initiatives. The findings enrich the existing knowledge on sustainable luxury by shedding light on how luxury brands can enhance their influence on consumers and community welfare through the adoption of integrated sustainable practices.*

3.1. Introduction

> *"Real luxury is based on authenticity and sincerity – the product is almost secondary to the experience. But if your products are not in sync with a higher set of values, then you aren't going to survive in this business".*
>
> François-Henri Pinault, Kering CEO.

In the last 20 years, the pressure exerted by the regulations toward sustainability has grown and keeps growing day by day. Consequently, sustainability practices are getting more and more attention from all stakeholders, whose concerns about environmental and social issues have reached new heights, resulting in growth expectations and more complex needs (Freeman & Velamuri, 2008). Notably, consumers are becoming more aware of how their consumption choices can influence the environment and the community they belong to. This is especially true in the cases of Millennials and Generation Z, who among all consumer groups have shown a sensitivity to sustainable behaviors (Batat, 2019a; Kapferer & Michaut-Denizeau, 2020). When Millennials and Gen Z look for products, they value companies that promote equity, inclusion, diversity, and social impact. They prefer brands to do better, not just "less bad" (D'Arpizio et al., 2022).

As a result, companies can no longer rely on implementing sustainable standards or doing marketing activities purely to improve their reputation through CSR. Young consumers expect companies to integrate sustainability into operations at the corporate level (D'Arpizio et al., 2022). The integrated CSR approach enables companies to transform their business models to include ethical, environmental, and social dimensions in their values, methods, codes, and actions (Freeman et al., 2010). Implementing an integrated CSR model empowers businesses to provide authentic, credible, and fair services to their employees and communities. However, according to sustainable luxury research (Athwal et al., 2019; Kunz et al., 2020), few studies explain how luxury brands integrate sustainability into their corporate strategies and business models to effectively contribute to individual and collective well-being. This chapter tries to fill this gap by exploring the CSR activities of luxury brand companies. These endeavors applied the CSR integrated framework that leveraged the stakeholder theory of Freeman (2010) providing the guidelines to identify the sustainable activities performed by luxury brand companies.

The chapter is structured as follows. First, we introduce the concept of CSR. Then, by explaining the differences between residual and integrated CSR, we describe the CSR framework that guides the analysis of the CSR actions implemented by luxury brand companies. There are three main categories of CSR activities, according to the framework: standards and norms, strategic philanthropy, and integrated outputs. While companies implement a more residual approach to CSR with standards and norms, CSR efforts grow when companies move toward strategic philanthropy and integrated outputs.

3.2. Foundations of corporate social responsibility

Despite years of intense academic research and institutional work, finding a globally accepted and comprehensive definition of CSR is still tricky. Several business experts and academics stated that CSR is a dynamic and ever-changing concept (Jin & Lee, 2019; Mosca & Civera, 2017b; Vallester et al., 2012).

The first practices related to the sustainable and responsible management of the business date back to the Industrial Revolution (Carroll, 2015; Visser, 2010). In the mid 1800 public opinions started to recognize the need to solve social problems in factories, such as wages, bad working conditions, and child labor. Then, the awareness about the role of sustainability increased when the first American corporation was born in the 1920s. At that time managers realized that their actions and decisions affect not only the lives of their shareholders, [1] but also the well-being of employees, customers, and, more generally, of society. Thus, in 1947 the first code of business ethics was born. Then, in the 1950s the corporate social responsibility concept entered the business lexicon (Brondoni, 2014). In 1953, Bowen, who is considered the father of CSR, gave the first definition of CSR. In his book titled "Social Responsibility of the Businessman", the author stated that CSR was a set of mandatory rules that both managers and business owners had to observe when pursuing policies, making decisions, or elaborating strategic actions to meet the expectations and values of society. His vision of CSR reflected the awareness that companies could no longer ignore the significant impact of business on communities (Carroll, 2009). However, up to the 1950s, the increasing interest in CSR was not followed by practical implications, while remaining linked to a purely theoretical field.

Further attempts to define CSR were made in the 60s when the birth of the first environmental movements generated increasing pressure against the exploitation of natural resources (Visser, 2010). At that time, public opinion recognized the fundamental role of companies in environmental and social disputes. Thus, in the 1960s Davis (1976) outlined CSR as a set of actions and management decisions that should go partially beyond the mere economic interest. It was only in the 1970s that concrete CSR programs within companies began to focus on diverse activities rather than solely on philanthropy (Muirhead, 1999).

The decade that goes from the 1970s to the 1980s was characterized by an intense debate on the real responsibilities of business, as a trade-off between economic interests linked to the company's owners and social interests that concern the well-being of employees, consumers, communities, and institutions. Johnson (1971) postulated that a company, making strategic decisions, had to balance various interests: economic, social, environmental, and employee welfare. Particularly, in the 1970s and 1980s the contribution to CSR definition came by two opposed theories: Shareholder Theory (Friedman, 1970) and stakeholder theory (Freeman, 2010).

Friedman, who first conceptualized the shareholder theory in an article published in the New York Times Magazines said that "the social responsibility of business is to increase its profits". He thought that company and responsibility were placed solely on the economic level, and companies did not need to perform any other achievement except the interests of the shareholders, the people for which the company was formed. According to Friedman (1970), all the meanings and implications of CSR depended on the willingness of companies to give up a part of their economic gain to achieve social objectives.

In contrast to the shareholder theory, Freeman introduced the stakeholder theory, which has become a landmark in defining a more holistic vision of CSR since the 1980s. As stated by Freeman (2010), the main mistake of previous theories regarded the idea that the sole purpose of business was to make profits to satisfy the shareholders (Freeman & Dmytriyev, 2017). By introducing the stakeholder theory, Freeman emphasized a new approach to managing business that required balancing the needs of all stakeholders. Stakeholder theory considers the company as an open social system aimed at realizing the interests of its owners while meeting the expectations of all other stakeholders. Notably, he divided stakeholders into two categories: primary and secondary stakeholders. The primary stakeholders are suppliers, consumers, investors, employees, financial institutions, associations and the community. They represent the groups of people or organizations whose relationship with the company is fundamental for the survival of the company itself. Instead, the secondary stakeholders are the competitors, media, public opinion, and public institutions. Secondary stakeholders influence the company's activities, but they are not essential to the survival of the enterprise. He stated that companies must try to meet the needs of all their stakeholders, not just those of shareholders. The result is a concept of CSR characterized by a broad expansion of the responsibilities of companies, which go beyond their borders and cannot be limited to maximizing profits. Therefore, the stakeholder theory affirms that the company, with its activities, is responsible for generating and increasing wealth, not only for itself, but, above all, for society and, consequently, for the economic system (Carroll, 2009). This holistic vision of CSR proposed by Freeman represents a valuable guideline that nowadays leads companies – no matter the sector or country of origin – to adopt socially responsible behaviors that favor all stakeholder well-being.

3.3. From residual to integrated CSR

As emerged from paragraph 3.2, from being initially considered an expensive and unnecessary practice, CSR has become one of the most accepted concepts within the business world. Today most companies establish specific guidelines and divisions dedicated to managing sustainability.

But an overarching question is: "To what extent can companies take actions that lead to stakeholder well-being?". According to scholars, in most cases, companies implement superficial CSR actions with the intent of enhancing corporate reputation and meeting stakeholder demands, rather than contributing actively to well-being by reformulating the traditional business model in a more sustainable way (Civera et al., 2019; Hoque et al., 2018). Freeman calls this kind of sustainable approach residual CSR. Residual CSR, for instance, is when companies limit their CSR efforts to actions aiming at meeting voluntary or compulsory rules imposed by governmental organizations. Due to its poor effects on society's well-being, residual CSR activities have been recognized as ineffective means of achieving a good level of sustainability commitment within a company.

Thus, Freeman (2010) suggests performing integrated CSR to reach a tangible, positive CSR development. In contrast to residual CSR, integrated CSR is rooted in stakeholder theory. By performing integrated CSR actions, companies go beyond simply responding to society's demands. In integrated CSR, company efforts aim to integrate environmental and social issues into everyday business strategies (Silvestre & Fonseca, 2020). Therefore, it is only through an integrated CSR approach that a company can simultaneously meet both stakeholder interests and its financial goals. Leveraging on the definition of residual and integrated CSR proposed by Freeman et al. (2010), this chapter uses a framework proposed by Mosca and Civera (2017b) as a reference model to distinguish activities that can be considered effective CSR integration or not. The framework structures the integration of CSR into three dimensions: standards and norms, strategic philanthropy, and integrated output (Figure 1).

Figure 1. The integrated CSR Framework

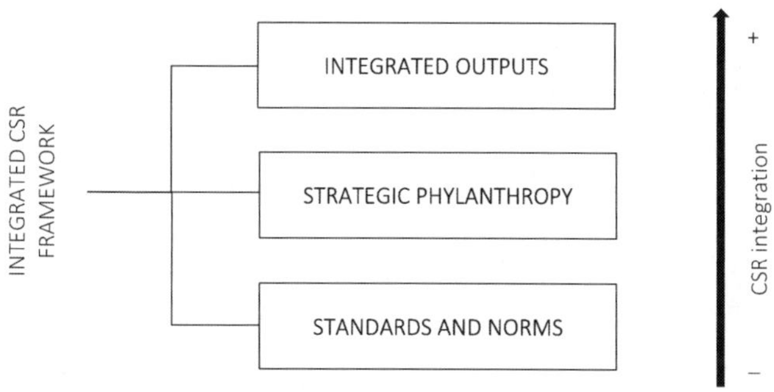

Source: Adapted from Mosca & Civera (2017b).

The first dimension, standards and norms, include all national and international standards that a company can implement for the environment, quality, ethics, people, and accounting. Over time, due to the growth of competition and the increasing attention to sustainability from public opinion, most standards became compulsory. Thus, standards and norms now remain a residual tool at the service of communication (Mosca & Civera, 2017b) and are not a source of competitive advantage for luxury brand companies. The second dimension, strategic philanthropy, marks a step forward in CSR's integrated business model. The term "strategic" applied to this field emphasizes a philanthropic approach that is tied and consistent with the company's core business (Porter & Kramer, 2002). Hence, strategic philanthropy involves supporting causes of social concern pursued by third sector organizations or causes in the arts, culture, and sports that are relevant and coherent to the company's core business. The more related and consistent these activities are with the company's core business, the more the CSR approach can be integrated.

Finally, the third dimension of the integrated CSR framework, integrated outputs, is the maximum expression of the integration of CSR into the core business of companies and aims to redefine the business model itself. Integrated outputs represent a concrete integration of social, ethical, and environmental practices into products/services, processes, and policies, going beyond the simple integration of ethical and social values into the mission and vision of companies. This means, for example, adopting principles of circular economy, like the reconfiguration of the materials used for production, or recycling. Moreover, it entails a new way of dealing with stakeholders, towards a cooperative decision-making process, and defining programs and policies aimed at promoting the involvement of the communities, empowering them, and increasing their autonomy, especially in long and complex supply chains. Thus, the company's CSR efforts grow when a company moves from a residual approach with standards and norms to a strategic philanthropic effort and then integrated outputs.

We use the integrated CSR framework to create a checklist (Table 1) that helps us analyzing CSR's activities of luxury brand companies. More details about the methodology approach for the checklist's creation can be found in Appendix 2.

Table 1. The checklist for testing the integration of CSR of luxury brands

Dimensions	Factors
1. Standards and norms	Environmental standards Quality standards People standards Economic and social reporting
2. Strategic philanthropy	Sponsorship of artistic or cultural initiatives Donations Cause related marketing Creating and managing foundations Community project Employee volunteering time donations
3. Integrated outputs	The use of new or recycled raw materials Traceability of the supply chain Capacity to reduce the use of materials, energy, or water, and to find more eco-efficient solutions Reducing environmental emission Employees' training and development policy Welfare policies to benefit employees Code of Ethics

Source: Adapted from Mosca & Civera (2017b).

3.4. Standards and norms for sustainability in the luxury brand market

Companies that operate in the luxury market started to feel compelled to contribute to society's well-being by meeting a set of national and international standards concerning the sphere of the environment, quality, ethics, employees, and economic and social reporting. As previously anticipated, this dimension of the integrated CSR framework is no longer a source of competitive advantage, but it represents a minimum requirement for companies with the ambition of competing globally. While standards and norms require companies to meet specific environmental, social, and economic metrics, they do not imply changes in strategies at the corporate level. Table 2 shows a general overview of the standards included in the checklist. Then the chapter explores more in-depth each standard category.

Table 2. Standards and norms in the luxury brand market

Dimensions	Factors	Example of Standards
1. Standards and norms	Environmental standards	ISO14001, ISO5001, LEED certification, GOTS, FSC
	Quality standards	ISO9001, ISO22716
	People standards	SA8000, ISO45001, Global Compact
	Economic and social reporting	GRI, AA1000, SASB

Source: Authors' elaboration.

3.4.1. Environmental standards

Environmental standards are voluntary or compulsory rules designed by national or international organizations for environmental protection including, for example, prohibitions of specific activities, monitoring schedules, and permits for land or raw materials used. Luxury companies apply different environmental standards that range from general measures, such as ISO, to other certifications related to specific sectors (Table 3).

Concerning the ISO standards,[2] the certifications are not mandatory, but voluntary. Some organizations decide to implement the ISO standards for the benefits they provide to the company itself, while others use the ISO certifications as residual CSR marketing tools that show companies' commitment to better energy management. ISO14001 is an international standard that defines the minimum requirements for the environmental management system. This standard demonstrates that the organization has an adequate management system to monitor the environmental impacts of its activities, and systematically seeks improvement in a consistent, effective, and sustainable way.

ISO 5001 is an international standard that attests to the efficient use of energy thanks to the development of an energy management system. Companies that hold the ISO 5001 ensure the development of a well-defined energy strategy that includes consumption analysis, setting of objectives, targets and programs, operational control, performance monitoring and measurement.

Then, most luxury companies applied for the LEED certification, an acronym for Leadership in Energy and Environmental Design, a voluntary certification program developed by the US Green Building Council, which can be applied to any type of building and covers the entire life cycle of the building, from the design to the construction. The LEED certification promotes a sustainability-oriented approach, recognizing the performance of buildings through energy and water saving, reduction of CO_2 emissions, improvement of the ecological quality of the interior, of the materials and resources used, quality of the design, and the location's choice.

Considering luxury apparel, companies seek to align with the Sustainable Development Goals (SDGs) of the 2030 Agenda by applying some environmental standards that safeguard animal welfare. The most common include the Global Organic Textile Standard (GOTS), the Sustainable Fibre Alliance for Cashmere (SFA), the Leather Working Group Certification (LWG) and some standards proposed by the Textile Exchange[3] (The Responsible Alpaca Standard, the Responsible Mohair Standard, the Responsible Wool Standards and the Organic Content Standard). Another standard adopted by most luxury apparel companies is the Global Recycle Standard (GRS), which certifies the use of recycled materials in compliance with environmental and social criteria. Companies that operate in the hard luxury sector, instead, meet the voluntary standard proposed by the Responsible Jewellry Council (RJC) that works with members worldwide to create a more sustainable supply chain. Finally, the perfumes and cosmetics sector companies meet the Union for Ethical Biotrade Certification (UB-ET), which aims to ensure companies respect ethical sourcing practices for ingredients and the Roundtable on Sustainable Palm Oil (RSPO), on palm oil sustainability.

Finally, most luxury brand companies are FSC-certified, which means luxury companies make products and packaging from sustainably managed forests that benefit society, the environment, and the economy.

Table 3. List of environmental certifications adopted by luxury brand companies

Logo	Standard	Purpose
ISO 14001:2015	ISO 14001	The ISO 14001 international standard defines the minimum requirements for the environmental management system.
ISO ISO 50001	ISO 5001	The ISO 5001 ensures the development of a well-defined energy strategy.

continued

Logo	Standard	Purpose
	LEED	The Leadership in Energy and Environmental Design (LEED) recognizes the performance of buildings through energy and water saving, reduction of CO_2 emissions, improvement of the ecological quality of the interior, quality of the materials resources, design, and the location's choice.
	GRS	The Global Organic Textile Standard (GOTS) defines the requirements for organic textiles. The standard certifies textiles are made with sustainable raw materials, ecologically and socially responsible manufacture, and labelling.
	GOTS	The Global Organic Textile Standard (GOTS) defines the requirements for organic textiles. The standard certifies textiles are made by sustainable raw materials, ecologically and socially responsible manufacture, and labelling.
	RAS	The Responsible Alpaca Standard (RAS) ensures that farmers and ranchers meet animal welfare, land management, and social requirements.
	RMS	The Responsible Mohair Standard (RMS) ensures that farmers and ranchers meet animal welfare, land management, and social requirements.
	RWS	The Responsible Wool Standard (RWS) ensures that farmers and ranchers meet animal welfare, land management, and social requirements.
	OCS	The Organic Content Standard (OCS) is a voluntary international standard that establishes the requirements for chain of custody and third-party certification of organic materials.
	SFA	The Sustainable Fibre Alliance (SFA) standard ensures the production of internationally traded cashmere is carried out exclusively by using sustainable practices, reducing environmental impact, and ensuring fair financial compensation for all parties involved along the supply chain.

continued

Logo	Standard	Purpose
LEATHER WORKING GROUP	LWG	The Leather Working Group (LWG) is a global multi-stakeholder community committed to responsible leather production.
Regenerative Organic Certified™	ROC	The Regenerative Organic Certified™ (ROC) is standard for food, textiles, and personal care ingredients. ROC™ farms and products meet high standards in the world for soil health, animal welfare and farmworker fairness.
rj RESPONSIBLE JEWELLERY COUNCIL	RJC	The Responsible Jewellery Council is the global membership and standards body for responsible jewellery throughout the entire supply chain – from mine to retail.
CERTIFIED SUSTAINABLE PALM OIL RSPO	RSPO	The Roundtable on Sustainable Palm Oil (RSPO) is the leading convening body that develops and sets the standards for palm oil sustainability and enables palm oil certification.
FSC	SFC	The FSC (Forest Stewardship Council) ensures that products come from responsibly managed forests that provide environmental, social, and economic benefits.
UNION FOR ETHICAL BIOTRADE SOURCING WITH RESPECT	UBET	UEBT is a non-profit organization that supports ethical sourcing. Companies certificated UBET employed ethical ingredient sourcing from biodiversity in their efforts to restore the environment and ensure a brighter future for humans. The purpose of Ubet is to support the creation of a world where biodiversity and all people can prosper.

Source: Authors' elaboration.

3.4.2. Quality standards

According to Kapferer (2010), by nature, luxury companies adhere to sustainable quality standards by manufacturing in-house, rather than outsourcing production, to maintain quality standards throughout the entire supply chain. Joy et al. (2010) also agree that the link between luxury and sustainability depends on the durability and quality of luxury goods.

Although luxury companies meet quality standards by nature, from non-financial reporting, it emerges that most luxury companies adhere to

ISO 9001. This standard represents the international reference for the Quality Management System (QMS) to respond simultaneously to the need for increasing the effectiveness and efficiency of processes and improving the competitiveness in the markets through the improvement of customer satisfaction and loyalty.

The primary purpose of ISO 9001 is, in fact, the pursuit of customer satisfaction for the products and services provided, as well as the continuous optimization of business performance, by ensuring the maintenance and improvement of the quality of its goods in the long term.

Thanks to the strong consumer orientation, the implementation of this standard ensures the supply of products and services in line with the market requirements. The standard does not specify what quality-related goals are or how to meet customer needs but requires organizations to define those goals and continually improve their processes to achieve them.

Considering luxury companies that compete in the perfume and cosmetic market, most meet ISO 22716. It is the first international standard that sets the principles for the application of good manufacturing practices in companies that produce cosmetic products. ISO 22716 applies to the production, control, storage, and shipping processes of cosmetic products. It does not apply, however, to research and development and product distribution activities.

3.4.3. People standards

People standards help luxury companies to certify the extent of their positive impact on people both in terms of human rights and human resource management.

Regarding human rights, all luxury brands adhere to the current primary legislation and guiding principles proposed by the United Nations. Most luxury companies act following the United Nations Global Compact, the Universal Declaration of Human Rights and OECD Guidelines for Multinational Enterprises (Table 4).

Moreover, most companies adopt the SA 8000 which shows when companies meet certain requirements that attest to socially responsible behavior in different areas related to child labor, prevention for the health and safety of workers, freedom of association and bargaining, discrimination, disciplinary procedures, working hours, and remuneration.

Considering employee management, we found most luxury companies act according to ISO 45001 which replaces, from March 2018, the previous OHSAS[4] 18001. ISO 45001 aims to improve occupational safety and health performance, as this standard requires organizations to look beyond short-term issues related to workers' health and safety and to consider what society, in general, expects from the organization in terms of responsibility. It applies to all organizations that want to formalize a management system that aims to eliminate or reduce the risks of accidents when performing their activities. In other words, this standard attests that companies adopt risk management criteria related to the health and safety of employees.

The people standards also include the code of conduct. This document is a charter of moral rights and duties that defines ethical and social norms that people who work inside the company or collaborate with it must observe. It is a voluntary and non-binding instrument under the law that constitutes a statement of values and intentions that the organization intends to pursue. The code of conduct introduces a clear and explicit definition of ethical and social responsibilities that allows the prevention of irresponsible or unlawful behaviors of people who work in the name of or on behalf of the company. In most cases, the company imposed its code of conduct not only on its employees but also on suppliers. A supplier code of conduct's major objective is to ensure financial and social transparency throughout the supply chain to create responsibility for everyday workplace issues like environmental effects, employee health and safety, and human rights.

Table 4. List of people standards adopted by luxury brand companies

Logo	Standard	Purpose
SA8000	SA8000	The SA8000 acronym of social accountability is an international ethical standard aimed at certifying certain aspects concerning CSR that includes the respect for human rights, labor law protection against child exploitation, safety, and health in the workplace.
ISO 45001:2018	45001	The ISO 45001:2018 outlines the specifications for an occupational health and safety (OH&S) management system and provides instructions for its application, enabling organizations to provide safe and healthy workplaces by proactively enhancing their OH&S performance and preventing work-related injury and illness.
United Nations Global Compact	United Nations Global Compact	The United Nations Global Compact promotes human rights, regulates the entire supply chain labor standards, protects the environment, and combats corruption.

continued

Logo	Standard	Purpose
	Universal Declaration of Human Rights	The Universal Declaration of Human Rights (UDHR) is a document drafted by delegates from all around the world with varying legal and cultural backgrounds to define the fundamental human rights to be universally safeguarded.
	OECD Guidelines for Multinational Enterprises	The OECD Guidelines for Multinational Enterprises help ensure that MNEs act in harmony with the policies of the countries in which they operate and with societal expectations.

Source: Authors' elaboration.

3.4.4. Economic and social reporting

The corporate sustainability disclosure landscape has become increasingly complicated over time. Clarity and simplification were demanded by companies and investors. Thus, some international non-profit organizations created sustainable performance reporting standards to conform to the non-financial reporting procedures of all companies in the world. Economic and social reporting aims to provide companies and stakeholders with reporting procedures designed to evaluate and compare sustainable performances.

As emerged from our analysis, most luxury brands meet the Global Reporting Initiative (GRI) and the reporting method offered by the Sustainability Accounting Standards Board (SASB) However, we can find companies that decided to create their own economic and social reporting tools (Table 5).

The Global Reporting Initiative (GRI) is an independent international organization founded in Boston in 1997, currently based in Amsterdam, and a pioneer in reporting related to sustainable efforts of companies of all sizes, sectors, and countries of the world. Adopting a multi-stakeholder approach, the GRI has created one of the most internationally recognized frameworks for sustainability reporting. It proposes a series of guidelines for the detection of environmental, social, and governance performances of companies, helping to make them comparable. In this way, the GRI principles represent a valid comparison tool, useful to different categories of corporate stakeholders to carry out their investment assessments.

As previously anticipated, the other reporting standards are proposed by the Sustainability Accounting Standards Board (SABS) founded in 2011. The SASB Standards define the subset of environmental, social, and governance issues that have the highest impact on companies' financial performance, by dividing them into 77 industries. Thus, the main difference between GRI and SASB refers to the area of application. While the GRI Standards are designed to be used by organizations in any sector, the SASB Standards are sector-specific and identify distinctive disclosure topics for each of the 77 industries.

Moreover, in the case of Kering, the company created an innovative economic and social reporting tool called the Environmental Profit & Loss (EP&L). The EP&L is designed to quantify and value the environmental effects of a company's operations as well as those of its supply chain management. The tool indicates important areas where a business can prioritize and concentrate its efforts to reduce its impact on the environment in which Kernig's brands operate. Every year, Kering posts the EP&L methodology and the Group's consolidated EP&L results on its website to share information with stakeholders.

Finally, the ongoing changes related to sustainable reporting represent a tricky issue for companies that should stay up to date to implement the most recent legislation. Now, we find companies such as Rolex and Chanel that have decided not to publish their sustainability reports. However, in Europe, the Corporate Sustainability Reporting Directive (CSRD), scheduled to be implemented by the beginning of 2024, will increase the number of companies required to report on sustainability. Notably, it mandates non-financial disclosure to all companies with more than 500 employees and more detailed reporting requirements on companies' impact on the environment, human rights, and sustainability risks.[5] Thus, luxury companies that have not provided stakeholders with sustainable reporting requirements yet, need to set new procedures dedicated to social and economic reporting to remain in line with the current European legislation.

Table 5. List of economic and social reporting certifications adopted by luxury brand companies

Logo	Standard	Purpose
GRI	GRI	The Global Reporting Initiative (GRI) is an independent organization founded in Boston in 1997 that provides companies with a universal common language to describe their sustainable efforts.
SASB	SASB	The Sustainability Accounting Standards Board (SABS) is a non-profit organization founded in 2011 in the US to identify the subset of environmental, social, and governance issues most relevant to sustainability that are reasonable to impact a company's operational and financial performance and risk profile.
KERING	EP&L	EP&L is the system created by the Kering Group to identify environmental risks and opportunities for the company. This system enables Kering to make more informed decisions about how it interacts with stakeholders and can better support natural capital.

Source: Authors' elaboration.

3.5. Strategic philanthropy activities pursued by luxury brand companies

Strategic philanthropy represents a further step of CSR integration after the standards and norms, as at this stage companies have chosen to broaden their objectives from the mere application of rules to support causes of social interest, cultural initiatives, or sports events. In other words, strategic philanthropy includes all actions that help the company to give back to stakeholders, including sponsorship, donations, cause related marketing, community projects, managing a foundation, and employees volunteering (Table 6).

The term "strategic" used in this field emphasizes the presence of a philanthropic approach closely connected and consistent with the company's mission and core business. Thus, social causes supported should be chosen in areas where the company can maintain a competitive advantage.

Table 6. Strategic philanthropy activities in the luxury brand market

Dimensions	Factors
2. Strategic philanthropy	Sponsorship of artistic, cultural, or sporting initiatives Donations Cause related marketing Creating and managing foundations Community projects Employee volunteering

Source: Authors' elaboration.

3.5.1. Sponsorship of artistic, cultural, or sporting initiatives

When implementing a sponsorship, the company's purpose is to link its brand to the values and emotions of a certain sports team or of a famous person, to improve the positioning and the opportunities to reach the target audience.

In the context of strategic philanthropy, most luxury companies perform sponsorships that link their name and image to institutions focused on causes of social interest in the field of arts, culture, or sport. This approach allows the company to develop effective CSR communication while representing a way for non-profit organizations to raise funds.

> **Ferragamo** – *Currently Ferragamo is the main sponsor of "Corri la Vita", a non-competitive sporting event hosted annually in Florence. Founded in 2003 and organized by Associazione "Corri per la Vita Onlus" this event aims to support public health facilities related to the fight against breast cancer, by providing women with psychological care, physical and social rehabilitation, prevention, training, and palliative care.*
>
> *In the previous 20 editions, the event has collected and distributed over 7,901,000 euros, bringing together almost 449,174 participants, and allowing quality assistance to over 500,000 women.*

3.5.2. Donations

The term donation indicates an action that allows an individual to transfer a patrimonial asset or his/her right to another person without any return consideration. In the case of strategic philanthropy, donations involve the free contribution of luxury brand companies to non-profit organizations or other institutions that support causes of social interest.

The contribution might consist of money or might be a material contribution.

Kering Group and LVMH Group – *On 15th April 2019, a fire broke out in one of the most famous and iconic buildings in Paris, the medieval cathedral of Notre Dame. The two bells' towers and the main structure were saved, but the fire caused extensive damage to the roof, the fleche, and a part of the furniture.*

The cathedral has a huge value not only for French people who have an emotional connection with the building (the highest monument in Paris before the Tour Eiffel was built in 1899) but also for tourists who consider it one of the best monuments of the French capital. Every year Notre Dame attracts over 12 million visitors, whose number reached a pick in 2014 when 14,300 million people visited it. Considering the role of Notre Dame as a cultural symbol of France, also the biggest luxury brand conglomerates, Kering and LVMH decided to participate in its restoration, aiming at demonstrating their support to the nation they belong to. Both Kering and LVMH are French luxury conglomerates that have always demonstrated their commitment to supporting the community where they operate.

On the one hand, Kering Group said: "This tragedy strikes all the French and beyond all those who are attached to spiritual values. Faced with such a tragedy, everyone wants to revive this jewel of our heritage as quickly as possible". On the other hand, LVMH Group stated: "The Arnault family and the LVMH group would like to show their solidarity at this time of national tragedy and are joining up to help rebuild this extraordinary cathedral, which is a symbol of France, of its heritage and of French unity". Both Kering and LVMH contributed to Notre Dame's restoration by donating 100.000 euros each.

3.5.3. Cause related marketing

The cause related marketing consists of a relationship between luxury companies and non-profit organizations to promote an image, a product, or a service benefiting each other.

To be transparent and useful, CRM activities must become a strategic choice of the company, and not just a short-term promotional marketing operation, unrelated to the ethical behavior of the company.

We can define four forms of cause related marketing:

- Transactional CRM: financial and/or material resources related to the turnover resulting from the collaboration are provided to the non-profit organization.

- Promotion CRM: the product of the luxury company is used as a means for the transmission of the message and the cause supported by the non-profit organization.
- Licensing CRM: the non-profit organization offers its own brand in exchange for a corresponding economic quantification.
- CRM Joint Fundraising: the for-profit company guarantees support to the non-profit cause by acting as an intermediary for fundraising between its customers and the non-profit organization.

Omega – *Omega is a company owned by the Swatch Group. Since 2011 Omega has been collaborating with Orbis International, a non-profit organization dedicated to saving eyesight worldwide. The partnership between Omega and Orbis was created to provide high-quality ophthalmological treatments in the most remote areas of the world. By leveraging on this collaboration, in 2017 Omega decided to launch new the Speedmaster 38 MM watch called "Orbis". With every watch sold, OMEGA will donate a portion of the revenues to Orbis International. Moreover, for every young patient undergoing a life-changing treatment, Omega provides a cuddly teddy bear branded with Omega "Speedmaster Orbis".*

3.5.4. Creating and managing corporate foundations

Although corporate foundations are becoming increasingly common, there remains a lack of a definitive and universally accepted definition for corporate foundation (Gehringer, 2021).

According to the report titled "Foundation giving trends 2021", the term corporate foundation refers to charitable foundations established and funded by the corporate sector, through company endowments, covenants or annual gifts. Thus, the corporate foundation is an autonomous and incisive tool that companies use to demonstrate a concrete and long-term commitment to solving real problems. Corporate foundations offer the opportunity for the company to be actively involved in projects that have a positive impact both within the community and the company.

The number of corporate foundations has increased dramatically year after year. According to the Foundation Center's database, there were over 5,000 corporate foundations in the United States in 2020. The study titled "Corporate foundations in Italy", conducted by the Bracco Foundation and the Sodalitas Foundation in 2019, counted 111 corporate foundations in Italy in 2019. Moreover, the study also provided an in-depth understanding of the evolutionary path of this innovative philanthropic strategy in Italy. According to this research, the corporate foundation needs to meet three essential characteristics. First, it must be created by a business organization. Then the corporate foundation must be a separate legal entity from the founding companies. Finally, the founding company must have a significant presence in the corporate foundation governance.

In recent times, another wide-spreading type of foundation consists of the so-called family foundation, as it is directly managed by family members. This type of foundation acts in a way that is indirectly related to the core business of the founders' activity. In fact, in most cases, the family foundation performs functions unrelated to the economic well-being of companies to which they refer. However, in fulfilling their social or environmental mission, family foundations could generate effects that in the long term can impact positively on the productivity and profits of the related company.

In the luxury brand market, the corporate foundation represents an emerging element of strategic philanthropy. Considering luxury marketing, almost all companies create a corporate foundation. As shown by Table 7,[6] which collects a long list of foundations created by luxury brand companies, the foundation goals can be grouped into three main areas:

- Corporate foundation aiming at supporting the culture and art.
- Corporate foundation dedicated to community well-being through initiatives related to cancer care and prevention, women empowerment, and community building in underserved communities.
- Corporate foundation focused on transmitting brand heritage's savoir-faire.

Table 7. List of foundations in the luxury brand market

Name	Topic	Mission	Foundation Year	Group	Country
Estée Lauder Companies Charitable foundation	Community well-being	Improving the well-being of our diverse global communities, with an emphasis on women and girls. Foundations' efforts are focused on three main pillars: health, education and the environment, and make annual grants to organizations in the United States and around the world that align with these pillars.	1946	Estée Lauder Companies	United States

continued

Name	Topic	Mission	Foundation Year	Group	Country
Fondation Cartier pour l'art contemporain	Culture and Art	Bringing contemporary art to the largest audience possible, stimulating curiosity by promoting the discovery of young artists or the unveiling of works by world-renowned artists, and commissioning work from artists to enrich its expansive collection.	1984	Richemont	Switzerland
Loewe Foundation	Community well-being	Promoting creativity, supporting educational programs and safeguarding heritage in the fields of poetry, dance, photography, art and craft.	1988	LVMH Group	Spain
The Omega Foundation	Community well-being	Savings capacities of families living on modest incomes through various micro-financing programs, including Calmeadow, SmartSAVER and EcoSAVER.	1992	The Swatch Group	Switzerland
Fondazione Prada	Culture and Art	Enhancing and promoting culture, art and design in Italy and abroad.	1993	Prada Group	Italy
Cologni Foundation for the Métiers d'Art	Community well-being	Supports and carries out several cultural, scientific and educational programmes to promote, encourage and bridge outstanding crafts safely into the future.	1995	Richemont	Switzerland
Fondation L'Oréal	Community well-being	Empowering women to shape their future and the world.	1998	L'Oréal	France
The Cristóbal Balenciaga Foundation	Brand heritage's savoir-faire	Promoting, developing and publicize the enormous importance of the figure and work of the couturier Cristóbal Balenciaga Eizagirre in the world of fashion and particularly haute couture, and in artistic creation in general.	1999	Kering Group	Spain
The Tiffany & Co. Foundation	Community well-being	Promoting the responsible Mining, Coral Conservation, Urban Parks and the Decorative Arts.	2000	LVMH Group	United States

continued

Name	Topic	Mission	Foundation Year	Group	Country
Ralph Lauren corporate foundation	Community well-being	Supporting cancer care and prevention, protecting the environment, fostering advocacy & access, and strengthening community resilience.	2001	Ralph Lauren corporate foundation	United State
Fondazione Alda Fendi – Esperimenti	Culture and Art	Organization of art exhibitions.	2001	LVMH Group	Italy
Fondazione Ferragamo	Brand heritage's savoir-faire	Offering young people, who focus their activity on fashion, design and the highest forms of Italian handcraftsmanship, opportunities of professional growth and training, in line with values and principles at the root of Made in Italy concept.	2003	Ferragamo	Italy
Fondation Pierre Bergé – Yves Saint Laurent	Culture and Art	Preservation of haute couture and ready to wear clothing and accessories, organization of exhibitions, support of institutions and cultural projects.	2004	LVMH Group	France
Fondation de la Haute Horlogerie	Brand heritage's savoir-faire	Promoting and spreading the reputation of watchmaking excellence around the world.	2005	Richemont	Switzerland
Louis Vuitton Foundation	Culture and Art	Promoting and supporting art (especially the contemporary one) to make it accessible to the broadest possible audience.	2006	LVMH Group	France
Fondation Azzedine Alaïa	Culture and Art	Preserving and showcasing the work of Azzedine Alaïa, and the many works from the disciplines of art, fashion, and design that he collected over the course of his lifetime, to organize exhibitions and to support cultural and educational activities.	2007	Richemont	Switzerland
Fondation d'entreprise Hermès	Brand heritage's savoir-faire	Transmitting know-how, create works, protect the environment, and encourage solidarity gestures.	2008	Hermès	France

continued

Name	Topic	Mission	Foundation Year	Group	Country
Burberry Foundation	Community well-being	Promoting the STEAM agenda, tackling educational inequality, reducing waste, and supporting social and economic development.	2008	Burberry	United Kingdom
Kering Foundation	Community well-being	Combatting violence against women through partnerships with local NGOs and awareness campaigns to support women survivors of violence.	2008	Kering Group	France
Coach Foundation	Community well-being	Giving back to community by partnering with local non-profit organizations that support local and global communities.	2008	Tapestry Group	United States
Fondazione Brunello e Federica Cucinelli	Community well-being	Supporting any initiative that enhances knowledge, the protection of the territory and monuments, the values of tradition, the spiritual and everyday values of man.	2010	Brunello Cuccinelli	Italy
Capri Holdings Foundation	Community well-being	Supporting diversity, inclusion and equality throughout the fashion industry.	2021	Capri Holdings Foundation	United States
Versace Foundation	Community well-being	Promoting the organization's activities, aimed at supporting the Lgbt+ community (lesbian, gay, bisexual, transgender, queer, intersex, asexual, etc.). The foundation will collaborate with various philanthropic organizations to preserve the history and culture of the community and promote its improvement in terms of well-being, safety, and equality.	2022	Capri Holdings Foundation	Italy
Hugo Boss Foundation	Community well-being	The scope of the charitable activities of the Company will be extended to new partners, particularly in the fields of climate and environmental protection.	2023	Hugo Boss	Germany

continued

Name	Topic	Mission	Foundation Year	Group	Country
Cartier Charitable Foundation	Community well-being	Improving the lives of vulnerable communities in low-income countries, with a particular focus on women and children.	x	Richemont	Switzerland
The Pvh Foundation	Community well-being	Giving back to communities around the world.	x	The Pvh Corporation	United States

Source: Authors' elaboration.

3.5.5. Community projects

The community project describes all the company's activities implemented to empower the community where the company conducts its businesses. While in the past most companies decided to outsource to developing countries like India, Thailand, East Europe, and China, to produce at the lowest cost by exploiting the local raw materials and labor, today the behavior is different. Once becoming aware of the damages caused by the heedless use of natural resources and exploitation of the local labor, an increasing number of companies started to take to heart the well-being and growth of communities where company activities are managed.

The community projects implemented by luxury brand can be grouped into different categories, depending on the company's activities. Examples of activities designed to support local communities are the following:

- project aiming at safeguarding the local savoir-faire;
- programs for empowering minorities;
- actions to support the local community's economic growth.

LVMH Group – *The French luxury conglomerate with its companies provides a significant contribution to growth and progress in the nations and regions where they operate and makes sure that it consistently goes hand in hand with close relationships with local authorities, especially on initiatives connected to culture, education, and employment. Particularly, the Group keeps encouraging the growth of entrepreneurship. An example of LVMH's efforts to support local communities is the creation of the "Never Stop Never Settle Society". It is a growth accelerator for the next generation of African American entrepreneurs, established in the US following the partnership between Hennessy and the Marcus Graham Project. Moreover, LVMH'S Maisons collaborates with other non-profit groups like the Asian American Business Development Center, the Hispanic Federation, and One Hundred Black Men to encourage regional businesses run by members of minority communities. For example,*

Sephora. Through its acceleration program, has assisted 67 female-founded firms in North America, Mexico, and Brazil since it began in the US in 2016.

3.5.6. Employee volunteering

Employee volunteering, also called corporate volunteering, is an employer-driven initiative in which employees volunteer for a good cause for the local community. It is an opportunity that companies can use to express their responsibility to employees, the community, stakeholders, and the surrounding environment.

Employee volunteering is a practice strongly supported by the European Commission, which has introduced the European Employee Volunteering Awards to reward entrepreneurial endeavors in corporate volunteering. As part of this project, the European Commission has published The Employee Community Engagement Measurement Workbook, which is an operational guide that lists the most common forms of corporate volunteering.

According to the study of Mosca and Chiaudano (2022), most luxury brand companies encourage employees to participate in volunteering activities, including LVMH, the Estée Lauder Companies, Compagnie Financière Richemont, PVH Corp., Hermès, Tapestry, Shiseido, and Capri Holdings.

The most common activities implemented by luxury brand companies consists of:

- Working days volunteering: staff spent working hours carrying out specific tasks or projects with no profit, such as mentoring activities for individuals, environmental projects, restoration/maintenance of buildings belonging to non-profit associations, etc.
- Paid roll giving: an initiative aimed at employees of public and private companies that consists of a free donation, withheld monthly from the paycheck, whose amount is equivalent to one or more hours of work. This donation, which is materially withheld from the employee's monthly paycheck, is then allocated to the non-profit organization (s) designated by the employee.

Tiffany – *The US brand Tiffany Inc. which now belongs to the LVMH group, in line with its commitment to giving back to the community where the company operates, supports an employee giving and volunteer matching program called "Care". Through this program, Tiffany Inc. matches donations (dollar for dollar) and donates $20/hour for personal* *volunteer hours that employees contribute to eligible non-profit organizations, up to a combined annual matching donation of $1,000 per employee each calendar year. In 2023 the program was valid for people working in the United States, Canada, the United Kingdom, Ireland, Australia, New Zealand, and Hong Kong.*

Burberry – *Burberry's employees are encouraged to devote up to three working days a year to community service. The iconic British Brand encourages employees to organize and participate in community outreach activities, including cooking classes, sports training, or recycling waste. In 2020, approximately 30% of Burberry's employees resulted committed to volunteer activities, by delivering 1,000 hours to charitable causes.*

According to the company, in addition to helping the community, employees' volunteering enhances workplace skills, builds community connections, motivates employees, and enhances personal fulfilment. The community project describes all the company's activities implemented to empower the community where the company conducts its businesses. While in the past most companies decided to outsource to developing countries like India, Thailand, East Europe, and China, to produce at the lowest cost by exploiting the local raw materials and labor, today the behavior is different. Once becoming aware of the damages caused by the heedless use of natural resources and exploitation he local labor, an increasing number of companies started to take to heart the well-being and growth of communities where company activities are managed.

3.6. The integrated outputs

The integrated output dimension represents the highest level of sustainability integration. At this stage, "be sustainable" is not an intent or a promise. On the contrary, the company puts into practice sustainability by performing a series of activities that improve the well-being of all stakeholders, both primary and secondary ones from the employees to the customers.

The integrated output dimension includes social, ethical, and environmental activities related to products or services, processes, and policies that request a redefinition of the business model, starting from the integration of ethical and social values in the mission and vision statement.

An example of a luxury company that is permeated by sustainable values and principles is Stella McCartney. The company's commitment to sustainability is evident in all its collections and an integral part of its philosophy that helps Stella McCartney to be an up-to-date company while acting responsibly and honestly.

Basically, reaching the highest level of sustainable integration we named integrated outputs in our model, means setting different activities that include the reconfiguration of the production process, a new way of approaching the supply chain, waste and emission reduction, and welfare policies to benefit employees and other stakeholders. Table 8 shows the main factors related to the integrated CSR outputs dimension that the paragraph deeply analyzes with examples in the following subparagraphs.

Table 8. List of integrated outputs in the luxury brand market

Dimensions	Factors
3. Integrated outputs	The use of sustainable raw materials
	Traceability of the supply chain
	Capacity to reduce the use of materials, energy, or water, and to find more eco-efficient solutions
	Reducing environmental emission
	Employees' training and development policy
	Welfare policies to benefit employees
	Code of Ethics

Source: Author's elaboration.

3.6.1. The use of sustainable raw materials

The need for sustainable products and services requires luxury brands to constantly rethink production processes, which are traditionally guided by profit maximization through cost reduction. This modus operandi that has characterized company activities for a long time strongly damaged the environment by causing waste, the exploitation of natural resources, and harmful emissions. Thus, companies, including luxury ones, have started to make huge investments to use new raw materials, in an attempt to safeguard the environment and communities where they operate.

Among the innovations introduced, luxury brand companies increased their commitment to offering fabrics made by upcycling or recycling processes. Both processes limit their negative impact on the environment by reusing waste.

On the one hand, recycling is the conversion of waste into reusable material. This technique consists of downgrading the waste into raw inputs and then using them in a new industrial process. On the other hand, the upcycling process means "prolonging the life of old objects by creatively reusing and reshaping them into new products" (Kamleitner et al., 2019, p. 77).

Thus, upcycling represents a step forward, as it does not limit to return of an object to the same function as the process of recycling does. On the contrary, the upcycling method, as suggested by the definition, means reusing objects without losing value to create a product of higher quality.

Moreover, to reduce toxic waste, most luxury companies started to favor products made with compostable and environmentally friendly raw materials. The materials are defined as compostable when following their degradation, they take the form of a natural fertilizer, called compost. Consequently, even in the event of disposal, products made from compostable raw materials do not hurt the environment or the surrounding ecosystem but can be processed easily and safely.

Finally, luxury companies take care of issues related to the environment by reducing or eliminating the usage of animal fur. Some companies like Burberry, Prada, Michael Kors, and Gucci have left the use of fur-origin materials by proposing exclusively false fur alternatives.

Salvatore Ferragamo – *Salvatore Ferragamo is a luxury high-end company founded by the homonym Italian shoe designer in the 1930s. Today the company is strongly committed to implementing sustainability into its business model at the corporate level by introducing some sustainable collections.*

- **Multicolor Eyewear Capsule:** *colorful sunglasses made from environmentally friendly materials. The glasses are made with materials derived from wood and waste from agricultural industries. Even the packaging is made of 50% pre-consumer recycled plastic.*
- **Icon-Up:** *iconic women's shoes and belts made by combining the innovative principles of circularity and material recovery with the brand's heritage and DNA.*
- **Earth Top Handle Bag:** *a bag made of cork, which has obtained ISO 14067 Certification – Product Carbon Footprint.*
- **Rainbow Future Sandals:** *Rainbow Future is a hand-finished wedge in real wood that is part of the prestigious Ferragamo's Creations line. It is made of organic crocheted cotton that has been certified to meet the stringent environmental and social GOTS. The leather lining is finished without the use of water or carbon dioxide emissions (Layertech technology). Ferragamo has enlisted the support of Treedom, which will plant 100 orange trees in the countryside around Catania, one for each pair of Rainbow Future.*

- **Capsule Collection Orange Fiber:** *a sustainable capsule collection of womenswear, thanks to the collaboration with Orange Fiber, the innovative start-up that develops vitamin yarns from citrus waste.*
- **Capsule Collection 42 Degrees:** *a tribute to the rainbow as a natural phenomenon linked to the Sustainable Thinking project, it is made entirely from sustainable and Italian materials.*
- **F-80 Skeleton:** *responsible re-edition of the F-80 Skeleton timepiece. The strap is made of materials with a low environmental impact. The watch cushion is made of bioplastic material obtained 100% from sugar cane. F-80 Skeleton meet the ISO 14067 standard requirements. Employee volunteering, also called corporate volunteering, is an employer-driven initiative in which employees volunteer for a good cause for the local community. It is an opportunity that companies can use to express their responsibility to employees, the community, stakeholders, and the surrounding environment.*

3.6.2. Traceability of the supply chain

The supply chain consists of a network of individuals or organizations that either contribute directly or indirectly to the fulfilment of customer demands. All the participants focus on value formation along the supply chain to ensure final customer satisfaction, while enhancing their profitability.

Traceability refers to the ability to follow the product from the first stage of the supply chain, as raw material, until the last step when the product is available for purchasing.

On one side, traceability helps the company avoid disappearances, extraversion, and product losses by reducing the risk of profit loss. On the other side, consumers take care of traceability, because it ensures safety and the highest possible quality by registering the various stages of the production process. Thus, the need for traceability arises from companies' need for greater profits and customers' requests for high-quality products.

In managing effectively, the supply chain to provide consumers with all information about the product they consume, companies generally follow the GS1 (Global Traceability standards), which request companies features that enable the identification of the product, its historical data, and its interconnections as shown in Figure 2.

Figure 2. The request of the GS1 (Global Traceability standards)

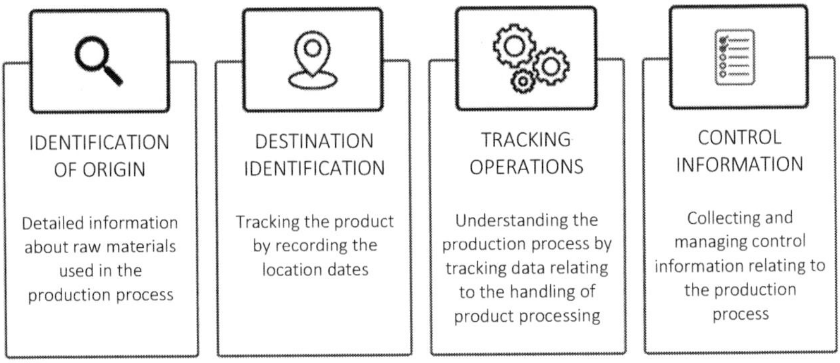

Source: Authors' elaboration.

Particularly, luxury brand companies consider traceability a critical step in the sustainability path and for this reason implement several actions. Examples of sustainable practices are:

- Using cutting-edge techniques to increase transparency, such as the QR codes that enables each client to quickly get complete product information, including all traceability and material certification information.
- Evangelizing and disseminating information with suppliers.
- Ensuring the use of certified materials along the whole value chain.
- Membership of organizations devoted to supply chain traceability.
- Creation of assessments of the raw materials to monitor traceability.

Compagnie Financière Richemont SA – *Compagnie Financière Richemont SA is a conglomerate located in Switzerland that owns several world-leading companies in the hard luxury sector. Some of the most prestigious brands related to jewelry and watches belong to this conglomerate including Cartier, Van Cleef & Arpels, IWC Schaffhausen, Jaeger-LeCoultre, Officine Panerai, Piaget, Vacheron Constantin, Montblanc, Alfred Dunhill, and Chloé.*

The sustainability report published by Compagnie Financière Richemont SA in 2022 reveals that the group is truly committed to supply chain traceability of some core raw materials used in the production process of jewels and watches.

Regarding gold, 99.6% of the gold currently purchased by the conglomerates is COC-certified. In addition, the group has the ambition to source 100% traceable gold by 2025. In this endeavor, Compagnie Financière Richemont SA is working to fully integrate transparency criteria into the selection process of suppliers. New suppliers must disclose their sources to help the group to improve the visibility of the supply chain.

Furthermore, the group ensures that diamonds are not "blood diamonds" (traded to fund conflict in war-torn areas). For this reason, 89% of diamonds supplied by Compagnie Financière Richemont SA are RJC COP-certified.

3.6.3. Capacity to reduce the use of materials, energy, or water, and to find more eco-efficient solutions

Another relevant practice, implemented by luxury brand companies to safeguard the environment for future generations, consists of the introduction of the waste management system.

It consists of the implementation of a set of policies, procedures, and methodologies aimed at managing the entire waste process, from the production to the logistics.

Waste minimization is usually achieved through better product design and proper process management. The process of waste minimization consists of optimizing the resources, re-using waste material, improving quality control, and monitoring processes.

In 2005, the European Commission promoted the process of reforming the waste discipline by proposing a legal framework that controls the entire waste cycle, with an emphasis on recycling procedures.

Moncler – *Moncler is a luxury company founded in 1952 in France that specializes in clothing and accessories. Today, guided by Remo Ruffini, the Group employs a circular approach to develop solutions for recycling its waste in constant dialogue with partners and organizations. Considering the textile processing scraps, the company is strongly committed to reusing and recycling processes, with a particular focus on nylon processing waste. In 2021 Moncler introduced the Zero Waste Project. It consisted of classifying and assessing all the obsolete materials, including fabrics and components contained in the Moncler warehouse. As a result of this activity, a more accurate view of inventories has been obtained, allowing new collections to be produced by reducing the generated waste.*

In addition to textile scraps, other solutions are implemented to manage packaging and office waste. In 2021, Moncler and Stone Island recycled or recovered approximately 98% of the waste produced in Italy and at Moncler's Romanian factory. Group offices and stores are equipped with special waste sorting containers, and employees are informed of the importance of properly recycling/recovering waste or disposing of it in a residual manner. Waste sorting includes paper, cardboard, wood, plastic, and IT equipment.

3.6.4. Reducing environmental emissions

In June 2021, the EU adopted a European Climate Law, aiming to reach net zero greenhouse gas emissions (GHG) in the EU by 2050. Consequently, emissions reduction has become a crucial aspect that luxury brand companies are carefully managing. Companies must implement systems to contain harmful emissions to the environment. Notably, CO_2 emissions represent one of the worst aspects caused by the industrial plants that pollute and release into the surrounding environment the highest amount of carbon dioxide.

After the Paris Climate Agreement of 2015, several institutions including governments, environmental organizations, NGOs are committed to reducing CO_2 and all other dangerous emissions by suggesting alternative models of industrial production.

Companies can adopt several practices for lowering environmental emissions that can be grouped into alternative energy sources and energy saving. The first one refers to the usage of clean energy such as wind or solar energy. The second one, instead, consists of a series of practices aimed at minimizing the consumption of energy when performing a company's activities.

In addition to these practices for reducing environmental emissions, recycling, together with waste minimization, contributes decisively to energy savings and the reduction of pollution.

In 2019 the European Green Deal, emphasizing the need to transform Europe's economy into a circular economy, enforced the European Commission's vision of a climate-neutral economy by 2050 and increased the attention on GHG emissions.

The Estee Lauder Company Inc. – *It is an American conglomerate located in New York that operates in the beauty & cosmetics sector by providing the market with makeup, skincare, fragrance, and haircare products. The company includes in its portfolio several famous brands including La Mer, Jo Malone London, Clinique, and Tom Ford Beauty.*

In recent times, The Estee Lauder Company Inc. has made its contribution toward sustainability by implementing several practices aiming at reducing harmful emissions.

To lower the negative impact of the production processes on the environment, in 2018 the company set the goal of reducing direct and indirect greenhouse gas (GHG) emissions by 50%, by 2030. In addition, it implemented an emissions reduction program to cut (60% per unit revenue in 2030) the emissions caused by transportation, distribution, and business travel.

In this endeavor, the strategy adopted by The Estee Lauder Company Inc. includes several activities:

- *On-site and off-site renewable energy projects (wind energy, solar installations).*
- *Energy-saving initiatives such as lighting retrofits, air flow and temperature management system and occupancy sensors.*
- *Integrated solutions with suppliers to reduce transportation and distribution emissions.*
- *Product-packaging formats that require lower GHG emissions.*
- *Retail design and operations focused on reducing energy usage. It consists of the implementation of a set of policies, procedures, and methodologies aimed at managing the entire waste process, from the production to the logistics.*

3.6.5. Employee's training and development policies

Training and development means providing staff with the essential skills and knowledge to satisfy the company's goals and business plans (Johnson et al., 2001). However, training and development are not concerned exclusively with how to carry out specific tasks. On the contrary, training and development include a series of initiatives for instilling commitment and a sense of belonging of employees to the company. For example, luxury brand companies organize training with newly hired employees to share companies' values. In other cases, luxury companies build academy to teach human resources the brand savoir-faire, such as Brunello Cucinelli. Some companies agree that training and development plans represent a valuable tool also to attract and retain top talents.

Prada Group – *Prada Group is an Italian company specializing in fashion and leather goods that owns some iconic brands, including Miu Miu, Church's, Car Shoe, the historic Pasticceria Marchesi and Luna Rossa.*

All the brands are managed with a strong commitment to respecting the value of each individual and human rights. Moreover, aiming to support stability in employment relationships and long-term investment in human resources, Group Prada takes care of employees by implementing training and development policies. Throughout the 2000s, the Prada Group has implemented learning paths for its employees, creating an internal Academy that combines conventional courses, on-the-job training and online learning. The activities provided by the group can be grouped into three main areas, and each one provides employees with specific activities:

1. **Learning and developed Academy.** *The learning and development academy deals with training courses focused on managing complexities present in different business environments. The courses are targeted to*

the country where they are delivered to meet the specific needs. This group of courses includes activities that assist managers in their crucial role of ensuring the well-being of their teams, by creating a feedback culture and the dissemination of social and environmental issues among employees.

2. **Industrial Academy.** *The Industrial Academy's main objective is to continuously improve the technical and craft skills of employees, allowing them to become increasingly more proficient in their jobs and move freely within their scope, while experimenting with new tasks, resulting in an improved overview of the operating processes.*
3. **Store Academy.** *The Store Academy includes courses designed to strengthen the professional skills, brand knowledge, and customer service orientation of Prada store staff, with the support of experienced store personnel.*

In 2021 about 56% of Prada's employees received at least one hour of training.

More in detail, a total of 122,410 hours of training were delivered to 81,268 participants in 2021, approximately 42% of which were delivered online.

3.6.6. Welfare policies to benefit employees

It is the set of contractual or unilateral initiatives aimed at increasing the well-being of workers and his/her family through different practices that consist of a monetary amount or other kinds of benefit, ranging from kindergartens to culture bonuses. The involvement of employees facilitates a greater adherence to company objectives and increases the level of engagement and the quantity and quality of work within the organization. Guaranteeing employees' wellbeing generates the development of more responsible employees who, in turn, raise awareness of the overall responsibility of the community by establishing a virtuous circle. Finally, the welfare policies represent an opportunity for companies that desire to intercept talented people. In fact, beyond the compensations, workers pay attention to the environment or atmosphere in which a company's employees work, looking for team cohesion, trusting relationships, and initiatives that safeguard the work-life balance.

Cucinelli – *Brunello Cucinelli S.p.A is an Italian fashion house founded by the homonymous entrepreneur well-known for producing fine cashmere knitwear in the medieval village of Solomeo. Over the years Brunello Cucinelli S.p.A. has developed multiple initiatives in line with the Humanistic Enterprise*[7] *principles.*

For the entrepreneur, stable working relationships based on trust and a sense of belonging to the company are crucial. For this reason, Brunello Cuccinelli pays particular attention to welfare policies that benefit the employees. The initiatives implemented by the company are several and can be grouped into different areas:

- **Work-life balance improvement:** *Brunello Cucinelli company safeguards employees' well-being, to ensure a proper work-life balance. Staff members do not clock in or out, and working hours are established from 8 a.m. to 5:30 p.m. During the lunch break scheduled for an hour and a half, employees can use the company restaurant and outdoor spaces, to immerse themselves in the natural surroundings of the company park, or otherwise return to their homes and have lunch with their families.*
- **Management of working spaces:** *Regarding the working environment, the company's ambition is not only complying with hygiene and safety standards imposed at the regulatory level but also offering a high level of comfort in terms of personal well-being, thus assessing indicators inherent in air quality, indoor temperature, and natural light. Special care is given to the aesthetics of both indoor and outdoor spaces, making sure that every employee has the opportunity, during the working day, to look up and look at the park outside.*
- **Employees' empowerment:** *Strongly convinced that culture is the fundamental nourishment of the human spirit, Brunello Cucinelli company created the "Why culture flourishes" bonus. It consists of €500 per year that each employee can use for subscriptions to magazines, cinema, theatre, the purchase of books, participation in training courses and kindergarten expenses for young children. In July 2021, the bonus has been extended to most of the foreign offices including Taiwan, Dubai, and Singapore.*
- **Healthcare assistance:** *The company provides insurance that allows workers to take advantage of various medical services, with special discounts. In addition, the company also has agreements with different medical offices. Starting in 2021, additional health insurance was included for surgeries. In this case, an additional ceiling has been made available to cover the costs of the surgery for both Brunello Cucinelli S.p.A. employees and their family members (meaning spouses and dependent children up to age 26).*
- **Employees' well-being practices:** *Further elements of the welfare plan are the marriage allowance, compensation for the births of children, the provision of meal vouchers, and from 2021 the possibility for employees in Italy of subsidized financing for home renovation (Superbonus 110%). Concerning this last point, Brunello Cucinelli S.p.A. signed a specific agreement with a leading banking institution to support employees in managing financing and insurance aspects. Finally,*

all human resources of the Group are entitled to parental leave, according to the terms (duration) provided by the local legislation. Particularly, in 2021, worldwide 77 employees (6 men, 71 women) took parental leave: the rate of return to work during the year was 91% (96% in 2021). 91% (96% in 2020), while the retention rate was 89% (90% in 2020).

3.6.7. Code of Ethics

The Code of Ethics is a document consisting of a set of principles, designed to guide members of the organization to carry out their activities honestly and with integrity. It is publicly disclosed and thus addressed to interested parties to learn about how the company operates. The code of ethics describes the organization's core values that guide decision-making and establishes general guidelines to help people apply their judgment regarding appropriate behavior in each situation in the environment where the company operates. The code of conduct originates from the code of ethics and converts the rules into specific guidelines to be followed by members of the organization.

Hermes – *"For more than six generations, the values of craftsmanship have shaped Hermès development and, at the same time, its relationship with the world.*

In line with the company's vision, Hermès' ambition in terms of sustainable development involves ensuring the authenticity of the object and the application of our house's ethics to all aspects of our business.

The house's values are formalized in a code of ethics, updated in 2018 and available in twelve languages" (Code of Ethics the Essential, 2019). The values on which Hermès was founded are collected in the Group's Code of Ethics shared with all employees working at the Maison. The document aims to uphold some fundamental ideals that improve interactions among employees, as well as with clients, suppliers, and the larger environment in which Hermès operates. The company created an internal committee aiming at supervising the dissemination of it. It is the set of contractual or unilateral initiatives aimed at increasing the well-being of workers and his/her family through different practices that consist of a monetary amount or other kinds of benefit, ranging from kindergartens to culture bonuses. The involvement of employees facilitates a greater adherence to company objectives and increases the level of engagement and the quantity and quality of work within the organization. Guaranteeing employees' well-being generates the development of more responsible employees who, in turn, raise awareness of the overall responsibility of the community by establishing a virtuous circle.

Finally, the welfare policies represent an opportunity for companies that desire to intercept talented people. In fact, beyond the compensations, workers pay attention to the environment or atmosphere in which a company's employees work, looking for team cohesion, trusting relationships and initiatives that safeguard the work-life balance.

3.7. To what extent luxury brand companies are sustainable?

As shown by Figure A2.1 (Appendix 2) most luxury companies provide stakeholders with their non-financial disclosures to make them aware of the sustainable practices implemented.

In most cases, the documents show in detail the actions undertaken, the expected goals, and the SDG(s) to which the action refers. However, there is a lack of clarity for readers in discerning whether these actions reflect a comprehensive integration of sustainability or merely adherence to established standards.

This chapter seeks to assist readers in distinguishing instances where a luxury brand's actions represent the effective integration of CSR. To achieve this, we utilize a checklist (Table 1) based on the integrated CSR framework (Figure 1) previously introduced. This checklist aids in identifying when actions demonstrate a move beyond mere compliance with CSR standards towards a more integrated CSR approach.

The results of the current research (Table 9) confirmed that luxury brands are working extremely hard to create more sustainable businesses to improve the well-being of employees and communities. In the following part of the chapter, we analyze more in details the main CSR practices performed considering each dimension of CSR framework to give a general overview about CSR integration in the luxury brand market.

Considering the first dimension of the CSR framework, called standards and norms, luxury brands seem to be meeting all the rules promoted by national and international organizations. This applies to standards that provide practical tools to manage environmental and quality responsibilities and those related to people management and reporting systems. Considering the fast-changing legislation about sustainability, luxury brand companies need to monitor the landscape of standards. For example, the future challenges that luxury brands need to face concern the introduction of the European Sustainability Reporting Standards (ESRS). They are created by the European Financial Reporting Advisory Group (EFRAG) to make corporate sustainability and environmental social governance reporting within the EU countries more accurate, common, consistent, comparable, and standardized.

However, the integrated CSR framework remarked that standards and norms are primarily expressed through residual CSR (Mosca & Civera, 2017b), leading to stand-alone practices that enhance corporate reputation and respond to stakeholder pressure instead of creating a process for continuous improvement (Hoque et al., 2018). As a result, the implementation of rules and norms has a limited impact on society, necessitating more efforts from businesses to further incorporate CSR into their corporate strategies. Particularly, the strategic philanthropy dimension represents the further step of integration of CSR into the business model.

Considering the second dimension of the CSR framework – strategic philanthropy – our chapter revealed that there is an increasing amount of commitment to philanthropic activities among luxury brand companies. Notably, the critical function of corporate foundations and strategic alliances has developed as tools that allow businesses to take sustainability seriously. Concerning foundations, each luxury brand is taking the lead on its foundation, by engaging in several initiatives that explore sustainable ways to enhance community well-being, from preserving the environment to empowering individuals. Regarding partnerships, luxury brands supported charitable initiatives or social events to encourage customers to view the company as sustainable, because it was involved in the community.

However, while recognizing that tools of strategic philanthropy are closer to integrated CSR practices than the mere application of standards, their fulfilment does not imply a fundamental change in the business model of luxury companies. On the contrary, strategic philanthropy initiatives still consist of additional activities that do not reside at the heart of corporate strategies.

Finally, we examined the efforts made by luxury brands to incorporate outputs that show a tangible integration of social, ethical, and environmental principles into their goods and services, operations, and policies (Mosca & Civera, 2017b).

Regarding products, using resources that have a positive influence on communities and the environment, such as packaging made from wood sourced only from responsibly managed forests, has become a focus in the production processes.

Luxury businesses are concentrating their efforts on developing collections utilizing sustainable raw materials from animal breeding that do not employ cruel treatment of animals, or recycled technologies that lessen the impact on the environment and the usage of natural resources. Moreover, they also want to be more environmentally friendly. Luxury brands are pushing the use of certified ecologically friendly production methods, encouraging the decrease of harmful chemical consumption, reusing or recycling energy and water, and minimizing waste as ways to show that they care about the environment. Regarding policies, the adoption of the code of conduct by suppliers and business partners provides luxury companies with a useful framework for disseminating sustainable principles and fostering stakeholder engagement.

But even while the way luxury brands integrate outputs shows more exceptional efforts to engage in sustainable practices, there is still a lot of work to be done.

First, luxury companies need more commitment to community projects. In other words, companies operating in the luxury brand market are asking to increase the number of actions aiming at empowering the community where the company manages its businesses. In fact, in some cases, the financial disclosure reveals that not all companies are still committed to contributing with concrete and effective actions to empower community minorities or improve the economic conditions of an area.

Second, when it comes to items, the dedication to sustainability is still frequently restricted to capsule collections created in partnership with start-ups and does not apply to the complete line of goods.

As a result, we expect high-end companies to include all the outputs in their range of sustainable products. To improve on this, the business model must be reformulated with an ethical and humanistic perspective that integrates the effectiveness of the company's social mission with its operational efficiency.

Finally, another issue concerns the supply chain. According to Karaosman et al. (2020), most companies have introduced a code of conduct to clarify the sourcing and traceability of raw materials, regarding issues linked to nature, biodiversity, animal welfare, and local communities. However, this practice is a weak attempt to support suppliers' endeavors to become more sustainable. Luxury companies need to enforce their influence on supply chain sustainability by using more practical measures that ensure radical changes in the activities of all stakeholders. However, as most luxury companies have started to integrate new technologies, such as blockchain, to improve supply chain traceability, we expect them to be on the right track.

Table 9. The integration of CSR of luxury brands emerged from this study

Dimensions	Factors	%
1. Standards	Environmental sustainability standards	100%
	Quality standards	80%
	People standards	90%
	Economic and social reporting	90%
2. Strategic philanthropy	Sponsorship of artistic or cultural initiatives	65%
	Donations	100%
	Cause related marketing	100%
	Community project	50%
	Creating and managing foundations	70%
	Employee volunteering time donations	70%
3. Integrated outputs	The use of new or recycled raw materials	100%
	Traceability of the supply chain	50%
	Capacity to reduce the use of materials, energy or water, and to find more eco-efficient solutions	100%
	Reducing environmental emission	100%
	Employees' training and development policy	90%
	Welfare policies to benefit employees	90%
	Code of ethics	100%

Source: Authors' elaboration.

Notes

1 The shareholders are people who own shares in a company and, as a result, get part of its profits and can vote on how the business organization is governed. A stakeholder is a person or an organization that has an interest in a company and can either affect or be affected by the business.

2 Founded in 1947 in Geneva, the International Organization for Standardization (ISO) is an independent, non-governmental international organization that produces international and voluntary standards, that support innovation and provide solutions to global challenges. From the consumer's point of view, ISO standards assure consumers that a certain product or service is safe, reliable, and of good quality. From a company perspective, ISO standards represent strategic tools that reduce costs, minimize waste and mistakes, and increase productivity.

They also allow access to new markets and partnerships, as in several cases a certain ISO certification is required to start collaborating or to operate in a certain market. https://www.iso.org/home.html.

3 The Textile Exchange is a global non-profit that promotes climate change actions in the apparel and textile sectors. From the very beginning of the supply chain, this non-profit organization directs and assists a growing community of brands, retailers, manufacturers, farmers, and other stakeholders committed to climate action toward more ethical production.

4 OHSAS is the acronym of the Occupational Health and Safety Assessment Series. The OHSAS 18001 standard was issued in 1999. The certification attests to the voluntary application, within an organization, of a system to ensure adequate control of the safety and health of workers, in addition to compliance with mandatory standards. With the publication of an international standard (ISO 45001 – "Occupational Health and Safety Management Systems – Requirements with guidance for use") in March 2018, OHSAS 18001 was withdrawn and replaced by ISO 45001.

5 Considering the financial reporting future development of standards, in 2021 the European Commission proposed the Corporate Sustainability Reporting Directive (CSRD) that defines the rules and requirements for companies reporting on sustainability impacts, opportunities, and risks. Under the proposed CSRD, the European Financial Reporting Advisory Group (EFRAG) approved the final version of the ESRS, marking another important step in the creation of a new sustainability reporting system in Europe. The CSRD which mandated sustainable reporting for companies with more than 500 employees, will significantly expand the number of companies required to report on sustainability from the current 12,000 to over 50,000.

6 Table 7 contains a list of corporate foundations collected by the non-financial disclosure. Each foundation is analyzed considering the name, topic, mission, foundation year, luxury company it belongs to and country of origin.

7 The Humanistic Enterprise is defined on the website of Brunello Cucinelli by using these words: "I believe in a humanistic enterprise: business should comply in the noblest manner with all the rules of ethics that man has devised over the centuries. I dream about a form of humanistic modern capitalism with strong ancient roots, where profit is made without harm or offence to anyone, and part of it is set aside for any initiative that can really improve the condition of human life: services, schools, places of worship and cultural heritage".
https://www.brunellocucinelli.com/en/humanistic-enterprise.

Chapter 4

SOCIAL REPORTING AND THE IMPACT OF CSR PRACTICES ON LUXURY COMPANIES' FINANCIAL PERFORMANCES

Fabrizio Mosca and Valentina Chiaudano

ABSTRACT: *This chapter is focused on environmental, social, and governance (ESG) and social reporting within the luxury brand market. This exploration examines the importance of matching sustainability performances with stakeholders' expectations and investigates the current commitment to social reporting in the high-end market. Moreover, the chapter responds to the need for deeper exploration into the impact of CSR on financial performance.*

4.1. Introduction

> *"Our success is only valuable if it is virtuous. This is about acting for the common good and ensuring that our success has a positive impact beyond our immediate sphere".*
>
> Bernard Arnault, founder, chairman, and CEO of LVMH Louis Vuitton Moët Hennessy.

The shift from a shareholder-centric approach to a stakeholder-centric approach had profound implications for how companies conducted business. It emphasized the importance of considering the ethical and social consequences of business decisions, valuing relationships with stakeholders, and striving for a more balanced and sustainable approach to corporate operations (Freeman & Gilbert, 1988).

Stakeholder theory's emphasis on a broader array of stakeholders and their interests led to the recognition that companies have responsibilities not only to their shareholders but also to society. This perspective acknowledged that businesses play a vital role in shaping the communities in which they operate and have ethical and social obligations beyond generating profits (Godfrey et al., 2009).

In line with the stakeholder-centric approach, the topic of sustainable finance has gained increasing interest in recent years.

The assessment of economic and financial risks, involving an examination of a project's financial viability and its ability to meet financial obligations, should also consider the broader impact of the company's activities on the local community. The growing demand for information about environmental risks, their effects on the local community, and an understanding of the company's strategic direction led to the development of models for environmental, social, and governance (ESG) analysis.

By encompassing environmental, social, and governance dimensions, ESG metrics provide a structured framework for evaluating a company's sustainability performance. Consequently, ESG metrics have gained prominence in response to increasing demand from investors and stakeholders who advocate a shift from a sole focus on financial bottom-line figures to a more comprehensive and ethical assessment of the cultural, environmental, and managerial aspects within organizations (Alkaraan et al., 2022).

By considering the relevance of reporting sustainability performances in line with stakeholders' expectations, this chapter explores ESG and social reporting in the context of the luxury brand market that remains unexplored by the current literature.

Moreover, the authors answer the call for further investigation of the financial impact of CSR in the luxury context (Kunz et al., 2020). Utilizing the differentiation between internal and external CSR dimensions, this chapter investigates the impact of CSR actions on luxury firms' financial performance. The results add to the discussion surrounding CSR involvement in the luxury sector by offering empirical evidence of the discernible financial impact of CSR initiatives aimed at various stakeholder groups.

4.2. The meaning of ESG for businesses

In line with the increasing knowledge expectations of investors, market regulatory authorities have intervened to require companies to provide transparent communication not only on traditional economic aspects but also on non-financial information related to environmental and social issues, respect for human rights, and the fight against corruption (Saini et al., 2022). This shift emphasizes the development of a broader reporting perspective. The growing need for information regarding environmental risks, their impact on the local community, and an understanding of the strategic direction chosen by the company are the basis of the development of ESG indicators (Chen & Xie, 2022).

The concept of ESG factors has its roots in the 1987 Brundtland Report by the World Commission on Environment and Development. This report was a key milestone in discussions about environmental issues and how they relate to global social and economic disparities. It stressed the importance of balancing economic growth with environmental protection and introduced the widely accepted idea of sustainable development, which means ensuring that our current actions do not harm the ability of future generations to meet their needs (Brundtland, 1987). Initially, sustainability was mainly about protecting the environment, as seen in the principles outlined in the 1992 Rio de Janeiro Declaration; over time, however, it became clear that sustainable economic growth should also consider social and governance factors in both the public and private sectors. This evolution led to the official integration of the three pillars of sustainable development (environmental, social, and governance) in 2004, marked by the introduction of the term "ESG" in the Who Cares Wins report by the United Nations Global Compact Initiative.

Companies are and will increasingly be legally required to implement ESG factors, which have become an approach through which investors evaluate companies. The adoption of these factors entails the following:

- **Environmental pillar**. Companies need to comply with and report on environmental sustainability KPIs understood as their impact on climate change and the energy sources used.
- **Social pillar**. Companies need to respect and report on KPIs related to employee relations, workplace safety, fair compensation policies, consumer protection, respect for human rights and labor rights, and gender equality and participation.
- **Governance pillar**. Companies need to disclose their governance model and report on how the company is governed and managed (management model structure; relationships with stakeholders; adoption and concrete implementation of procedures aimed at preventing negative behaviors such as corruption, fraud, money laundering, and false social communications).

4.3. Luxury companies and ESG

As previously mentioned, the ESG factors provide a structured approach to evaluating and promoting sustainability within organizations (Ahmad et al., 2023). Investors and stakeholders increasingly consider a company's ESG performance as an indicator of its long-term perspective and resilience in a rapidly changing world (Kapil & Rawal, 2023). Companies that prioritize sustainability and perform well in ESG are often better positioned to manage risks, attract investors, and foster positive relationships with their stakeholders, contributing to their overall sustainability goals (Bahadori et al., 2021). Figure 1 presents a visual representation of the ESG performance of luxury brands by considering each ESG dimension. For our analysis, we focused on brands listed in the Deloitte Power of Luxury Goods report published in November 2022, specifically those included in the Refinitiv DataStream Asset4[1] platform; we also included Essilor Luxottica. Despite not being featured in the Deloitte report, Essilor Luxottica stands as one of the foremost and highly influential companies in the eyewear industry. Thus, our analysis includes 42 luxury brands. To calculate the efforts in sustainability in the luxury market through the lens of ESG, we determined the average ESG performance of the sample by evaluating each of the ESG pillars. The data were extracted using Refinitiv DataStream Asset4 [1] in October 2023. The results contradicted the idea that sustainability can be more related to environmental preservation than to the two other pillars (Boström, 2012). In fact, the social environmental pillar score (average = 60.33) was not higher than the social pillar score (average = 62.80). Moreover, the governance pillar score (average = 57.45) did not differ significantly from the other two. The balance among the three pillars means that luxury businesses are addressing the challenges and opportunities related to all three sustainability pillars in a balanced and appropriate manner. This is generally a positive outcome, as it demonstrates an overall commitment to sustainability rather than an excessive focus on one aspect at the expense of others. However, since evaluating sustainability performance requires a detailed and specific assessment of data and practices within each pillar, we provide below some details of the categories that compose the three pillars.

The analysis of the environmental pillar's category indicates that luxury companies have cultivated the capacity to reduce their consumption of materials, energy, and water, while also exploring eco-efficient solutions through improvements in supply chain management. Even the emission score average reveals companies' dedication to efficiency in reducing environmental emissions in their production and operational processes. Nonetheless, regarding their environmental dedication, the average score for product innovation suggests that there is still room for improvement. Specifically, luxury brand companies can augment their capacity to alleviate environmental impacts and burdens for their customers, potentially opening new market avenues through innovative environmental technologies and processes, or eco-friendly product designs.

Figure 1. ESG performance of luxury brand companies

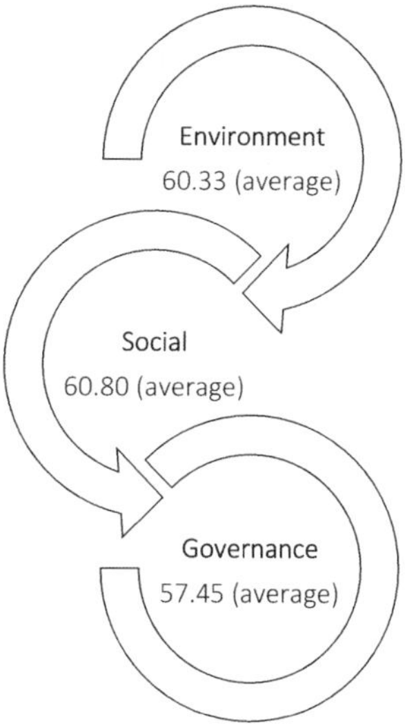

Source: Authors' elaboration.

When assessing the social dimension, luxury companies demonstrate a strong performance in terms of both employee engagement and satisfaction, in addition to their dedication to safeguarding public health and upholding business ethics. Additionally, they adhere to fundamental human rights conventions. Nonetheless, the product responsibility score average suggests that companies should enhance their capacity to manufacture high-quality products and services, while also integrating considerations for customers' health and safety, data integrity, and confidentiality.

In conclusion, an examination of the categories about the corporate governance pillars reveals that luxury companies have adhered to sound corporate governance principles and strengthened their commitment to incorporating economic, social, and environmental dimensions in their daily decision-making processes.

4.4. Social reporting and luxury brand management

Over time, a multitude of sustainability reporting frameworks and standards have emerged, serving as comprehensive guidelines, norms, and protocols defined to establish specific requirements and regulate how companies address ESG practices (Adams & Abhayawansa, 2022). The sustainability reporting principles can be categorized based on their focus, spanning economic, environmental, social, and governance issues, as well as their approach, which can either be general or sector-specific. Each of these standards is adept at crafting documents tailored to specific audiences, catering to well-defined groups or stakeholders. Among the most frequently employed standards for sustainability reporting, we find (Afolabi et al., 2022):

- Global Reporting Initiative (GRI) standards.
- Sustainability Accounting Standards Board (SASB).
- International Integrated Reporting Council (IIRC).
- Climate Disclosure Standards Board (CDSB) framework.
- Task Force on Climate-Related Financial Disclosures (TCRFD) recommendations.

While the proliferation of these globally recognized standards underscores the strong interest in this field, it can also present a formidable challenge for those preparing sustainability reports. They must navigate the intricate task of selecting from this multitude of standards. To assist luxury brand managers engaged in sustainability reporting, our study conducts a content analysis of non-financial disclosure documents from luxury brands to identify the predominant sustainability reporting frameworks within the luxury brand sector.

The study reveals that the standards proposed by GRI standards are the most widely adopted in the luxury brand market (Table 1). The GRI is an independent international organization established in Boston in 1997 following the environmental disaster caused by the Exxon Valdez oil spill. Its core objective is to help organizations achieve transparency and take responsibility for their impacts (Global Reporting Initiative, 2023). The GRI offers companies a set of guidelines to report their sustainable performance to shareholders encompassing areas such as emissions, human rights, and product responsibility. The first version of the guidelines (G1) dates to 2000, effectively establishing the initial global framework for sustainability reporting. This initial version underwent several updates, with G2 in 2002, G3 in 2006, and G4 in 2013, leading to the 2016 version. In recent years, the GRI has shifted its focus from merely offering guidelines to establishing the most widely recognized global standards for sustainability reporting. In fact, in 2021, the GRI released an update to its Universal Standards published in 2016. These new Universal Standards (GRI 1, GRI 2, and GRI 3) are set to replace the prior standards officially from January 2023. The current structure of the GRI standards is as follows (Figure 2):

- Universal Standards (GRI 1, GRI 2, GRI 3) can be applied to all organizations and provide the utmost level of transparency regarding an organization's effects on the economy, environment, and people.

- Sector Standards aid in recognizing the most prominent effects within a sector and align with stakeholders' expectations of sustainability reporting. They elucidate the sustainability landscape specific to a sector, delineate the probable focal areas for organizations driven by the sector's foremost impacts, and compile a roster of pertinent disclosures that the sector should incorporate into its reporting.
- Topic Standards encompass disclosures for conveying information about various subjects. These include standards for waste management, occupational health and safety, and taxation. Each standard encompasses an introductory explanation of the subject matter and includes specific disclosures about how an organization handles the related effects and impacts.

Compagnie Financière Richemont, Essilor Luxottica, Prada Group, Salvatore Ferragamo, TOD's, and Cucinelli are examples of companies that adopted the GRI standards to report sustainable performance in 2022.

Figure 2. Overview of GRI Standards framework

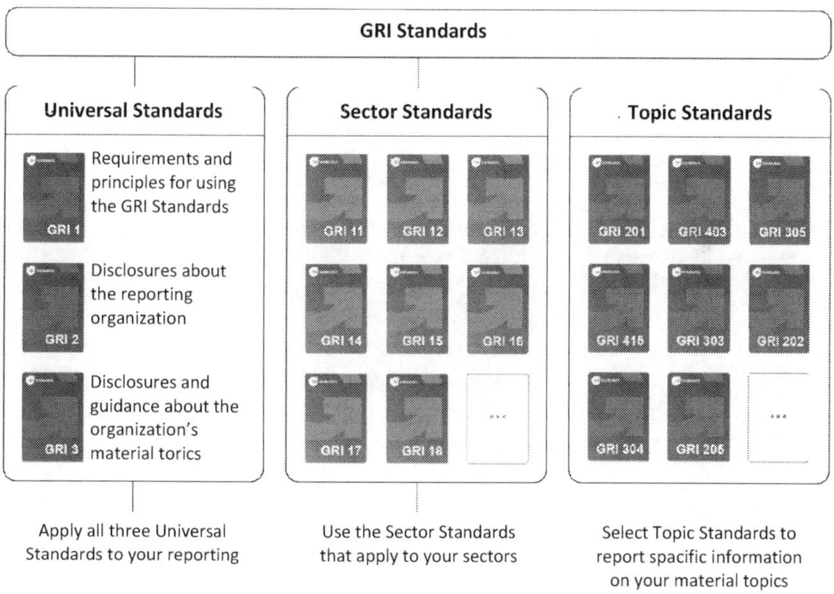

Source: GRI Standards.

The second most widely embraced sustainability reporting framework within the luxury brand market is the SASB standards (Guillot, 2020). These standards empower organizations to deliver industry-specific disclosures regarding sustainability-related risks and opportunities that may reasonably impact the company's cash flows, access to financing, or cost of capital in the short, medium, or long term. SASB standards pinpoint the sustainability-related concerns most pertinent to investors' decision-making across 77 industries. SASB's research begins with five overarching sustainability dimensions and subsequently applies an industry-specific perspective. The five dimensions of sustainability included in the SASB framework consider the environment, leadership and governance, social capital, human capital, and business model and innovation (Figure 3). The SASB principles also guide the creation of the materiality map.[2]

Since 2019, Capri Holdings has reported in line with SASB's Standard for the apparel, accessories, and footwear industry as defined by SASB's Sustainable Industry Classification System (SICS). Canada Goose declares that the Standards Board describing the consumer goods/apparel, accessories, and footwear sector guides the disclosure to investors of the company's financial material sustainability information.

Figure 3. SABS dimensions and items

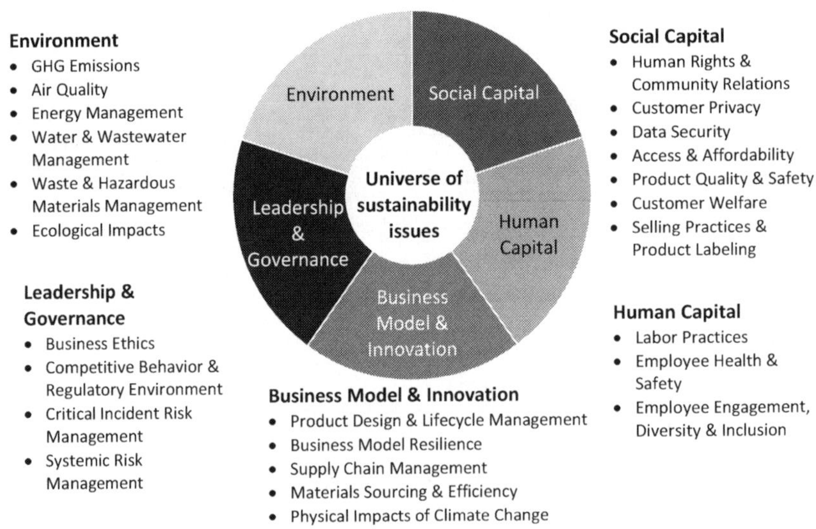

Source: Global Reporting Initiative (2020).

While the GRI and SASB frameworks are the most prevalent in the high-end market, other reporting models are also available. In particular, many luxury companies combine GRI and SASB reporting with the TCRFD. This framework provides a set of guidelines for companies that need to report their sustainability performance, with a particular focus on environmental issues.

Nevertheless, the reporting environment is constantly evolving. The IFRS Foundation is currently developing the International Sustainability Standard Board (ISSB) intending to meet the emerging information needs of investors, while the European Council on 28 November 2022 definitively approved the Sustainability Reporting Directive, also known as the Corporate Sustainability Reporting Directive (CSRD). The Directive aims to ensure at the European level a transition to an economic and financial system increasingly in line with the United Nations Sustainable Development Goals (SDGs) and the European Green Deal. The new Directive requests that companies indicate the impacts that the company generates in terms of sustainability, as well as how sustainability factors influence the development, activities, and performance of the company. Consistent with this objective, the CSRD introduces more detailed transparency requirements regarding the environmental, human rights, and social impacts of businesses, also given the type of corporate sustainability information.

The innovations introduced by the CSRD do not only concern the content of sustainability information. The Directive has broadened the scope of companies required to report. The number of reporting companies is expected to increase from the current 11,700 to approximately 50,000 at the European level. The Directive has also stipulated that the mandatory information must be included within the management report, eliminating the possibility for Member States to allow companies to communicate the required information in a separate document from the management report. To make the sustainability information of entities subject to the Directive more comparable, it must be provided following the European Sustainability Reporting Standards (ESRS), which are being developed by the European Financial Reporting Advisory Group (EFRAG). These standards are issued by the European Commission through Delegated Acts and will definitively define the requirements under which companies must prepare this information.

Table 1. Reporting frameworks in the luxury brand market

Company's Name	Reporting Framework
LVMH Moët Hennessy-Louis Vuitton	Own sustainability framework, OEDC
Kering	GRI, EP&L
The Estée Lauder Companies Inc	GRI, SASB, TCFD
L'Oréal Luxe	GRI
Compagnie Financière Richemont	GRI
Chow Tai Fook Jewellery Group	GRI
The Swatch Group Ltd	GRI
PVH Corp	GRI, SASB, TCFD
Tapestry, Inc.	GRI, SASB, TCFD
Shiseido Company, Limited	GRI, SASB, TCFD
Ralph Lauren Corporation	GRI, SASB, TCFD
Capri Holdings Limited	SASB, TCFD
Prada Group	GRI
Pandora	GRI
Hugo Boss	GRI
Burberry Group plc	TCFD
Coty Inc	OECD
Titan Company Limited	IIRC, SASB, TCFD
Moncler SpA	AA1000, GRI, SASB, OECD TCFD, The Fashion Pact and DIST forum
G-III Apparel Group, Ltd	Not applicable
Fossil Group, Inc.	GRI, SASB, TCFD, SDGs
L'Occitane International SA	HKEX and ESG reporting guide
Salvatore Ferragamo SpA	GRI
SMCP	GRI
Pola Orbis Holdings Inc.	GRI
Onward Holdings Co., Ltd.	Not applicable
Kalyan Jewellers India Limited	Not applicable
Farfetch Limited	GRI
TOD'S SpA	GRI
Inter Parfums, Inc	Not applicable
Brunello Cucinelli SpA	GRI
Canada Goose Holdings Inc	SASB
Aritzia Inc	Not applicable

continued

Company's Name	Reporting Framework
Guangdong CHJ Industry Co., Ltd	GRI
Samsonite International	ESG
Movado Group, Inc.	GRI
Ted Baker plc	Not applicable
Grupo de Moda Soma	GRI
Aeffe SpA	GRI
PCJewelleyLtd	Not applicable
Mannai Corporation	Not applicable
EssilorLuxottica	GRI

Source: Authors' elaboration 2023.

4.5. The relationship between the CSR and the financial performance in the context of luxury

Having examined ESG metrics, their connection to stakeholder theory, and their application in assessing sustainability performance in the luxury brand market, this section employs ESG criteria to assess how sustainability practices impact the financial performance of luxury brands. The examination of CSR's impact in the luxury sector has not received as much attention as in the non-luxury context. While some studies in this field have highlighted the potential positive effects of CSR on financial performance (Broccardo et al., 2023; Sharma & Mishra, 2018; Thomas & James, 2012), it is important to note that these studies are primarily centered on the hospitality industry or are limited to single case studies. Consequently, there remains a compelling need for further investigation by examining a broad sample of luxury brands to determine whether the luxury industry exhibits a clear and discernible positive or even negative relationship between CSR practices and financial performance (Kunz et al., 2020). Given this existing research gap, our study seeks to elucidate the impact of sustainability on financial performance by calculating whether both internal and external CSR initiatives positively impact the financial performance of luxury companies (Figure 4). Considering the correlation between CSR and the stakeholders' concept, as advocated by Carroll (1991) and influenced by stakeholder theory (Freeman, 2010), earlier studies introduced a distinction between the internal and external CSR dimensions (Schons & Steinmeier, 2016; Tang et al., 2012). In this context, internal CSR concerns actions directed at stakeholders within a firm's boundaries (e.g., employees, managers, owners), while external CSR concerns actions targeting stakeholders typically outside the organization (e.g., society, government, customers, suppliers, creditors, and shareholders). This distinction aligns with the theoretical framework of neo-institutional theory (Hawn & Ioannou, 2016), which posits that firms can pursue two types of action to establish legitimacy: internally focused actions aimed at signalling conformity to legitimized structures and externally focused actions intended to defend the organization's public image by making pro-social claims (McDonnel & King, 2013). While most studies examining the relationship between CSR and financial performance have assessed CSR activities using comprehensive measures (Buallay et al., 2020; Salehi et al., 2018), some scholars argue that adopting an approach that distinguishes between internal and external CSR actions can provide valuable insights into deconstructing CSR practices. This approach helps to separate the two distinct components of the resource accumulation process that leads to value generation within a firm (Hawn & Ioannou, 2016).

To test the impact of internal and external CSR actions on firms' financial performance, ordinary least squares (OLS) regression models are used.[3]

For our internal CSR assessment, we employed the workforce score (WORKscore), derived from the social pillar score available in the Refinitiv DataStream database. This metric evaluates various aspects of a company's performance, including the promotion of job satisfaction, the establishment of a safe and healthy work environment, the encouragement of diversity and equal opportunities, and the provision of growth opportunities for its employees.

To assess our examination of CSR initiatives oriented toward external stakeholders, we employed an additional social metric referred to as the community involvement score (COMscore). This metric evaluates a company's commitment to improving its position as a socially responsible corporate entity. It considers various factors, including the company's active engagement with the community through activities such as contributions, volunteerism, philanthropic initiatives, and investments in the local community.

In our examination of financial performance, we considered two widely recognized accounting metrics for evaluating company performance: return on assets (ROA) and return on sales (ROS). A higher ROA typically indicates superior firm performance (Saeidi et al., 2015; Wang & Sarkis, 2017). On the other hand, ROS provides a means of comparing the profitability of companies of varying sizes without factoring in capital investments (Nirino et al., 2019). Additionally, we incorporated a market-based measure, Tobin's Q, calculated as the ratio of a company's market capitalization plus total assets minus the book value of shareholders' equity, divided by total assets. Tobin's Q serves as an indicator of how investors assess a company's potential to generate future economic earnings, making it a forward-looking metric that can serve as a proxy for growth prospects. Consequently, it appears better suited for capturing the anticipated future influence of CSR on financial performance (Hillman & Keim, 2001).

The calculation shows a positive correlation between employee-focused CSR initiatives and luxury firms' financial performance but a negative correlation between philanthropic efforts and luxury firms' financial performance. We argue that luxury companies actively engaging in policies aimed at enhancing the well-being, equitable treatment, and inclusivity of their employees reap benefits in terms of both operational efficiency and assessments by capital markets. The pursuit of internal CSR initiatives, which may be linked to normative commitment due to their lower external visibility (Tang et al., 2012), plays a crucial role in integrating responsible corporate practices into the day-to-day operations of organizations. Consequently, these findings align with the anticipated positive outcomes associated with the adoption of an integrated CSR approach (Mosca & Civera, 2017b), wherein stakeholders' interests are promoted and woven into the fundamental business framework (Fiandrino et al., 2019).

By considering the correlation between philanthropic efforts and luxury firms' financial performance, previous research has contended that philanthropic initiatives can also be strategically integrated into a company's core operations (Porter & Kramer, 2002). However, in recent years, luxury companies have faced increased scrutiny due to unethical practices or greenwashing. Consequently, we posit that highly visible initiatives and communication strategies, which involve elaborate ceremonies to establish legitimacy, may be perceived by both customers and investors as greenwashing behavior.

As indirect confirmation of the risk of a negative perception of ESG initiatives, without denying the relevance of actions underlying CSR, some recent remarks by global investors (e.g., Carry Fink, CEO of BlackRock, October 2023) have highlighted that ESG themes have been overly emphasized by numerous corporations. This implies that a company's involvement in CSR activities is primarily aimed at creating an impression of genuine CSR values (Mahoney et al., 2013) or is merely a response to external pressure following a negative event. Furthermore, CSR activities primarily motivated by external pressures are likely to result in less integrated CSR efforts and can be easily detached from the company's day-to-day operations (Basu & Palazzo, 2008). This detachment prevents the realization of the benefits associated with an integrated CSR approach (Freeman et al., 2010). Additionally, many external stakeholders lack insight into a firm's actual actions, making it challenging to verify whether CSR actions are symbolic or substantive (Schons & Steinmeier, 2016). In this context, philanthropy can be readily associated with symbolic gestures and can have a negative impact on a firm's financial performance (Walker & Wan, 2012).

Figure 4. The impact of internal and external CSR on financial performance

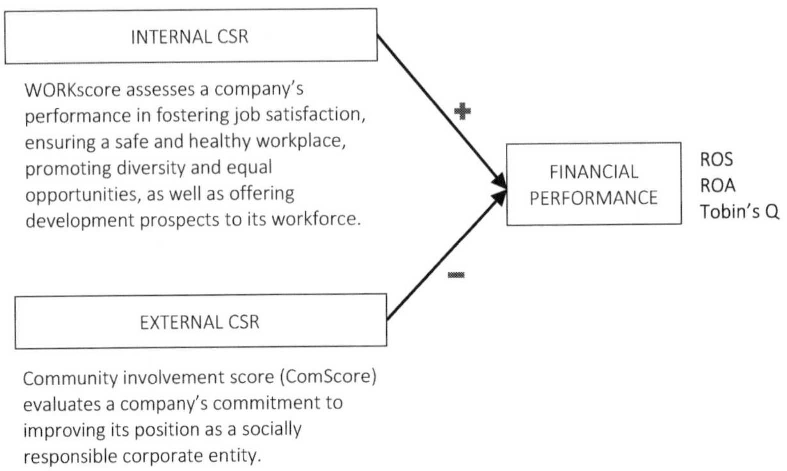

Source: Authors' elaboration from Gordano & Chiaudano (2022).

By highlighting the distinct impacts of two types of social activity (employee and community-focused) on a luxury firm's financial performance, we contribute to the existing body of research that has explored the link between CSR practices and firms' performance. Our findings suggest that relying solely on a comprehensive CSR score or the widely used distinction between ESG dimensions as the dependent variable may overlook the outcomes of various CSR actions implemented to secure organizational legitimacy and competitive advantage.

The luxury business offers a valuable context for this analysis, as the beneficial effects of CSR practices by luxury firms have been the subject of debate (Davies et al., 2012; Janssen et al., 2017; Kapferer & Michaut-Denizeau, 2014; Torelli et al., 2012). Our results carry significant implications for managers, providing guidance on crafting a CSR strategy that positively influences a firm's performance. Particularly, the noted negative effects on the financial performance of CSR engagement through donations and charitable initiatives serve as a cautionary signal for managers, suggesting that seeking legitimacy through symbolic actions directed at more distant stakeholders and external charitable causes may be a pitfall that diminishes market value and profitability. Consequently, we advocate a strategic approach to philanthropy that emphasizes its alignment with the company's core business. In contrast, a firm's commitment to sustainable practices, especially in how it treats its employees, is highlighted as actions that yield positive financial outcomes. We propose that such actions not only increase perceptions of the company's intrinsic motivations for engaging in CSR but also enable the firm to reap the rewards of a more substantive and integrated CSR approach.

Notes

1 Refinitiv DataStream is a financial data platform provided by Thomson Reuters that offers a comprehensive collection of historical and real-time financial market data and economic time series. Specifically, Refinitiv DataStream's ASSET4 compiles company-specific ESG metrics, with a subset of 186 measures considered the most relevant and comparable within each industry. These metrics are categorized into ten categories, which then contribute to the calculation of scores for each ESG pillar and, ultimately, the overall ESG score. The categories that form each ESG pillar include resource use, emissions, and innovations for the environmental pillar; workforce, human rights, community, and product responsibility for the social pillar; and engagement, shareholders, and CSR strategy for the governance pillar. The final ESG score reflects the company's performance, dedication, and efficacy in ESG matters, all based on publicly disclosed information.

2 The materiality map is the outcome of the materiality analysis process, resulting from a collaborative effort between the company and its stakeholders. The process of defining the materiality matrix begins with stakeholder engagement, which involves engaging with and interviewing representatives from various stakeholder groups to understand their areas of interest and priorities regarding ESG topics. Based on the insights gathered from these interactions and discussions, applying a materiality analysis helps create a list that enumerates all the most pertinent aspects related to the organization's economic, environmental, and social sustainability goals.

3 To investigate the impact of CSR on luxury brand performance, we used Deloitte's Global Power of Luxury Goods report, which features the top 100 companies in terms of revenue. Then we extracted data concerning ESG performance from Refinitiv DataStream. After filtering out companies with missing data on the Refinitiv DataStream database, our final sample comprised 42 luxury firms. We sourced information on these companies' ESG commitments from Refinitiv DataStream ASSET4. In

our internal assessment of CSR, we utilized the workforce score (WORKscore). In addition, we incorporated a social metric known as the community involvement score (COMscore). In the evaluation of financial performance, we took into account two distinct accounting-based metrics: return on assets (ROA) and return on sales (ROS). Furthermore, we integrated a market-oriented indicator, Tobin's Q, calculated by dividing a company's market capitalization plus total assets minus the book value of shareholders' equity by total assets. Consistent with previous studies, we incorporated the following control variables into our analysis: company size, quantified by taking the logarithm of total assets and annual sales revenues; the ratio of total debt to total assets (leverage), serving as a proxy for financial risk; and beta, used as an indicator of a stock's systematic risk. To test the impact of internal and external CSR actions on a firm's financial performance, the following ordinary least squares (OLS) regression models were carried out:

$$ROA = \beta 0 + \beta 1WORKscore + \beta 2COMscore + \beta 3ln\_assets + \beta 4ln\_revenues + \beta 5LEV + \beta 6BETA + \varepsilon$$

$$ROS = \beta 0 + \beta 1WORKscore + \beta 2COMscore + \beta 3ln\_assets + \beta 4ln\_revenues + \beta 5LEV + \beta 6BETA + \varepsilon \ TOBINQ = \beta 0 + \beta 1WORKscore + \beta 2COMscore + \beta 3ln\_assets + \beta 4ln\_revenues + \beta 5LEV + \beta 6BETA \ \varepsilon$$

Chapter 5
COMMUNICATING CSR IN THE LUXURY MARKET

Fabrizio Mosca and Valentina Chiaudano

ABSTRACT: *The chapter contributes to the literature about sustainable communication in the luxury market by exploring how luxury brand companies communicate their sustainable performance online. The online context considers luxury companies' presence on corporate websites and their profiles on social media platforms. Results show that most luxury brands have created a section dedicated to sustainability on their websites where they communicate not only their promises about sustainability but also their performances.*

5.1. Introduction

"Luxury must be kind and mindful. We must restore economic and social dignity to manual labor".

Brunello Cucinelli, Italian entrepreneur

Nowadays, companies are judged on their ethical, social, environmental, and economic behavior, more than they have ever been before (Latapí Agudelo et al., 2019). Public opinion tends to condemn all businesses that ignore negative effects on society and the environment to pursue "profit at any cost". Therefore, a business that creates exclusively value for shareholders is no longer acceptable. Contrarily, there is a widespread belief that businesses are essential to preserving and promoting sustainable development, or the capacity to meet the requirements of the present generation without compromising the ability of future generations to meet their own needs. Thus, CSR has become an important aspect of creating a positive corporate image that enhances competitiveness and differentiation (Freeman, 2017). In this context, the global luxury players and the key people involved in governance have understood that they can no longer ignore their environmental and social responsibilities, and an increasing number of them have started to show more commitment toward the achievement of sustainable goals. However, from current literature reviews, sustainable luxury research lacks studies that explain to what extent luxury brands effectively communicate sustainability, especially online, both on their websites and on social media (Athwal et al., 2019; Kunz et al., 2020). The available literature on the subject has focused more on exploring the compatibility between sustainability and luxury (Kunz et al., 2020), than on the analysis of the topic in the online environment. For this reason, online communication of sustainability in the luxury market offers room for further research.

In this chapter, we contribute to the literature on sustainable communication in the luxury market by providing insights into how luxury brands communicate sustainability on their website and social media. In this endeavor, first, we provide the reader with a background about luxury communication and the challenges of online communication strategies in the luxury market. Then, the focus shifts to the main issues of matching sustainability and communication for luxury brands. Finally, the chapter explores to what extent luxury brand companies communicate their sustainable goals in the online sphere. The online context considers their presence on corporate websites as well as their profiles on various social media platforms. Results show that most luxury brands have created a section dedicated to sustainability on their websites where they communicate not only their commitments but also report on their performances. Considering social media, LinkedIn results as the main communication channel used to show luxury brands' attention to sustainability. Their contents on LinkedIn are mainly focused on world preservation, inclusion, materials and production processes. Furthermore, the analysis reveals that the circular economy is a very debated topic online, indicating that it is no longer perceived as an alternative business standard but as a real effort for all luxury brands.

5.2. Fundamentals of luxury brand communication

In recent years communication has gained a pivotal role as a source of competitive advantage (Kotler et al., 2019). Communication, in fact, helps companies to be a part of a system of relationships among actors that exchange information, feelings, images, and moods through different channels (Duncan & Moriarty, 1998). The aim of communicating is to define a strategy that, using the most appropriate channels, makes corporate communication effective in strengthening consumer interest in the brand, product, and service as well as the company's reputation. For the reasons mentioned above, communication is considered an activity of great strategic value, which is not only an integral part of branding strategies, but one of the main strategic drivers to maintain a competitive advantage overall. Communication can be defined as the "voice" of the brand or company, the tool that allows businesses to establish a dialogue and a relationship with their public. Thus, before activating a communication strategy, it is necessary to gain knowledge of the market, the target audience, and the type of language suitable to be used, to avoid mistakes that could damage brand positioning (Kotler et al., 2019).

If managing communication strategies is critically related to all industries, it remains a sensitive issue in the luxury brand market. Luxury companies do not adopt the same style and content used by mass-market firms. According to Kapferer and Bastien (2009), luxury companies must follow a set of strict guidelines to implement proper communication.

5.2.1. Techniques for communicating in the luxury brand market

The critical aspect of communicating in the luxury market depends on respecting and responding to the rules of luxury brand positioning to convey messages that evoke luxury brand attributes (Pantano et al., 2018). Therefore, channels identified for communication campaigns must be able to convey the same intrinsic attributes of the luxury brand (Dall'Olmo Riley & Lacroix, 2003). To bring out these attributes, the communication strategy can make use of several factors: the simple visual or text description of the main luxury brand traits, the description of the experience that the association with the brand guarantees, and the representation of the values associated with the brand in question. Other elements that luxury companies leverage when communicating are the places, people and legends that have made the brand unique and timeless, i.e., the elements related to the heritage attribute (Mosca, 2017). From a technical point of view, among advertising techniques, the most used by luxury brand companies is visual seduction to evoke the allure, refinement, prestige, and dreamlike dimension of the luxury brand (Kapferer, 1997). Authors such as Kapferer and Bastien (2009), theorize the rules to follow to generate content in line with the expectations of luxury brand consumers. The elements indicated by the authors are analyzed as follows.

- **Communicating the dream**

  The purpose of luxury brand communication is not to sell the product but to allow the consumer to participate in the brand's values and thus the dream universe associated with the brand (Kapferer, 1997). Furthermore, luxury brand communication is not limited to the creation of the dream, but it includes the need to maintain it over time by revealing the scarcity of the luxury product: the more exclusive the product is, the more the dream dimension is reinforced.

- **Not communicating the price**

  The high price is an attribute that identifies luxury goods. However, the communication focused on price risks weakening the dream dimension created around the brand.

  Not disclosing information about money also includes a lack of reference to financial results, unless strictly necessary for the stock market listing: when buying a luxury product, the consumer must feel part of the dream universe and not be concerned with the company's turnover.

- **Communicating the luxury codes that identifies the brand**

  Communication should not focus on a single product. On the contrary, communication should create a system of codes that identify the brand and all the products associated with it by using consistency in the aesthetics of communication. The system of codes is necessary considering the long time that passes between the moment consumers get in touch with the brand's product and the moment they decide to buy it.

- **Communicating differently from the mass market**

  As luxury brand communication aims to create a distinct brand dream, the content and tools utilized by luxury companies should be carefully chosen and targeted toward consumers who appreciate storytelling and content centered around the brand's heritage.

  This emphasis on exclusivity and brand heritage explains the initial reluctance of luxury brand companies to establish a strong online presence. The online environment offered accessibility to a wide audience, potentially compromising the brand's exclusivity during communication (Chevalier & Mazzalovo, 2012).

5.2.2. The challenges of online communication in the luxury market

While most mass-market businesses have approached digital technologies since the advent of Web 2.0, luxury firms avoided digitalization for diverse years. They agreed that having an online presence could damage the image of the company (Table 1). Academics and professionals frequently pondered the questions: "How can luxury companies preserve their ability to sell a dream with an online presence? How can a luxury company long-term safeguard its reputation in the online environment?".

At first, the literature provided several reasons for Web 2.0's incompatibility with luxury. According to some authors, the fundamental characteristics of luxury, such as exclusivity, premium price, prestige, and scarcity, stand in stark contrast to the guiding principles of Web 2.0, whose goal was to be completely accessible (Chevalier & Mazzalovo, 2012; Okonkwo, 2010). Another hurdle to digitalization was the absence of multimodal experiences due to the lack of physical touch between customers and sellers in the online environment.

The digital integration, however, was a decision that luxury brand firms had to make. In September 2016 a report by Barton et al. (2016), titled "Digital or Die: The Choice of Luxury Brands" clearly explained that adopting digital technology was a must for luxury brand firms if they wanted to be in business for a long time and attract the younger luxury consumers. The report revealed that the true force behind luxury brand digitalization was younger customers. Differently from the elderly generations, youngsters were not satisfied with the mere offline presence of luxury brands but requested various ways to engage with brands directly online, as well as for enhanced social media experiences (Baker et al., 2018). Digital technologies were effective tools for engaging luxury consumers since they can strengthen brand awareness and loyalty by using content (Kim & Ko, 2010). Furthermore, social media intensifies the brand experience by allowing the consumer to have experiences connected to the brand universe. Digital technologies can positively influence purchase intention, and optimize the service offered to luxury brand consumers when communicating about it (Mosca & Civera, 2017a).

Today, luxury brand consumers request digital experiences seamlessly integrated across all touchpoints of the customer journey, since they are ready for phygital interactions. The creation of such experiences implied that managers of luxury companies need to effectively combine traditional media like television, radio, periodicals, and billboards with new digital technologies by maintaining coherence across all channels. In other words, it is important to transmit online the same messages that are delivered offline by traditional means of communication. Figure 4.1 shows the infrastructure that companies need to manage to perform digital and traditional channel integration.

In the current and fast-changing environment, a new challenge impacts luxury brand communication strategies, as nowadays luxury brands are dealing with the task of implementing CSR communication. Given its roots in solidarity, egalitarianism, and frugality, communicating about sustainability is a big issue for luxury brand companies that used to focus communication on emotion, excess, social distinction, self-enhancement, and dreams. Thus, luxury companies need to understand the potential of digital technologies to engage with consumers when communicating about sustainability.

Table 1. The digitalization of luxury market: the phases

First phase (2000) Digital skepticism	Second phase (2005-2010) Digital segregation	Third phase (2011-2015) Multichannel integration	Fourth phase (2016-2023) Omnichannel integration
Managers and consumers are skeptical about the possibility of adopting digital in the luxury brand market	Digital adoption is recognized as a necessity, but there are difficulties with integration	Integration between physical and digital channels: the birth of the multi-channel experience	Luxury companies create phygital experiences to all consumers

Source: Adapted from Mosca & Chiaudano (2019).

Figure 1. Traditional and social media in the luxury market [1]

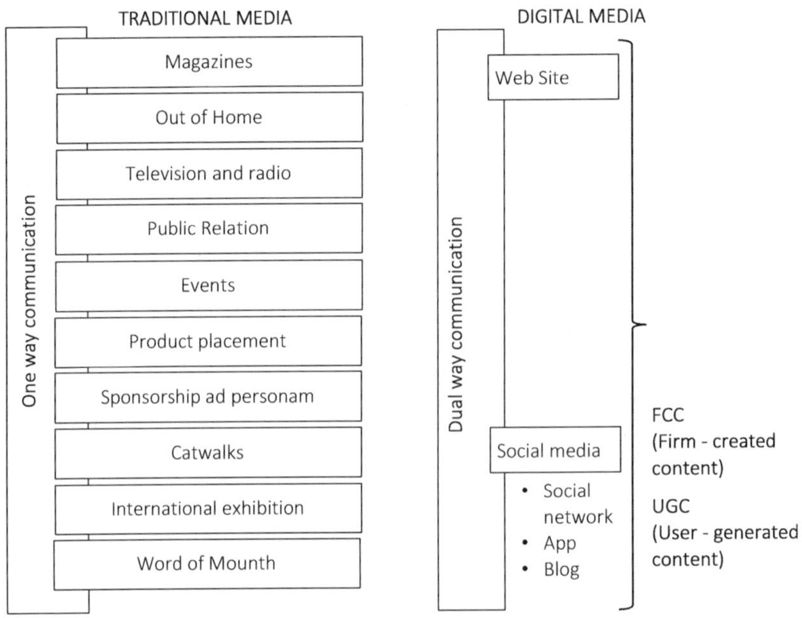

Source: Adapted from Mosca et al. (2021).

5.3. Issues for communicating sustainability in the luxury market

Both reports and academic studies agree that communicating CSR has risen in importance for luxury firms. First, CSR communication meets stakeholders' desire to be aware of luxury companies' socially and environmentally responsible and ethical organizational practices. Then, sustainability-focused communication can positively impact consumers' perceptions and evaluations. As explained by Luo et al. (2021) sustainable information can be an essential consumption driver for more environmentally friendly consumers. Furthermore, Amatulli et al. (2021) confirm that leveraging communication on sustainability rather than providing mere product information increases consumers' willingness to buy luxury brand products. However, companies cannot take for granted that messages related to ethics and sustainability can only increase stakeholders' positive perceptions (Jahdi & Acikdilli, 2009). Such communication can instead increase skepticism and mistrust (Civera et al., 2018), damaging corporate, brand reputation and consumer perceptions. Torelli et al. (2012) state that the perceived compatibility of luxury brand values with CSR communication is critical in how consumers respond to CSR activities. When consumers perceive that something is wrong or that there is a mismatch between actions and luxury brand value, they respond with lower evaluations than they would give if the brand provided no CSR information. Even Sthapitat et al. (2017) demonstrate that the perceived fit between the luxury brand and CSR activities impacts consumers' evaluation.

Thus, the literature offers some recommendations on CSR content that aligns with the values expressed by luxury brands. From the literature, it emerges that communicating about sustainable and philanthropic programs should not alter the authenticity of luxury brands (Cervellon, 2013). While environmental donations such as planting trees or philanthropic deeds like donating to fight poverty positively impact customers' perceptions (Karatzas et al., 2019; Amatulli et al., 2021) also demonstrate that consumers have a positive attitude towards communication about sustainable business processes, such as recycling, upcycling, sustainable alternatives, or waste-reducing production methods. This finding is consistent with De Ven (2008) and Hur et al. (2014), who agree that a higher trust in the perceived authenticity of CSR messages is evident in the communication of actual performances.

Finally, Civera et al., (2016) give us interesting insights on how to perform effective CSR communication. In their paper, the authors empirically demonstrated that the best CSR communication relies on companies' ability to implement an integrated CSR communication, which represents the alignment of social responsibility promises (typically expressed by companies' mission, vision, and long-term goals) and CSR performances. "The more the promises (in terms of values and ethical principles) are aligned with the performance achieved by the company..., the more the CSR function will have created social value and the communication function, will have contributed to positive repercussions to the company's financial performance (Werther & Chandler, 2005) and company's reputation".

Figure 2 helps graphically represent the integrated CSR communication as the equilibrium between the prevalence of pure social intents (corporate social responsibility; axis A) and the pure marketing goals and contents communication (integrated firm communication; axis B). The imbalance can result in two opposite negative scenarios that generate a negative evaluation of the company, according to the customer's point of view. The first situation, called over-communication, happens when CSR serves as a straightforward engine for enhancing and safeguarding consumer reputation. In this case, the company conveys messages with inconsistent ethical content that generates false perceptions of the brand. The maximum expression of over-communication is greenwashing,[2] which refers to the communication strategies aimed at constructing a deceptively positive image of the company in terms of its environmental impact to attract consumers or to divert public attention away from the negative environmental effects of the company's activities (Jahdi & Acikdilli, 2009). The second situation caused by the imbalance between CSR promises and CSR action is called under-communication. In this case, the organizations achieve good CSR results but decide not to communicate them to the public for fear of getting the communication strategy wrong. This is a typical case that can occur when luxury companies decide to not communicate due to the incompatibility between luxury and sustainability. However, the choice to not communicate about sustainability can be interpreted as a desire to conceal unethical actions or broken promises and, therefore, consumers may lose confidence in the company.

Having established that the best way of communicating CSR in the luxury brand market is via integrated CSR, the next section analyzes the communication channels for sustainability in the luxury market.

Figure 2. The model of integrated CSR communication

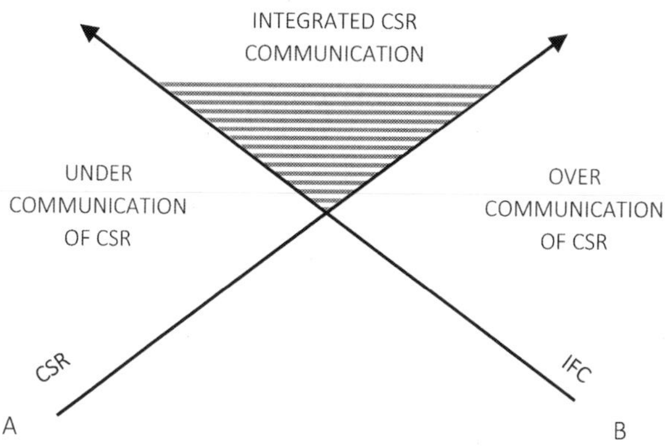

Source: Civera et al. (2018).

5.4. Communication channels for sustainability in the luxury market

Ziek (2009), in his paper titled "Making Sense of CSR Communication" identified seven key techniques that businesses may employ to share details about their CSR operations both internally and externally: annual report, annual shareholders letter, organizational codes, non-financial reporting, information on philanthropy, indexes, and the webpage about sustainability. When considering where companies post information about sustainability, the literature reveals that non-financial reporting appears as a standard tool for communicating corporate social responsibility goals to stakeholders. As Cerin (2002) stated: "This report offers a previously unavailable window into corporate environmental and social strategy and performance". Even if it was not mandatory, almost all big corporations chose the non-financial report as a primary tool to support evidence about their dedication to environmental and social initiatives. The same considerations can be applied to the luxury brand market, where the non-financial report became the primary channel to communicate CSR activities. Research conducted by Mosca & Chiaudano (2022) shows that almost all top luxury brands included in the Deloitte Power of Luxury Goods 2022 provide stakeholders with non-financial reports. In the sample investigated, only Chanel, Rolex, and Lao Feng Xiang Co Ltd. still do not produce a sustainability report.

Although communication of sustainability uses the report as a primary tool, some authors agree that it has some main limitations (Confetto & Covucci, 2021; Wells et al., 2021). First, CSR communication on financial reports is focused exclusively on results defined at the conglomerate level rather than analyzing single brands' CSR activities. This fact is confirmed by the study of Wells et al. (2021) who found inconsistencies due to the lack of brand-level reporting, by analyzing the non-financial disclosure of Kering and LVM. Furthermore, as suggested by Confetto and Covucci (2021), sustainability reports suffer from low power of engagement both as a communication vehicle and for the type of content delivered. In a world where the audience is more interactive, the strategic challenge for luxury firms is to develop communication strategies that inform stakeholders about sustainable activities and goals by offering a higher level of involvement and making more accessible and more attractive information (Chomvilailuk & Butcher, 2018; Lim & Greenwood, 2017 and Rossi & Tarquinio, 2017). In fact, in recent times the audience of sustainable reports is not limited to institutions, but it also includes consumers who are increasingly interested in sustainable actions. Thus, to provide consumers and other stakeholders with the aforementioned style of communication, luxury brand companies need to exploit new tools of communication beyond the traditional non-financial report. The online environment is widely acknowledged by many scholars and marketing professionals to be an effective channel for creating more engaging messages about sustainability. This holds also true for luxury brands whose presence on websites and social media may increase information and distinctive communications about sustainability.

5.4.1. Website CSR communication of luxury brand companies

As previously anticipated, planning CSR communication requires careful consideration of both the message to be delivered and the channels used to inform the public (Wong & Dhanesh, 2017). Despite the sustainability report being the primary communication tool for sustainability, the advent of the Internet made it possible for companies to leverage online channels such as websites and social media to communicate their social and environmental efforts and projects (Eberle et al., 2013; Lodhia, 2006). Differently from traditional tools, online channels play a significant role in creating business-stakeholder interaction, as they allow people to connect with brands in an "inexpensive, simple, and fast" way (D'Andrea et al., 2022; Jose & Lee, 2007). Web 2.0 has made it possible to merge various types of content and make it interactive, extensive, and demanding. According to D'Anolfo et al. (2017) and Luo et al. (2021), companies' websites are particularly effective in communicating about sustainability, as they allow luxury companies to customize and update the content addressed to their target audience differently from traditional media that support the creation of static and not engaging contents (Da Giau et al., 2016; Herzig & Godemann, 2010; Luo et al., 2021). Moreover, in contrast to social media where some contents are user-generated, websites offer the advantage of delivering messages firm-created, and thus more reliable. The authors conclude that the use of a website generates a positive impact on consumer behavior, leading to increased trust in the brand, and giving rise to positive word of mouth. Hence, creating and managing websites represents for luxury companies an opportunity to share their actions and performance aiming at creating environmental well-being (D'Anolfo et al., 2017; Luo et al., 2021).

However, to what extent do luxury brands use websites to communicate about sustainability?

Considering the level of visibility of sustainable activities on luxury companies' websites there are three possible scenarios:

1. Do not report any information about sustainable efforts on the website.
2. Limiting communication about sustainability to posting information about sustainability in combination with other messages. In this case, companies do not create a section exclusively focused on sustainability. For example, information about sustainability is included in the press or news.
3. Reserving for sustainability a subcategory of the "About Us" or "Corporate" label that appears in the menu, website's header, or footer. In this case, the communication of luxury brands about sustainability is profuse and well-developed ranging from the non-financial report to the in-depth insights about sustainable practices.

Table 2 shows companies that decided to reserve an appropriate level of visibility to sustainable activities and those that make sustainable actions not visible. It emerges that most of the companies analyzed created a section dedicated to sharing their sustainable actions and non-financial reports. Only a few companies still do not provide consumers with information about sustainability.

Table 2. Website communication of luxury companies

Brand	Sector	Group	Website section for sustainability
Porsche	Automotive	Volkswagen Group	Corporate (Sustainability)
Gucci	Leather Goods	Kering	Gucci Equilibrium, Code of Ethics
Louis Vuitton	Leather Goods	LVMH	World of Louis Vuitton (Sustainability)
Chanel	Leather Goods	No	Home (Corporate sustainability)
Cartier	Jewelry	Kering Group	The Maison (Commitments)
Hermes	Leather Goods	No	Maison Hermès (Sustainable development)
Ferrari	Automotive	Exor	Corporate (Sustainability)
Rolex	Watches	No	Rolex.org
Dior	Fashion	LVMH	NO
Guerlain	Cosmetics	LVMH	Home (Our commitment)
The Estée Lauder Companies Inc.	Cosmetics	Estee Lauder Group	Home (Our commitment)
Tiffany & Co.	Jewelry	LVMH	Our company (sustainability)
Coach	Leather Goods	Tapestry	Our company responsibility and foundation)
Omega	Watches	Swatch Group	NO
Lancôme	Cosmetics	LVMH	Home (Commitment)
Burberry	Leather Goods	Burberry Group Plc	Company (Company responsibility, sustainability)
Ray-Ban	Accessories	Luxottica	NO
Prada	Leather Goods	Prada Group	Company (Foundation, Sustainability)

continued

Brand	Sector	Group	Website section for sustainability
Bulgari	Jewelry	LVMH	La Maison (Responsibility)
Clarins	Cosmetics	LVMH	About us (Our commitments)
Moncler	Fashion	Moncler Group	Corporate (Sustainability)
Yves Saint Laurent	Fashion	LVMH	Home (Sustainability)
SK-II	Cosmetics	Procter & Gamble	NO
McLaren	Automotive	McLaren Group	About (Corporate social responsibility)
Bentley	Automotive	Volkswagen Group	World of Bentley (100 Beyond)
Armani	Fashion	Armani Group	Our Company (Armani Value)
Givenchy	Fashion	LVMH	NO
Lamborghini	Automotive	Audi Group	Company (Sustainability)
Shangri-La	Hospitality	Kuock Group	About us (Community and social impact)
Rolls- Royce	Automotive	BMW Group	NO
TAG Heuer	Watches	LVMH	NO
Valentino	Fashion	Valentino	Corporate (Ethic Code)
Loewe	Fashion	LVMH	Home (Sustainability)
Celine	Fashion	LVMH	NO
InterContinental	Hospitality	InterContinental Group	Corporate (Responsible business)
Bottega Veneta	Leather Goods	Kering	Home (Sustainability)
Sulwhasoo	Cosmetics	No	NO
Aston Martin	Automotive	No	Corporate (Sustainability)
Shiseido	Cosmetics	Shiseido	Who we are (Savoir-faire beauty innovations for a

continued

Brand	Sector	Group	Website section for sustainability
			better world)
Cle de Peau Beaute	Cosmetics	No	News (Sustainability)
Van Cleef & Arpels	Jewelry	Richemont Group	NO
Salvatore Ferragamo	Leather Goods	No	Sustainable Thinking
Maserati	Automotive	Stellantis	NO
Tissot	Watches	The Swatch Group	NO
Jaeger-LeCoultre	Watches	Richemont Group	About us (Sustainability Jaeger-LeCoultre)
Dolce & Gabbana	Fashion	Capri Holding	Corporate (Ethic Code)
Kenzo	Fashion	LVMH	NO
Bobbi Brown	Cosmetics	No	Company (Sustainability and citizenship)
Longines	Watches	The Swatch Group	NO
Pola	Cosmetics	No	Company information (sustainability)

Source: Authors' personal elaboration (April 2023).

We use the integrated CSR framework to identify the topic related to sustainability communicated on luxury companies' websites. This framework helps us to understand whether luxury companies perform integrated marketing communication, which is considered the most effective approach for communicating sustainability. By analyzing the activities according to the CSR integrated framework, a balance between contents related to standards, strategic philanthropy, and integrated outputs[3] emerged (Table 3).

Considering standards and norms, social and environmental standards are the most widely communicated, followed by quality standards. The least communicated on the websites is the reporting standards, even if most luxury brands share the sustainability report in a specific section on their website. The most cited standards include the Paris Agreement, the European Green Deal, the 2030 Agenda with the 17 sustainable development goals (SDGs),[4] the United Nations Global Compact, quality standards related to processes and materials, norms concerning the health and safety in the workplace, equality, and inclusion standards, and the information related to the sustainable governance. However, standards and norms represent the basic effort when sharing information about sustainable activities (Carroll, 2021). Thus, focusing website communication on them is not an effective strategy to impress the audience.

The dimension of strategic philanthropy consisting of supporting causes of social interest appears to be enough communicated on luxury brands' websites. Carroll (2021) suggests that companies should be involved in philanthropic initiatives and consequently communicate about them, as they increase the reputation and trust toward the brand. Strategic partnerships, community projects, and donations are the most widespread activities of strategic philanthropy communicated online. Regarding donations, during the pandemic, companies supported their website section dedicated to sustainability with news about their donations to sustain the local community. On the contrary, the strategic philanthropy less featured in the sustainability web section are sponsorships to artistic and cultural initiatives, followed by the creation and management of foundations and voluntary donations of time by employees.

Finally, the topic of integrated output is largely communicated on luxury company websites. It consists of communication about concrete achievements linked to products and services (product features and recycled packages), processes (waste reduction, resource optimization, and cruelty-free testing), and policy implementation. Luxury brand companies, no matter their sector or size, focus the content delivered by their websites on recycled materials used for product creation. Supply chain traceability is also highly communicated and expresses the attention of companies to foster transparency that ensures suppliers and employees act responsibly. Few companies talk about policies implemented internally towards employees. Since usually the website is customer-centered, companies have probably preferred to communicate pro-society actions rather than internal improvement.

To conclude, from the analysis of luxury brand websites emerges other relevant evidence. The gap between luxury companies that communicate promises and the ones that have proven performances has decreased. In other words, luxury companies are inclined to implement integrated marketing communication.

Table 3. The main CSR topics communicated on the websites of luxury companies

Topic communicated	%
Environmental standards	66%
Quality standards	44%
Human resource standards	50%
Economic and social reporting	36%
Sponsorships to artistic or cultural initiatives	30%
Donations	50%
Cause related marketing	64%
Community project	46%
Creating and managing foundations	28%
Employee volunteering time donations	28%
The use of new or recycled raw materials	62%
Traceability of the supply chain	58%
Capacity to reduce the use of materials, energy, or water, and to find more eco-efficient solutions	60%
Reducing environmental emission	58%
Employees' training and development policy	30%
Welfare policies to benefit employees	36%
Code of Ethics	40%

Source: Authors' elaboration (2023).

For example, considering companies' impact on the environment, instead of declaring to be environmentally concerned, most luxury companies effectively support their promises by providing evidence of their achievements in reducing the consumption of heating, their investments in energy efficiency, the percentage of plastic, paper, and water reduction, and data about the positive impact on the environment when adopting more eco-efficient building design and construction methods. Moreover, luxury companies do more than simply communicate their intentions to support the art or minority groups, and provide evidence of activities to finance art & culture initiatives or to promote and donate to charities spread all over the world.

5.4.2. The social media for sustainability communication in the luxury market

Initially, luxury brand companies were skeptical about the opportunity to integrate social media platforms into their communication strategy. The authors agreed that the communication implemented through social media was more suitable for mass-market brands as it did not respect the selectivity of luxury brand communication dilution (Maman Larraufie & Kourdoughli, 2014). On the contrary, social media were perceived as inappropriate tools to preserve the elitism and exclusivity of luxury brand communication (Jahn et al., 2013). Furthermore, the dual-way communication of social media implied less control over the content posted by consumers, resulting in the risk of brand dilution (Maman Larraufie & Kourdoughli, 2014). However, luxury firms quickly recognized the compelling need for their presence on social media platforms. As a result, they proactively engaged in creating their accounts on the leading social media platforms. Altagamma (2020), highlighted Instagram and Facebook as the dominant social media choices within the luxury sector in 2019, with more than 80 percent of luxury brands from diverse industries actively maintaining accounts on these platforms. In recent years luxury brand companies directed their attention towards TikTok, which rapidly gained popularity among younger consumers. Now, TikTok is the most appreciated social media platform for executing campaigns targeted at engaging the new generation of consumers (Pangarkar et al., 2023)

Despite social media's recognized effectiveness in engaging luxury brand audiences, social media management still entails some challenges in the luxury industry. Specifically, maintaining control over the content posted through social media channels remains a significant concern, encompassing both firm-created content and user-generated content. On the one hand, user-generated content can lead to the uncontrollable dissemination of negative messages, potentially harming the brand's image dilution (Maman Larraufie & Kourdoughli, 2014). On the other hand, the incautious use of firm-created content can result in brand boycotts and reputational damage (Bellomi, I.J., & Kholod, T., 2023). The repercussions of Dolce & Gabbana's advertising campaign in China serve as a striking example. The literature provides insights by offering guidance on which types of content can lead to a significantly positive performance. It reveals that social media content around brands' heritage, craftsmanship, and origin of raw materials can have a more pronounced effect on consumers compared to those that emphasize hedonism and self-esteem (Chang et al., 2019; Maman Larraufie & Kourdoughli, 2014; Wang, 2022). Furthermore, luxury fashion brands have recently utilized content marketing strategies on social networks to drive their social responsibility initiatives (Castillo-Abdul, Pérez-Escoda et al., 2022). However, the topic of CSR communication through social media remains rather unexplored. To shed light on the emerging research field of CSR communication on social media in the luxury market context, our research explores:

a. The social media platforms most utilized by luxury brands to communicate sustainable activities.
b. The main topics that luxury companies communicate on social media when promoting and supporting their social responsibility initiatives.

5.4.2.1. Social media platform to communicate sustainability in the luxury brand market

As mentioned above, luxury brands have become increasingly aware of the growing importance of digital platforms, recognizing the potential of social media as a powerful tool for brand promotion and consumer engagement. Consequently, they have intensified their presence on popular social media platforms such as Facebook, Instagram, LinkedIn, and, more recently, TikTok. In our study, involving a sample of 50 luxury brand companies, LinkedIn emerges as the predominant platform utilized for communicating social and environmental responsibility initiatives within the luxury brand context. Notably, the number of sustainability-related posts published on LinkedIn surpasses those on Instagram and Facebook, which are primarily used for product and heritage-related communication. This distinction in content distribution can be attributed to the inherent nature of each social media platform. LinkedIn, with its focus on fostering professional connections in the business environment, exhibits a unique capacity to engage a broader spectrum of stakeholders through more specialized and technical forms of communication, compared to Instagram and Facebook. Table 4.4 presents an overview of luxury brands' efforts in communicating about sustainability on LinkedIn. It is noteworthy that Gucci stands out as the best in class of sustainability communication on LinkedIn.

Table 4. Social media and CSR in the luxury brand market

POSITION	BRAND	SECTOR	LINKEDIN PAGE	ACCOUNT ACTIVITY	SUSTAINABILITY POST NUMBER	SUSTAINABILITY SCORE	SUSTAINABILITY REPORT
1	Gucci	Leather Goods	✓	✓	33	5	✓
2	Porsche	Automotive	✓	✓	30	4,5	✓
3	Guerlain	Cosmetics	✓	✓	26	4	✓
4	Cartier	Jewelry	✓	✓	22	3,3	✓
5	Burberry	Leather Goods	✓	✓	22	3,3	✓
6	Shiseido	Cosmetics	✓	✓	22	3,3	✓
7	Rolex	Watches	✓	✓	18	3	x
8	Dior	Fashion	✓	✓	20	3	✓
9	Prada	Leather Goods	✓	✓	20	3	✓
10	Shangri-La	Hospitality	✓	✓	19	3	✓
11	Loewe	Leather Goods	✓	✓	18	3	✓
12	Lamborghini	Automotive	✓	✓	17	2,5	✓
13	Bentley	Automotive	✓	✓	16	2,4	✓
14	Hermes	Leather Goods	✓	✓	15	2,2	✓
15	Salvatore Ferragamo	Leather Goods	✓	✓	14	2,1	✓
16	Tiffany & Co.	Jewelry	✓	✓	12	2	✓
17	Louis Vuitton	Leather Goods	✓	✓	10	1,5	✓
18	Moncler	Fashion	✓	✓	9	1,5	✓
19	Ferrari	Automotive	✓	✓	8	1,2	✓
20	Aston Martin	Automotive	✓	✓	8	1,2	✓
21	Coach	Leather Goods	✓	✓	6	1	✓
22	Armani	Fashion	✓	✓	7	1	✓
23	Valentino	Fashion	✓	✓	6	1	✓
24	Maserati	Automotive	✓	✓	7	1	✓
25	McLaren	Automotive	✓	x	5	0,7	✓
26	Rolls- Royce	Automotive	✓	✓	4	0,6	✓
27	Intercontinental	Hospitality	✓	✓	4	0,6	✓
28	Bulgari	Jewelry	✓	✓	4	0,5	✓
29	Jaeger-LeCoultre	Watches	✓	✓	3	0,5	✓
30	Dolce & Gabbana	Fashion	✓	✓	3	0,5	✓
31	Bobbi Brown	Cosmetics	✓	x	2	0,3	✓
32	Chanel	Leather Goods	✓	✓	1	0,1	x
33	Yves Saint Laurent	Fashion	✓	✓	1	0,1	✓
34	Givenchy	Fashion	✓	✓	1	0,1	✓
35	TAG Heuer	Watches	✓	✓	1	0,1	✓
36	Kenzo	Fashion	✓	x	1	0,1	✓
37	Omega	Watches	✓	✓	0	0	✓
38	Lancôme	Cosmetics	✓	x	0	0	✓
39	Ray-Ban	Accessories	✓	x	0	0	✓
40	Celine	Fashion	✓	✓	0	0	✓
41	Bottega Veneta	Leather Goods	✓	x	0	0	✓
42	Cle de Peau Beaute	Cosmetics	✓	x	0	0	✓
43	Van Cleef & Arpels	Jewelry	✓	✓	0	0	✓
44	Tissot	Watches	✓	✓	0	0	✓
45	Longines	Watches	✓	✓	0	0	✓
46	Estee Lauder	Cosmetics	x	/	/	/	✓
47	Clarins	Cosmetics	x	/	/	/	✓
48	SK-II	Cosmetics	x	/	/	/	✓
49	Sulwhasoo	Cosmetics	x	/	/	/	x
50	Pola	Cosmetics	x	/	/	/	✓

Source: Authors' personal elaboration (April 2023).

5.4.2.2. The main CSR topics communicated by luxury brands on social media

After identifying LinkedIn as the main tool used to communicate sustainability in the luxury brand context, our study seeks to investigate the commonly discussed topics.

As Figure 3 shows, a strong connection emerges between the themes communicated by luxury brand companies and the Sustainable Development Goals (SDGs) published by the United Nations. The 17 Development Goals represent common goals to solve global issues: fighting poverty, eradicating hunger, combating climate change, achieving gender equality, reducing inequality, and preserving the world. Most luxury companies make huge efforts to pursue these goals and, as the research shows, communicate about them on their LinkedIn profile. Particularly, the communication topics about sustainability on LinkedIn can be grouped into three main categories that the chapter analyses in the following subparagraphs.

The topic of world preservation

Concerning the theme of "world preservation", it pertains to the online content of luxury brands that focuses on sustainable actions aimed at preserving the world for future generations. This involves communication regarding partnerships with global organizations and networks that combat major threats to world preservation, such as plastic pollution, climate change, overfishing, and poaching.

Regarding "events", this category encompasses conferences or parties organized by luxury brand companies to raise awareness about sustainability among consumers and stakeholders. For instance, these events may provide opportunities for consumers to interact with artisans, gaining insights into the culture of craftsmanship and the significance of heritage preservation. Additionally, event topics may include content related to luxury brands' participation in discussion panels organized by national or international organizations dedicated to promoting knowledge about sustainability.

The theme of inclusion

The theme most frequently addressed by luxury brands on their LinkedIn profile concerns their commitment to inclusion, which means supporting women, youth, communities, and employees through specific initiatives, programs, and activities.

The concept mostly discussed on LinkedIn is gender diversity and related actions taken to pursue inclusion, by reducing inequality following the fifth Sustainable Development Goal "Achieve gender equality and empower all women and girls". All luxury brands surveyed have emphasized on social media their commitment to ensuring equal conditions for women and men. They underline how women represent an important percentage of their workforce and show their commitment to women's empowerment by organizing a series of mentorship programs focused on tangible steps to promote gender equality. This topic is increasingly discussing by automotive sector brands that post on LinkedIn their efforts to raise awareness and bring women closer to the transportation sector and other activities in the STEM field. Moreover, to ensure equality among people, luxury brand companies also communicate their support to the LGBTQIA+ community. For example, luxury companies show their support for same-sex unions by communicating on LinkedIn that they actively participate in Pride Month or organize corporate initiatives aimed at supporting LGBTQIA+ employees.

The theme of inclusion also embeds communications related to the empowerment of the local community, which means supporting local people to preserve their natural resources and develop their communities. Most luxury brands commit to empowering and supporting the local community by promoting training programs in underdeveloped countries, in collaboration with nonprofit organizations. In other cases, luxury companies promote initiatives to gather funds that are donated to organizations supporting social causes.

Another kind of empowerment strongly discussed deals with the empowerment of younger generations. Most luxury brands communicate on LinkedIn initiatives whose aim is supporting the education of young people, such as donations to training institutions in collaboration with nonprofit organizations.

Finally, it is also considered workplace inclusion, namely the practice of creating a work environment where all employees feel welcome, respected, and valued regardless of their background, identity, or personal characteristics. Promoting inclusion in the workplace can have several benefits, including higher job satisfaction, improved employee morale and motivation, increased productivity, and reduced turnover rates. About this topic, most luxury companies communicated their willingness to join international organizations that support practices of equality and inclusion in the workplace.

The topic of sustainability for materials and the production process

Looking at the materials and production processes topic, nowadays, luxury brands are not limited to posting on LinkedIn content related to high-quality raw materials used, or about their choice of maintaining the production in the country of origin. On the contrary, when talking about raw materials and the production process, luxury companies desire to demonstrate their commitment to sustainability by showing results in compliance with SDG 7 "Adopting economical, reliable, sustainable, and innovative energy systems" and SDG 12 "Ensuring sustainable patterns of production and consumption". Most discussed on social media are the outputs related to luxury companies' commitment to reducing emissions and plastic use, recycling, resource management, and animal welfare. The types of initiatives posted on Linkedin depend on the specific sector or industry that the luxury brand belongs to. In the fashion industry, many luxury brands have announced on LinkedIn that they are permanently eliminating fur to ensure animal welfare. This is the case of Moncler and Dior. Other fashion companies focused their content on innovative and responsible materials they have introduced to safeguard the environment. Gucci frequently publishes posts on LinkedIn that show its eco-innovation activities underlying each new collection. Considering the cosmetic sector, brands communicate on LinkedIn their commitment to limiting the environmental impact in terms of manufactured components and packaging. Most cosmetics companies are vocal about their actions to reduce the use of plastic to achieve a future free of this material. At the same, we can find on LinkedIn the presence of posts related to circular economy (CE). In this case, brands communicate their activities for redesigning business processes and products to shift from the traditional linear business model to a more sustainable one.

Finally, luxury companies tend to signal their efforts to reduce their production processes' impact on the environment. The most communicated actions on LinkedIn are data on reducing CO_2 emissions and all initiatives to achieve carbon neutrality by shifting towards renewable energy sources. When luxury automotive companies post on their production processes, they deal with green transition, the hybridization of cars and the creation of full-electric models.

Figure 3. The main CSR topics communicated by luxury brands on LinkedIn

Source: Authors' personal elaboration.

5.5. A focus on circular economy communication

Nowadays, the business context has changed by shifting from the traditional linear economic model based on "take-make-consume-throw away" to a circular one. The European Parliament defines the circular economy as a model of production and consumption based on sharing, leasing, reusing, repairing, refurbishing, and recycling. The scope is to minimize the production of non-disposable waste by extending the life cycle of products (De Angelis et al., 2021). Even in the luxury market, the circular economy no longer appears as an alternative business standard that may or may not be adopted. New consumers and stakeholders ask companies to increase their commitment to producing more sustainable products by adopting the approach of the circular economy. This explains why the term "circular economy" appears in 95% of the sustainability reports published by luxury companies.

Particularly, luxury conglomerates like LVMH, Kering and Richmont are moving in this direction by serving as a benchmark for smaller ones. A striking and recent example is Kering, who by creating Gucci's Circular Hub is investing in the development of a "Circular Made in Italy." Particularly, Gucci's Circular Hub was created to accelerate the circular transformation of the fashion industry's production model in Italy, by involving the entire value chain, from raw materials and product design to the optimization of production and logistics processes.

By analyzing the online contents of luxury brand companies the circular economy practices can be categorized into some areas of intervention:

a) Research and innovation in circular-product design and processes, to spread the application of circular economy among other sector players. Luxury brands are committed to offering products made by using emerging techniques that underlie the circular economy practices. Most luxury brands focus on offering products made by upcycling and recycling processes. Currently, these emerging techniques are mostly applied to limited-edition collections. However, the scope of luxury brands is to expand the use of circular economy techniques to all collections soon. Considering the hospitality sector, companies developed programs to reduce food waste at every stage of the food & beverage process. This is the case of Hilton, which created the Hotel Kitchen Toolkit to monitor and limit food waste. We can find some practices of circular economy even in the automotive sectors. For instance, Ferrari has introduced waste management and advanced technical processes that reduce waste and reuse production waste, especially aluminium, while Porsche declared a strategic priority closing the materials cycle by using secondary or renewable raw materials.
b) Partnership with organizations that make the economy work for people, businesses, and nature by supporting circular economy integration into companies' business models. This is the case for fashion luxury brands that operate with the Ellen MacArthur Foundation (EMF). The EMF aims to spur companies in the luxury industry to embrace circular economy practices to produce more responsibly, minimizing resource waste and negative impact on Planet Earth. In partnership with the Ellen McArthur Foundation, Ralph Lauren is monitoring its activities by using a company-wide measurement tool called Circulytics. Instead, Estée Lauder partnered with the EMF foundation in 2022 to test circular alternatives to plastic wrap. Other brands that have collaborated with the EMF foundation include L'Oréal, PVH, Kering L'Occitane, Yoox-Net and Chloé. In the hospitality sector, Hilton collaborated with WWF on a new methodology for measuring waste.
c) Guaranteeing a second life to its products to extend the product lifetime. In recent times, most luxury brands increased their commitment to offering second-hand products available on digital platforms. For example, Hugo Boss allows customers to buy and return used clothing by making products available on the "Pre-Loved" resale platform. Since 2022, Michael Kors has extended the life of its products by offering to buy and sell pre-loved bags and accessories through its online marketplace in the United States. In honor of National Consignment Day 2022, Jimmy Choo has also embraced the circular customer expe-

rience, partnering with luxury resale marketplace TheRealReal.It offers its U.S. customers the opportunity to give their Jimmy Choo products a second life. In 2021 LVMH launched Nona Source, an online platform for the resale of materials, fabrics, and leathers not only to buyers belonging to LVMH Maisons but also to external ones. The attention of brands on circular economy is not limited to the fashion luxury companies but it involves other luxury sectors. In the watch industry, Watchfinder & Co., a brand belonging to Richmont conglomerates, was recognized at the Watch Pro Awards as the best-used goods retailer of the year.

d) Promoting rental practices. It is another way to extend the product's lifetime but is still not a very common practice among luxury brands. However, it is expected to increase in the next years. An example of best practice is Ralph Lauren, which embedded rental consumption as a pillar of its circular economy strategy. In fact, by implementing the Lauren Look platform, it extends the life of its products by offering consumers ways to rent.

e) Raising awareness among consumers on good practices to preserve the product. For example, Hugo Boss provides its customers with special guides to materials that contain practical information on quality, product care, and preservation. These guides encourage consumers to take care of their products to extend their lifetime. Even Jimmy Choo is committed to this activity and in addition, it offers a five-year repair service that backs on track Jimmy Choo's products.

Figure 4. Areas of intervention for circular economy

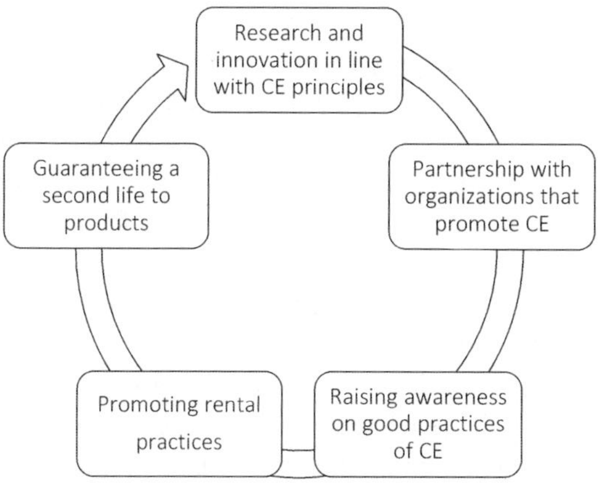

Source: Authors' elaboration.

5.6. Communication channels for sustainability in the luxury market

This chapter extensively explores the interplay between luxury and sustainability, specifically by emphasizing the dynamics of sustainability communication. In contrast to what happened in the past, the convergence of luxury and sustainability no longer raises skepticism; instead, it captures consumers' attention and interest in luxury brands. This shift in perspective is primarily propelled by the emerging generation of consumers who possess a heightened awareness of social and environmental concerns. When luxury brands communicate their sustainable products and practices, younger consumers tend to respond positively.

In the current era, one of the most discussed topics in luxury branding pertains to online communication of sustainability. This chapter aims to delve into this research area and offer readers valuable insights.

Particularly the main evidence that emerged from the chapter reveals:

1. Most luxury companies communicate sustainability through their corporate website. Luxury companies reserve for sustainability a subcategory of the "About Us" or "Corporate" label that appears in the main website menu. Their communication is profuse and well-developed, ranging from non-financial reporting to in-depth insights about sustainable practices.
2. In contrast to previous practices, luxury companies have shifted their approach to sustainability communication, moving beyond mere intentions and instead focusing on providing concrete information about their actions and performance. Consequently, the lexicon employed by luxury companies on online platforms has expanded to incorporate novel terms, such as recycling, upcycling, and fur-free, signalling their commitment to sustainable practices. This approach towards sustainability online communication helps mitigate the risk of greenwashing, ensuring transparency and credibility in their sustainability efforts. Furthermore, the dissemination of information on sustainable performance extends to both the company's official website and social media.
3. Luxury brand companies prefer LinkedIn to communicate about sustainability, and this might depend on the nature of the platform itself. More than any other social network, LinkedIn is apt to communicate with a wider range of stakeholders. The topics mainly discussed on LinkedIn are related to world preservation, inclusion, material, and production.
4. Circular economy is no longer viewed as an optional business approach.

In addition to being mentioned in 95% of luxury brands' sustainability reports, luxury companies strive to increase consumer awareness about the significance of the circular economy. The primary content they deliver focuses on innovations related to the circular economy partnerships involved in CE initiatives, as well as second-hand or rental practices.

Notes

1 Social media are communication channels that overcome the barriers of personal and mass media. Based on a dual-way communication form, social media has empowered users from passive targets of advertising to become active participants in conversations. Contents posted on social media can be divided into two categories: user-generated content (UGC) and firm-created content (FCC). User-generated content (UGC) refers to any content produced by consumers. User-generated contents are content posted online by users rather than marketing firms. Firm-created content (FCC) is any content that a business actively posts to its social media profiles to develop personal connections with customers.

2 Greenwashing is making inflated or fraudulent claims about the environmental or social benefits of a good or service for marketing or branding purposes. The concept was first introduced in the 1980s by environmental activist Jay Westerveld to refer to the hotel industry's practice of pushing patrons to reuse towels as a means of water conservation, while also engaging in more serious environmental detrimental practices (Becker-Olsen & Potucek, 2013).

3 Integrated outputs indicate a concrete integration of social, ethical, and environmental practices into products, services, processes, and policies. This entails, for instance, repurposing production materials to enable recycling and adopting a circular economy. It also entails developing a dialogue with stakeholders to begin a collaborative decision-making process and defining programs and policies aimed at encouraging community involvement, empowering them, and increasing their autonomy, particularly in lengthy and complex supply chains.

Chapter 6

THE BEST PRACTICES FOR A SUSTAINABILITY APPROACH: CASE STUDIES FROM DIFFERENT LUXURY SEGMENTS

Fabrizio Mosca and Valentina Chiaudano

ABSTRACT: *The chapter analyzes the best practices in the luxury market in terms of sustainable performance. As a result, it offers a more comprehensive understanding of the sustainable strategies employed by luxury brand companies, presenting the audience with a model for the proper implementation of sustainable practices that can contribute positively to overall well-being. The analysis facilitates the recognition of top corporate strategies across five luxury sectors to shed light on the primary initiatives undertaken within the integrated CSR framework, encompassing standards, strategic philanthropy, and integrated output.*

6.1. Introduction

> *"We judge the value of our results also by how we achieved them because long-term success comes from creating shared value".*
>
> Remo Ruffini, chairman and CEO of Moncler.

The global luxury brand market can be considered as the sum of diverse niches in which products and services are related to various aspects of daily life and communicate an elegant, refined, style-conscious, and quality-oriented way of living (Mosca, 2017). Traditionally, the luxury market was limited to only four sectors defined as personal luxury goods, because it refers to products designed for individual consumption and personal care. The personal luxury goods market includes apparel, leather goods, hard luxury (watches and jewelry), perfumes and cosmetics (Corbellini & Saviolo, 2009).

However, in addition to traditional luxury categories, other sectors, known as emerging luxury segments, have started to attract the interest of consumers (Wiedmann et al., 2007). The emerging luxury includes those services that prioritize the satisfaction of an experiential need over a material one. The emerging luxury market refers to luxury cars, luxury hospitality, fine wines & spirits, gourmet food & dining, high-quality design furniture & homeware, fine art, private jets & yachts, and luxury cruises (Chevalier & Mazzalovo, 2020).

Considering the study of sustainability in the luxury market, most studies focus exclusively on sustainable practices in the apparel sector and do not explore the other segments of the global luxury market (Kunz et al., 2020). For this reason, this chapter aims to explore the best practices of sustainability in the luxury brand market by considering not only the apparel related segment but other luxury segments that remain under investigation. Through the analysis of the case study, this chapter enables us to provide the best practices for sustainability implementation across five luxury segments: hard luxury, leather goods, cosmetics and perfume, apparel, and luxury cars. The best practices are detailed to provide insights into the key initiatives adopted alongside the three dimensions of the integrated CSR framework: standards, strategic philanthropy, and integrated output. [1]

In this paragraph, our ambition is to investigate how sustainability practices are embraced by brands belonging to different luxury brand segments.

Despite the interesting findings, the chapter presents several opportunities for further research development. Firstly, future research could consider a more extensive range of luxury brands to offer a more comprehensive perspective of best practices. Then, future studies might concentrate on emerging sectors within the luxury brand industry that so far have not received sufficient investigation For instance, future analyzes could expand to incorporate emerging luxury segments such as luxury hospitality, luxury furniture, or gourmet food.

6.2. Case selection

We adopt the case study analysis methodology, a research approach commonly used in management studies (Yin 2018) to reach our research goals. It consists of an in-depth analysis of the sustainability practices of 50 luxury brands included in the Brand Finance list published in 2022. [1] From the sample of 50 companies analyzed by using the integrated CSR framework (Freeman, 2010), [2] we have chosen those that have strategically designed their communication approach by showcasing their achieved results, as well as their dedicated commitments and objectives. These companies have managed to successfully integrate standards, philanthropic initiatives, and integrated outputs.

Specifically, we chose those companies that fulfill the following criteria:

- they demonstrate the highest level of effort in integrating sustainability into their business model;
- their website includes a dedicated section that focuses on sustainability;
- their communication strategy considers the principles of the Triple Bottom Line (economic, social, and environmental performance);
- their actions are aligned with the principles of the Stakeholder Theory, considering the interests of various stakeholders;

Table 1 shows the brands that we decided to analyze.

Table 1. Luxury brands considered in the in-depth analysis

Luxury brand	Group	Sector
Gucci	Kering	Leather Goods
Cartier	Richemont	Hard Luxury
Moncler	Moncler Group	Apparel
Guerlain	LVMH	Cosmetics & Perfume
Porsche	Volkswagen	Luxury Cars

Source: Authors' elaboration (2023).

The selected brands are analyzed as follows:

- Summary: essential information about the luxury brand company under investigation.
- Analysis of standards: understanding of the company's alignment with the minimum requirements demanded.
- Analysis of strategic philanthropy: an exploration of the company's efforts to support causes of social interest pursued by the third sector organizations or any other cause in the field of art and culture that is coherent with and relevant to the company's core business.
- Analysis of integrated outputs: definition of sustainable activities embedded in the luxury brand business model.

6.3. Case analysis

6.3.1. Gucci

Gucci was born in 1921 from the idea of Guccio Gucci, who founded a company focused on leather products and a small luggage store in Florence. In the 1930s, Guccio Gucci driven by his aristocratic hobby of horse riding, developed the distinctive icon of the horse bit. The brand's fame increased in the 1960s when jet-set personalities such as Jackie Kennedy, Liz Taylor, Peter Sellers, and Samuel Beckett began wearing Gucci. Those were the same years when the legendary logo with the two crossed Gs was created. During the following years, Gucci opened its stores from the US to the Far East, including Tokyo and Hong Kong. Then, the growth of Gucci speeded up when it became one of the leading brands of the François Pinault luxury conglomerate Kering.

Over the years, Gucci has maintained its traits of an Italian craftsman, exclusive and excellent quality brand. In addition to preserving its heritage, Gucci increased its attention to environmental and social issues, making sustainability one of its core values (Armitage et al., 2017; Bonacchi et al., 2012). Following Kerning's commitment to responsible business practices, in 2017 Gucci unveiled its 10-year "Culture of Purpose" sustainability strategy that supports a set of sustainable goals to be achieved by 2025. These goals spur the company to implement actions and initiatives to generate positive change for people and the planet. The Culture of Purpose is presented within the Gucci Equilibrium online platform, which links the brand's aesthetics and heritage with Gucci's commitment to generating positive change for people and the planet.

Standards

Through various initiatives, Gucci has aimed to align with different sustainability standards. Moreover, in line with the decision to become completely carbon neutral, the Maison has chosen to have all its fashion shows certified ISO 20121. This standard provides guidelines for designing a sustainable event in all its phases, including the use of sustainable materials, promoting materials that can be reused, recycled, or rented, preferring local catering, avoiding single-use plastic, donating surplus food, as well as increasing the use of green electricity and LED lighting, and choosing sustainable transportation options.

In 2019, the fashion house signed the Fashion Pact together with Kering, which is a significant commitment to address climate change collectively. One of the key issues highlighted in this pact is the consumption and waste of plastic. The goal is to eliminate single-use plastic from packaging by 2030 and to adopt more sustainable and circular alternatives, not only for products but also for stores and offices. The initiative includes plastic-free measures aimed at employees, promoting a plastic-free environment throughout the organization.

Since 2007, all Gucci stores have been certified with the SA8000 certification. It is the accredited international standard that meets the needs of organizations striving to differentiate themselves through their commitment to sustainable development, particularly in social issues Then, in 2019 Gucci also obtained the ISO 45001 certification for occupational health and safety. Moreover, Gucci protects the rights of LGBTQIA+ individuals and supports the UN's "LGBT Business Conduct" standards for companies. These standards include the elimination of any form of discrimination in the workplace, ensuring that there are no discriminatory practices toward customers, suppliers, and all stakeholders in business activities, and collaborating with business partners to address discrimination issues throughout the entire supply chain.

Considering the economic and social reporting standards, from 2011 Gucci has conducted an annual comparative analysis of environmental profits and losses by using the Environmental Profit & Loss (EP&L), a methodology developed by its parent company, Kering. This methodology is applied throughout Gucci's value chain, from sourcing to product manufacturing and retail, to highlight progress in terms of sustainability. The EP&L methodology allows Gucci to measure greenhouse gas emissions, air and water pollution, water consumption, land use, and waste production resulting from its business activities. Gucci's EP&L reporting data is included in Kerning's annual Universal Registration Document, which is the Group's annual report on financial and non-financial activities. The document presents data on the social and environmental impacts of the Kering Group's global operations, under the EU's legislative requirements for non-financial reporting.

Strategic philanthropy

To promote Gender Equality Gucci created the CHIME program in collaboration with Salma Hayek Pinault and Beyoncé Knowles-Carter. This program, by collaborating with 185 non-profit partners, including organizations like Equality Now, the Global Fund for Women, Ms. Foundation for Women, mothers2mother, and UN Women, has generated almost USD 21.5 million to back over 500 projects worldwide. In 2022 Gucci CHIME donated USD 500,000 to the UN Refugee Agency (UNHCR) to offer urgent assistance to refugees seeking safety from violence in Ukraine. Among its diverse range of initiatives, Gucci also provides support to refugees through employment prospects. Furthermore, Gucci shows its impact on society by implementing the Gucci Changemakers North America. It is an initiative that aims to increase inclusion and diversity within the fashion industry and across communities and cities in North America. Specifically, this program provides students and 40 organizations with grant funding and scholarship initiatives. In 2022, a total of 2,000 employees engaged in the Gucci Changemakers volunteering program, collectively contributing over 7,000 volunteer hours to support more than 100 NGOs across 55 cities worldwide.

Integrated outputs

"We look at the world around us in a holistic way and believe that it is our duty to be sustainable, responsible and accountable in everything we do". Building upon this statement, Gucci demonstrates a growing dedication to innovating products and embracing circular economy processes to enhance its environmental impact. For example, in 2022 the Scrap-less program enabled Gucci to prevent the utilization of 91,000 meters of leather and consequently to conserve energy equivalent to 477 MWh, refrain from using 75 tons of chemicals, including 10 tons of chrome, prevent the generation of over 73.4 tons of waste, and preserve 5.8 million liters of water. The Gucci-Up initiative instead helped Gucci to successfully repurpose 350 tons of surplus leather, 298 tons of textile remnants, and 67 tons of metal scraps. Furthermore, Gucci achieved significant progress in integrating sustainable materials into Gucci's collections. Specifically, in 2022 Gucci increased the utilization of organic or recycled cotton, organic, recycled, or responsibly sourced wool and cashmere, metal or chrome-free leather, organic silk, responsibly sourced precious metals, and paper from responsibly managed forest sources.

Considering the dedication to embracing more environmentally friendly energy management, Gucci reduced HG emissions in Scopes 1 and 2. In addition, Gucci effectively reached the milestone of sourcing 100% renewable energy for all stores worldwide.

The subject of traceability is also a matter of significant interest for Gucci. The brand demonstrates its strong commitment to raw material traceability by achieving an overall traceability rate of 97% in 2022. In 2022, 36% of our suppliers benefited from this initiative, amounting to a total of EUR 330 million.

Gucci firmly believes that supporting well-being pays attention to inclusion and diversity. For this reason, Gucci has a strong commitment to female leadership and monitors the gender pay gap. Moreover, Gucci was recognized as one of the 2022 Best Places to Work for Disability Inclusion by the Disability Equality Index. This acknowledgment underscores Gucci's commitment to creating enriching opportunities for individuals with disabilities within the company's workforce.

Gucci also places considerable emphasis on employee training, making investments in the advancement of skills and knowledge to uphold the creative heritage of Made in Italy products. Notably, Gucci strongly focuses on women's training, with 178 women having participated in training sessions since 2020.

Table 2. Integrated CSR framework applied to Gucci

Dimensions	Activities
1. Standards	ISO 20121, LEED certification
	ISO 9001
	SA8000, ISO 45001, LGBT Business Conduct standard, Code of conduct, Fashion Pact
	EP&L
2. Strategic philanthropy	Gucci Chime
	Gucci Changemakers North America
	7,000 volunteer hours to support NGOs
3. Integrated outputs	Use of organic or recycled cotton, organic, recycled, or responsibly sourced wool and cashmere, metal or chrome-free leather and organic silk, responsibly sourced precious metals, paper from responsibly managed forest sources
	Raw material traceability rate of 97%
	Capacity to reduce the use of plastic
	Reducing HG emissions in Scopes 1 and 2, 100% renewable energy
	Employees' training and development policy for preserving the craft
	Empowering women, diversity, and inclusion

Source: Authors' elaboration.

6.3.2. Cartier

Cartier was founded in 1847 by Louis Cartier in Paris and gained fame with the patronage of Princess Mathilde and Empress Eugenie. From that time, it started the tradition of kings, queens and emperors that will characterize the entire history of the French Maison including Italian, Greek, Spanish and Portugal cohorts. After opening its famous boutique in Paris and London, Cartier expanded to New York in 1909 and formed a partnership with Edward Jaeger in the 1920s. In 1972, it was acquired by investors led by Joseph Kanoui, and it is now part of Richemont. Cartier is known for iconic pieces like the "Bestiary" brooch and the Santos-Dumont wristwatch. In 2019, Forbes ranked Cartier as the fifth most valuable brand in the world, thanks to its commitment to offering jewelry pieces that transcend time. The company intends to show its attention to the future generation of consumers by embracing sustainability in every activity from purchasing activities to retailing, passing through manufacturing. Specifically, Cartier's commitment to sustainability is related to three major categories: business ethics, social performance, and environmental performance.

Standards

Cartier's policies are seamlessly aligned with Richemont. In 2005, Cartier proudly emerged as one of the 14 founding members of the Responsible Jewellery Council (RJC), an organization dedicated to promoting responsible practices in the jewelry industry. Hence, each customer is informed that all diamonds or precious stones used in Cartier's jewelry are sourced through ethical and responsible practices. Furthermore, Cartier requires all suppliers to adhere to Cartier's Corporate Responsibility Policy, which aligns with the fundamental rights of human beings and the dignity of individuals, as defined by the United Nations Universal Declaration of Human Rights.

Strategic Philanthropy

The Foundation Cartier Pour l'Art Contemporain, located in Paris, cultivates unexpected encounters among artists, scientists, philosophers, musicians, and architects. Cartier promotes donations through its philanthropic foundation, known as Cartier Philanthropy, which supports numerous charitable initiatives and works to improve the conditions of the most vulnerable individuals, particularly women and children living in less developed regions of the world. For example, it ensures access to clean water, adequate food, sanitary facilities, education, and medical care for children and their families. Additionally, as part of its commitment to gender equality, Cartier Philanthropy assists women who are victims of violence in accessing the knowledge, skills, and resources needed to rebuild their lives. The foundation is also active in emergency response, providing aid to save lives, alleviating suffering, and reducing casualties. Finally, it helps communities enhance their preparedness for emergency management. Moreover, Cartier demonstrates its dedication to empowering communities through the Women's Initiative. Established in 2006 in partnership with

INSEAD Business School, this global program aims to identify, support, and advance women entrepreneurs and their businesses.

Integrated Outputs

First, Cartier embraced circular economy principles by ensuring the option for all its customers to have any Cartier item repaired. In 1996, Cartier introduced the Cartier Tradition program. This program makes available for purchase Cartier creations that have been authenticated, documented, and if required, restored according to historical information preserved by the Archives.

The fight against conflict diamonds stands as an utmost priority for Cartier. Since its inception in 2003, Cartier has subjected all diamond purchases to the Kimberley Process Certification Scheme, which requires all sellers of cut diamonds to issue a written assurance, which is then passed along each time the diamond changes hand. This assurance declaration guarantees that the diamond originates from a conflict-free country.

Cartier has also a strong commitment to reducing the use of water, waste, and energy. Acknowledging the environmental and economic implications of lighting in its boutiques, Cartier has envisioned its lighting concept to strike a balance between necessity and environmental impact management. This drive led Cartier to be among the pioneers in adopting LED lighting. The implementation of this new lighting paradigm began in 2009 with table lamps and wall displays, followed by counters and wall lamps in 2010. From 2012 onward, Cartier's new boutiques have exclusively utilized LED lamps. Furthermore, in 2009, Cartier achieved a remarkable feat by attaining carbon neutrality. Subsequently, the brand took steps toward vertically integrating renewable energy production to fulfil the manufacturer's electricity requisites for production, lighting, heating, and air conditioning.

Another notable commitment for Cartier is the preservation of savoir-faire. The brand actively promotes the transmission of artisanal craftsmanship through initiatives such as the Maison des Métiers d'Art, the Institut Joaillerie Cartier, and the inclusion of one of the few remaining master carvers and glyptic experts in its workshops. Established in 2014, the Maison des Métiers d'Art endeavors to conserve, innovate, and disseminate artistic crafts, while the Institut Joaillerie Cartier, founded in 2002, aims to perpetuate and enhance jewelry craftsmanship through tailor-made training programs for skills refinement.

Finally, the brand promotes diversity and equal opportunity by implementing the DEI HR diagnostic, a tool used to monitor the implementation of initiatives in line with diversity and inclusion principles.

Table 3. Integrated CSR framework applied to Cartier

Dimensions	Activities
1. Standards	Repairing service for all Cartier piece Kimberly Certification, LEED certification The United Nations Universal Declaration of Human Rights, Code of Conduct
2. Strategic philanthropy	Partnership with UNICEF, Foundation Cartier Pour l'Art Contemporain, Cartier Philanthropy Women's Initiative
3. Integrated outputs	Repairing service for all Cartier piece Traceability of suppliers to guarantee diamonds from conflict-free country Reducing the use of water, waste, and energy Carbon Neutrality Employees' training and development policy for preserving the craft Promoting diversity and equal opportunity with DEI HR diagnostic

Source: Authors' elaboration.

6.3.3. Moncler

Moncler was founded in 1952 by René Ramillon, a French artisan producer of mountain equipment. The name "Moncler" is derived from Monestier de Clermont, the French mountain village where the company originated. Initially designed exclusively for mountain enthusiasts, in the early 1980s Moncler's clothing gradually evolved to suit everyday wear and urban settings, becoming a fashion phenomenon. During the 1990s, the company faced a challenging period due to wrong decisions in distribution channels, product placement in large retail centers, and a failure to effectively convey the brand's essence of luxury, quality, and fashion. In 2003, Remo Ruffini acquired the company and thanks to his leadership, the brand was restored to its previous standards, focusing on products, distribution, and communication to overcome its previous lack of positioning in the luxury sector.

In 2014, Moncler's revenue growth experienced a setback due to a scandal involving animal mistreatment. A television program accused Moncler of animal abuse, highlighting alleged inhumane methods used by the company's suppliers in the process of plucking geese for their feathers. This supply chain management failure had a significant impact on Moncler's reputation, prompting the company to understand the importance of ensuring good practices among suppliers. Moncler's corporate scandal led the company to adopt CSR disclosures, positioning the company among those striving for corporate legitimacy through sustainability investments and addressing stakeholders' concerns (Broccardo et al., 2023). Since 2015 Moncler has adopted a Sustainability Plan that aligns with the priorities defined in the 2030 Agenda for Sustainable Development. Today, its sustainability plan focuses on five strategic priorities: climate change, circular economy, responsible supply chain, diversity enhancement, and support for local communities. The plan is updated annually, considering the progress of the projects and the need to set new objectives in the pursuit of a continuous improvement perspective.

Standards

Moncler operates to increase resource efficiency. In this endeavor, the group implemented several efficiency measures., including the certification ISO 14001 for all plants and the LEED certification for all new plants and stores. Moncler also periodically subjects its commercial partners to audits to verify the management of the brands and the compliance with their principles of service and quality, by the ISO 9000 standard.

Regarding people standards, Moncler places great importance on the protection and promotion of health, safety, and well-being, considering them as fundamental values. To uphold this commitment, the company meets certain standards and adheres to diverse organizations that promote a secure and healthy working environment. Specifically, in 2016, Moncler obtained the OHSAS 18001 certification for its offices and stores in Italy, subsequently expanding it globally in 2019. Additionally, following the international standard ISO 45001, the company ensures a comprehensive health and safety management system.

Moncler also demonstrates its commitment to combat modern slavery, forced labor, and human trafficking by signing the Modern Slavery Act.

During the challenges posed by the pandemic, Moncler took proactive steps to support the clothing industry's supply chains by actively participating in the call to action initiated by the International Labor Organization (ILO). The company ensured the continuity of payment terms and methods, provided economic support to struggling stakeholders in the supply chain, and closely monitored compliance with ethical principles outlined in the Company and Supplier Code of Conduct. The focus was on human rights, worker health and safety, and environmental protection.

Finally, considering the accountability standards, the group writes the non-financial statement according to the GRI standards.

Strategic Philanthropy

Moncler is active in partnerships and donations. For several years, Moncler has been supporting UNICEF, which provides humanitarian assistance to children and their communities, and other associations such as UNHCR, the UN Refugee Agency, which safeguards the rights and well-being of refugees worldwide, and the Francesca Rava Foundation – NPH. These partnerships aim to protect the most vulnerable families living in some of the coldest regions in the world, where already extreme living conditions worsen during winter, making survival a daily struggle. Moreover, Moncler implemented collaborations with the most important universities and business schools in the world.

Moncler actively engages in activities to support the local communities where it operates, recognizing that the company's development can only thrive in harmony and with full respect for the community. These efforts stem from an ongoing dialogue and interaction between Moncler's local leaders at main sites and representatives of the communities or territorial authorities. The objective of this dialogue is to understand stakeholders' needs, expectations, and the impact of the company's activities on the population, thereby ensuring social consensus. Moncler's commitment to supporting the community is realized through various initiatives focused on key areas, including aiding populations during emergencies situations, supporting scientific research and prevention efforts, contributing to social development and poverty alleviation, and promoting arts and culture. Approximately EUR 2.7 million have been allocated by Moncler to support these endeavors aimed at benefiting the local communities.

Since 2018, Moncler has actively promoted corporate volunteering, recognizing its significance not only in fulfilling social responsibility but also in nurturing a culture of diversity and solidarity. Through partnerships with various nonprofit organizations covering a wide range of initiatives from environmental causes to social projects, Moncler has been driving impactful change. The company encourages every employee at its corporate locations across the globe to participate in the proposed volunteering activities, providing them with the opportunity to dedicate two days each year. This approach allows employees to choose from a diverse array of organizations, types of activities and dates, fostering a sense of empowerment and engagement. As a result of these efforts, 100% of the eligible workforce has been engaged in volunteering projects. Specifically,

241 employees have actively participated in volunteering programs in 2022, collectively contributing over 1,600 hours during their working hours. The main intervention area was represented by natural disasters and emergency response, followed by scientific research and social initiatives.

Moncler places great importance on the protection and promotion of health, safety, and well-being, considering them as fundamental values.

Integrated outputs

Some of the key principles of sustainability, such as the ability of products to endure over time, have always been part of Moncler's DNA. The high quality of the products and their timeless nature ensure an exceptionally long lifespan. In recent times, Moncler also contributed to the environment by committing to using recycled raw materials. Specifically, Moncler increased its feather recycling initiatives within its garments by introducing the DIST protocol that outlines the requirements for obtaining recycled feather certification. Moncler Group is also committed to reducing materials used for packaging, as well as researching and implementing lower-impact alternatives.

To decrease energy consumption and CO_2 emissions, Moncler is undertaking various initiatives across its stores, offices, logistic hub, and production facilities. These efforts range from the gradual replacement of traditional lighting systems with LED lamps to the implementation of Building Management Supervisory Systems for integrated and more efficient energy consumption management. The company is also employing electricity from renewable sources, utilizing eco-friendly computer equipment, and promoting the gradual integration of low-impact environmentally friendly vehicles into its fleet. Moreover, Moncler has initiated a series of activities aimed not only at assessing its water consumption impacts but also at analyzing water risk across its sites and throughout the supply chain. The objective of these efforts is to identify improvement actions and enhance water management practices.

Moncler has established audit activities concerning animal welfare and the traceability of down, following the DIST Protocol (Down Integrity System & Traceability) throughout the entire supply chain. The DIST Protocol, whose implementation began in 2015, governs the breeding methods of white geese, as well as the traceability and technical quality of down. Moncler exclusively procures down that has obtained the DIST certification. Among the foundational requirements that must be upheld at every level of the supply chain, the following are highlighted:

- Down must be sourced exclusively from white geese that are reared within the food supply chain of which down is a by-product.
- No form of live plucking or force-feeding of animals is permitted.

Training plays a pivotal role in the process of developing and enhancing individuals. It serves as a fundamental tool to foster the growth and consolidation of individual skills, facilitate a continuous upskilling of the essential knowledge required to keep up with ongoing business changes, and ultimately disseminate the values and strategy of the Group, supporting its cultural and organizational growth and evolution. Processes are designed to cater to the professional advancement of all individuals, enabling each employee to reach their full potential through opportunities based solely on skills, experiences, and potential. In 2022, an investment of over 1,708,000 Euros was made in training, resulting in the delivery of 170,843 training hours (a 44% increase in hours compared to 2021), benefiting over 5,400 employees.

Moncler's dedication to promoting and safeguarding the well-being of its employees goes beyond the scope of company activities and professional hazards. For all individuals employed on permanent or apprentice contracts at Moncler, a comprehensive range of benefits and services is provided. These include reimbursement of educational expenses, gift vouchers, leisure solutions, and wellness packages. The utilization of these services is also extended to family members. Moncler is actively engaged in forming partnerships with local healthcare centers to ensure that employees have access to high-quality medical facilities at advantageous rates. Throughout 2022, a dedicated psychological counseling service was introduced for employees across Moncler's Italian locations. Furthermore, employees at the corporate headquarters in Trebaseleghe (Padova), have received full financial support from the company for the nursery and kindergarten facilities.

In 2023, Moncler increased its commitment to the promotion of a culture of inclusion and the enhancement of diversity within the company.

Table 4. Integrated CSR framework applied to Moncler

Dimensions	Activities
1. Standards	ISO 14001, LEED certification ISO 9001 OHSAS 18001, ISO 45001, Modern Slavery Act, Code of conduct Non-financial disclosure (GRI)
2. Strategic philanthropy	Partnership with UNICEF, UNHCR, Francesca Rava Foundation Local community empowerment 1600 hours of employees volunteering in 2022
3. Integrated outputs	Feather recycling initiatives, low-impact packaging Down Integrity System & Traceability Zero Waste Project, activities to assess and reduce the water consumption, Adoption of renewable energy sources and improving operational efficiency Employees' training and development policy Benefits and personal services, advantageous rates from local healthcare centers, psychological counseling, promotion of inclusion and diversity culture

Source: Authors' elaboration.

6.3.4. Guerlain

Founded in 1828, Guerlain's origins trace back to its founder Pierre-Francois-Pascal Guerlain, who inaugurated the brand's first boutique in Paris. Leveraging a background in both medicine and chemistry, his groundbreaking approach yielded rapid triumphs, marked by a series of pioneering achievements. Guerlain can claim credit for pioneering scientifically grounded skincare, the introduction of kohl eyeliner and mascara, and a remarkable innovation in 1840: the inception of the first-ever lipsticks. Guerlain stands as a pioneering cosmetic brand in the realm of sustainability as well. Since 2007, the brand has embraced its role in safeguarding Nature in the pursuit of Beauty. With a resolute focus on preservation, Guerlain has placed the protection of the environment at the very heart of its endeavors.

Standards

With a profound connection between the Maison and Nature, serving as a genuine source of inspiration for Guerlain's creations, the company maintains specific standards aimed at preserving the environment. In pursuit of this goal, Guerlain actively collaborates with the Union for Ethical BioTrade (UEBT), a non-profit organization committed to advocating responsible sourcing that revitalizes nature and secures a brighter future for communities through ethical ingredient procurement from biodiversity. Furthermore, Guerlain upholds the protection of endangered species by adhering to the Washington Convention on International Trade in Endangered Species of Wild Fauna and Flora, commonly known as CITES.

Guerlain's dedication to environmental preservation is further underscored by the company's alignment with specific ISO standards. Notably, all of Guerlain's sites and subsidiaries hold ISO 14001 certification that attests to Guerlain's commitments to address environmental aspects, fulfill legal compliance obligations, and assess and evaluate risks and opportunities. Guerlain's products adhere to the ISO 16128 standard, ensuring a proportion of natural ingredients in line with Guerlain's eco-formulation approach. In terms of product assessment, Guerlain adheres to the ISO 14040/44 standard, enabling the evaluation and interpretation of the environmental impacts of any product or service throughout its entire lifecycle. This comprehensive approach encompasses considerations such as what materials are utilized, the origin and manufacturing process of components, transportation logistics, the distribution of the final product, and its eventual end-of-life considerations.

Strategic Philanthropy

As part of its commitment to biodiversity, Guerlain has been focusing on supporting bees, an indispensable creature for the food security of our planet. In 2011 the company created the "Guerlain for Bees Conservation Programme", which currently encompasses 10 partnerships and dedicated initiatives aimed at bees' preservation. Among the activities in favor of bees, by 2021 Guerlain has established funding for the "World Bee Day" whose 2022 edition collected one million euros. Furthermore, Guerlain collaborates with the Italian Consorzio nazionale apicoltori (CONAPI) on two projects: "Women for Bees", which trains eleven female beekeepers, and "Bee School", educating children about the role and importance of bees.

Finally, the Maison fosters engaged artistic and cultural collaborations, notably by participating in the "Art and Ecology" series at the Palais de Tokyo in Paris.

Integrated outputs

Guerlain's product takes care of the environment and biodiversity. The company shows a high commitment to developing eco-compatible and biodegradable products, eliminating the use of environmentally harmful ingredients, and reducing energy consumption during product manufacturing. The company created an index called the Formulation Eco-conceived (IFE) that evaluates the sustainability score of its products by considering six components: natural ingredients, traceability, environmental impact through biodegradability and eco-toxicity, sustainability, the substitution of controversial ingredients, and the quantification of the number of ingredients required.

Table 5. Integrated CSR framework applied to Guerlain

Dimensions	Activities
1. Standards	ISO14001, ISO16128, ISO14040, ISO14044, UBET certification
2. Strategic philanthropy	Partnership with UNESCO and artistic and cultural collaborations Aqua Allegoria del 2022 "Bee School", "Women for Bee" 1600 hours of employees volunteering in 2022
3. Integrated outputs	Recycling, Upcycling, Reuse of materials, eco-design "Bee Respect" traceability and transparency platform Recycling activities, reduction of water consumption and hazardous waste, consumption from renewable sources Reduction of GHG emissions in scopes 1 and 2 10,000 hours of training provided to employees, promotion of diversity and inclusion Employees' access to health services provided or covered by the company, improving employees' work condition

Source: Author's elaboration.

In line with what happens in the perfume and cosmetic sector, Guerlain puts attention on the traceability of its materials and shares all the details about the origin and lifecycle of its creations through "Bee Respect", a platform designed in 2019 to ensure transparency and to list the luxury brand's principal suppliers. Moreover, Guerlain also fosters employee well-being and development through various initiatives. First, the company celebrates talents and supports youth and equal opportunities. The company collaborates with the LVMH Institute of métiers excellence (ME Institute) to preserve and transmit to younger generations its unique savoir-faire. Then, in line with its idea of recognizing individuality, Guerlain is focused particularly on subjects of diversity and gender equality. Considering the diversity, Guerlains manages an inclusion program for people with disabilities, while in terms of gender equality women occupy 79% of executive positions, and they represent 74% of all personnel. Finally, the brand promotes employee well-being with its wellness program, offering fitness and training activities to all staff.

6.3.5 Porsche

Porsche's history starts in 1931 with the foundation of Porsche GmbH, a design studio and engineering firm situated in Stuttgart. Then, the founder Ferdinand Porsche and his son Ferdinand ("Ferry") launched the company in 1948, with a workforce of 200 employees. Since then, due to the visionary efforts of the founder and his son, the brand name "Porsche" has become synonymous with both sports and racer cars.

In 2012, following a period of financial fluctuations, Volkswagen Group finalized an agreement for the acquisition of Porsche which serves the luxury segment of the Group. Just one year later, Porsche introduced the innovative Porsche 918, a mid-engine hybrid supercar with unparalleled power and performance in the history of Porsche's road cars. In recent times, driving toward a greener horizon, Porsche has demonstrated a resolute commitment to sustainability, focusing on six key pillars: decarbonization, circular economy, diversity, partnerships, supply chain responsibility, governance, and transparency. This testament to Porsche's ethos radiates its dedication not only to engineering excellence but also to a harmonious coexistence with our planet's future.

Standards

Considering the standards, Porsche is dedicated to implementing the requirements outlined by ISO 14001, ISO 50001, and the EMAS Regulation. For instance, the Stuttgart-Zuffenhausen plant adheres to the ISO 50001 energy management standard, while other sites, including Porsche Leipzig GmbH, the Weissach research and development center, the central spare parts warehouse in Sachsenheim, and Porsche Werkzeugbau GmbH, conform both to ISO 50001 and ISO 14001. Porsche has also been certified with LEED (Leadership in Energy and Environmental Design) and BREEAM (Building Research Establishment Environmental Assessment Method) for buildings in Shanghai, London, and Atlanta. Concerning quality, Porsche's production processes are certified according to ISO 9001 standards.

In 2019, Porsche became the first automotive manufacturer to join the Value Balancing Alliance to develop a standardized method for measuring and evaluating the environmental and societal impact of corporate activities in monetary terms. Furthermore, at Porsche people are considered at the heart of the company. For this reason, Porsche rejects all forms of modern slavery by signing the Modern Slavery Act and promoting diversity and inclusion. The company expects both employees and suppliers to act according to its Code of Conduct, which outlines fundamental principles to ensure that activities are conducted lawfully.

Porsche publishes the Report in compliance with the GRI Standards of the Global Reporting Initiative (GRI).

Strategic philanthropy

Porsche provides global support to regions and communities in their efforts for environmental preservation, as well as in the establishment of favorable working and living conditions, and the promotion of social unity. Special focus is given to young individuals and those facing disadvantages, for whom Porsche has launched multiple partnerships with NGOs and other initiatives. Specifically, Porsche, in collaboration with UNICEF, launched the innovative Mobile Educational Training and Resource Unit (METRU) program. This initiative aimed to bring qualified instructors, educational kits, student packages, libraries, and sports equipment to young individuals in underprivileged areas. In collaboration with Michelin, Porsche is promoting sustainable natural rubber extraction through the CASCADE project (Committed Actions for Smallholders Capacity Development). Sports car manufacturers and tire producers are striving to enhance transparency and improve working conditions during rubber extraction. The initiative focuses on supporting numerous smallholders involved in rubber extraction in Sumatra, Indonesia. It aims to train over 1,000 smallholders to adopt more environmentally friendly and efficient production methods. Porsche and Michelin are jointly investing approximately one million euros in the project, which is expected to run until 2024.

In 2018, Porsche established its foundation, the Ferry Porsche Foundation which supports projects related to science, research, education, as well as training and development. It also promotes cultural and environmental initiatives and aids individuals facing social difficulties.

Furthermore, Porsche promotes The Porsche Hilft program, which is a volunteer platform created by the company as a digital placement platform that lists organizations and associations in need of volunteer support. Individuals and teams, including new employees and retirees of Porsche, can quickly and directly find areas where help is required. Each project and organization align with Porsche's sustainability strategy. Employees frequently utilize this service, and already hundreds of hours of volunteer commitment have been contributed.

Integrated outputs

Porsche is diligently working to achieve the goals set in its strategy, with significant emphasis on reduction targets for energy, CO_2, waste, water, and volatile organic compounds.

Electrification is the company's primary focus, with an investment of approximately 15 billion euros allocated until 2025. This investment encompasses electrification, digitalization, and sustainable production of its vehicles. As a result, Porsche is systematically expanding its range of electric mobility offerings. In line with this focus on sustainability, the company's corporate responsibility extends along the entire value chain. Consequently, the company is placing a strong focus on sustainability in its supplier management strategy. The sustainability assessment of its direct suppliers has become a mandatory criterion for contract awards since the introduction of the sustainability rating (S-rating). Additionally, the materials used in Porsche's products undergo systematic analysis to evaluate potential risks related to their origin, production conditions, or extraction of raw materials.

In terms of business process impact on the environment, Porsche continues to promote and increase the share of renewable energy generated on its sites. For example, in Leipzig, the company utilizes solar energy produced by a four-megawatt photovoltaic system. Cogeneration plants for electricity and heat, with an overall efficiency exceeding 83%, cover a significant portion of the remaining energy demand. Moreover, Porsche's new buildings exceed the minimum requirements for energy efficiency mandated by law. Since 2014, the company has successfully reduced water consumption per vehicle in its production activities by over 16%.

Porsche's dedication to its employees is evident in several ways. For over 10 years, the Porsche Aftersales Vocational Education (PAVE) program has provided highly skilled technical training to personnel. Employees undergo training at international sites in line with European standards and are subsequently appointed as members of Porsche dealer organizations and other brands within the Volkswagen Group worldwide. PAVE facilitates access to solid and top-notch professional training for young adults, particularly those facing disadvantages. This mutually beneficial initiative allows both the trainees and the Group to reap the rewards. Through long-term strategic school partnerships, professional training expertise is integrated at the local level.

The International Diversity Community was established to promote diversity. It serves as a forum that brings together all Porsche subsidiaries worldwide. The primary goal is to strengthen the global perspective on diversity and equal opportunities as part of the 2030 Strategy. The community fosters ideas for concrete implementation of diverse viewpoints within Porsche markets, facilitating learning from each other through dialogue and exchange. Moreover, Porsche is committed to ensuring a work-life balance for its employees and offers various measures and options to support them. For instance, local cooperation partners ensure that childcare facilities are available near the company's sites. Additionally, in case of emergencies, additional childcare places are available at daycare centers in Stuttgart. Parents also have the option to bring their children to work for a few hours. During summer, employees' children can attend a holiday program. Through its family service, Porsche provides free and personalized counseling and support on all aspects of family life, particularly for expecting parents and elderly care.

Porsche considers the individual needs of its employees and promotes flexible work options concerning workplace and working hours, providing a high degree of flexibility based on specific situations. This flexibility was further reinforced in 2021 with the introduction of the mobile work agreement, allowing up to 12 full days of mobile work per month.

Besides workplace safety systems and local medical assistance for employees, Porsche offers preventive health promotion activities at the workplace. Porsche Health Management provides courses on healthy eating, relaxation techniques, and effective self-management. Employees can also access individual physiotherapy advice at the workplace. Factory doctors assist in designing healthy and ergonomic workplaces, provide guidance to employees, and conduct preventive checks. Additionally, they help in organizing first aid and reintegrating employees into the workplace after illnesses.

Finally, the Proud@Porsche community represents an internal LGBTIQ network used by employees as a platform for networking and continuous dialogue.

Table 6. Integrated CSR framework applied to Porsche

Dimensions	Activities
1. Standards	ISO 14001, ISO 50001, LEED certification, BREEAM ISO 9001 Modern Slavery Act, Code of Conduct of employees and suppliers GRI
2. Strategic philanthropy	Collaboration with UNICEF, CASCADE project Ferry Porsche Foundation Volunteering platform
3. Integrated outputs	Electric vehicles Supplier management strategy Capacity to reduce the use of water Reduction of CO_2 emissions and waste Technical training for highly qualified employees Initiative to support the work-life balance, workplace safety system Code of Ethics

Source: Author's elaboration.

Notes

1 We choose the brands for analysis considering the list provided by Brand Finance in 2022 The list ranks the world's top brands based on their brand value.

2 As explained in Appendix 2, the integrated CSR framework supports our understanding of the degree to which luxury brands participate in integrated CSR activities, grouped into three categories: standards, strategic philanthropy, and integrated outputs. Standards imply less commitment to integrated CSR into the business model, while integrated outputs require companies to enhance their business model to make it more sustainable-oriented.

REFERENCES

Achabou, M.A., & Dekhili, S. (2013). Luxury and sustainable development: Is there a match?. *Journal of Business Research*, 66(10), 1896-1903.

Adams, C.A., & Abhayawansa, S. (2022). Connecting the COVID-19 pandemic, environmental, social and governance (ESG) investing and calls for 'harmonisation' of sustainability reporting. *Critical Perspectives on Accounting*, 82(102309), 102309.

Adıgüzel, F., & Donato, C. (2021). Proud to be sustainable: Upcycled versus recycled luxury products. *Journal of Business Research*, 130, 137-146.

Afolabi, H., Ram, R., & Rimmel, G. (2022). Harmonization of sustainability reporting regulation: Analysis of a contested arena. *Sustainability*, 14(9), 5517.

Ahmad, H., Yaqub, M., & Lee, S.H. (2023). Environmental-, social-, and governance-related factors for business investment and sustainability: A scientometric review of global trends. *Environment Development and Sustainability*.

Alkaraan, F., Albitar, K., Hussainey, K., & Venkatesh, V.G. (2022). Corporate transformation toward Industry 4.0 and financial performance: The influence of environmental, social, and governance (ESG). *Technological Forecasting and Social Change*, 175, 121423.

Altagamma. (2020). *Altagamma social luxury index*. https://altagamma.it/media/source/CS%20Altagamma%20Social%20Luxury%20Index_2020_DEF.pdf.

Amatulli, C., De Angelis, M., & Donato, C. (2021a). The atypicality of sustainable luxury products. *Psychology & Marketing*, 38(11), 1990-2005.

Amatulli, C., De Angelis, M., Korschun, D., & Romani, S. (2018). Consumers' perceptions of luxury brands' CSR initiatives: An investigation of the role of status and conspicuous consumption. *Journal of Cleaner Production*, 194, 277-287.

Amatulli, C., De Angelis, M., & Stoppani, A. (2021b). The appeal of sustainability in luxury hospitality: An investigation on the role of perceived integrity. *Tourism Management*, 83(104228), 104228.

Aria, M., & Cuccurullo, C. (2017). Bibliometrix: An R-tool for comprehensive science mapping analysis. *Journal of Informetrics*, 11(4), 959-975.

Arici, H.E., Cakmakoglu Arıcı, N., & Altinay, L. (2023). The use of big data analytics to discover customers' perceptions of and satisfaction with green hotel service quality. *Current Issues in Tourism*, 26(2), 270-288.

Arli, D., Gil, LDA., & Esch, P. (2020). The effect of religiosity on luxury goods:

The case of Chilean youths. *International Journal of Consumer Studies*, 44(3), 181-190.

Armitage, J., & Roberts, J. (2016). *Critical luxury studies: Art, design, media*. Edinburgh University Press.

Armitage, J., Roberts, J., & Sekhon, Y.K. (2017). Luxury products and services and the sustainable value chain: Six management lessons from Gucci. In M. Gardetti, (Ed.) *Sustainable Management of Luxury*. Springer Singapore, 259-279.

Arrington, D.W. (2019). Ethical and sustainable luxury: The paradox of consumerism and caring. *Engaging with Fashion*, 77-89.

Athwal, N., Wells, V.K., Carrigan, M., & Henninger, C.E. (2019). Sustainable luxury marketing: A synthesis and research agenda. *International Journal of Management Reviews*, 21(4), 405-426.

Bahadori, N., Kaymak, T., & Seraj, M. (2021). Environmental, social, and governance factors in emerging markets: The impact on firm performance. *Business Strategy & Development*, 4(4), 411-422.

Baker, J., Ashill, N., Amer, N., & Diab, E. (2018). The internet dilemma: An exploratory study of luxury firms' usage of internet-based technologies. *Journal of Retailing and Consumer Services*, 41, 37-47.

Baker, M.A., Davis, E.A., & Weaver, P.A. (2014). Eco-friendly attitudes, barriers to participation, and differences in behavior at green hotels. *Cornell Hospitality Quarterly*, 55(1), 89-99.

Banister, E., Roper, S., & Potavanich, T. (2020). Consumers' practices of everyday luxury. *Journal of Business Research*, 116, 458-466.

Bardhi, F., Eckhardt, G.M., & Samsioe, E. (2020). Liquid luxury. In F. Morhart, K. Wilcox, & S. Czellar (Eds.), *Research Handbook on Luxury Branding*. Edward Elgar Publishing, 22-42.

Barton, C., Bonelli, F., Gurzki, H., Pianon, N., Tsusaka, M., & Mei-Pochtler, A. (2016, September 22). *Digital or die: The choice for luxury brands. BCG Global.* https://www.bcg.com/publications/2016/digital-or-die-choice-luxury-brands.

Basu, K., & Palazzo, G. (2008). Corporate social responsibility: A process model of sensemaking. *Academy of Management Review*, 33(1), 122-136.

Batat, W. (2019a). How millennials and post-millennials are reshaping luxury. In *The New Luxury Experience: Creating the Ultimate Customer Experience*. Springer International Publishing, 187-210.

Batat, W. (2019b). *The new luxury experience the new luxury experience: Creating the ultimate customer experience* (1st ed.). Springer Nature.

Batat, W. (2020). Pillars of sustainable food experiences in the luxury gastronomy sector: A qualitative exploration of Michelin-starred chefs' motivations. *Journal of Retailing and Consumer Services*, 57(102255), 102255.

Batat, W., & Manika, D. (2020). Advancing transformative luxury research: Contributions to marketing theory about luxury, ethics, and well-being. *Journal of Macromarketing*, 40(4), 583-584.

Baudrillard. (1995). *Pour Une Critique De l'Economie Politique Du Signe*. Gallimard-Jeunesse.

BCG, & Altagamma. (2019). *2019 True-Luxury Global Consumer Insight*. https://media-publications.bcg.com/france/True-Luxury%20Global%20Consumer%20Insight%202019%20-%20Plenary%20-%20vMedia.pdf.

Becker-Olsen, K., & Potucek, S. (2013). Greenwashing. In S.O. Idowu, N. Capaldi, L. Zu, & A.D. Gupta (Eds.). *Encyclopedia of Corporate Social Responsibility*. Springer.

Bellomi, I.J., Kholod, T. (2023). *The Complexity of International Marketing: Pitfalls of Dolce & Gabbana Marketing Communication Strategy in China*. In E. Demir, M.H. Bilgin, H. Danis, F. D'Ascenzo, F. (Eds.). *Eurasian Business and Economics Perspectives. EBES 2022. Eurasian Studies in Business and Economics*, 26. Springer.

Berkup, S.B. (2014). Working with generations X and Y in generation Z period: Management of different generations in business life. *Mediterranean Journal of Social Sciences*.

Bernardi, A., Cantù, C.L., & Cedrola, E. (2022). Key success factors to be sustainable and innovative in the textile and fashion industry: Evidence from two Italian luxury brands. *Journal of Global Fashion Marketing*, 13(2), 116-133.

Berthon, P., Pitt, L., Parent, M., & Berthon, J.-P. (2009). Aesthetics and ephemerality: Observing and preserving the luxury brand. *California Management Review*, 52(1), 45-66.

Bertoli, G., & Resciniti, R. (2013). Made in Italy e country of origin effect. *Mercati & Competitività*, 2, 13-36.

Bhattacharya, A., Good, V., & Sardashti, H. (2020). Doing good when times are bad: the impact of CSR on brands during recessions. *European Journal of Marketing*, 54(9), 2049-2077.

Bof, & McKinsey & Company. (2022). *The State of Fashion 2022*. https://www.mckinsey.com/~/media/mckinsey/industries/retail/ourinsights/stateoffashion/2022/the-state-of-fashion-2022.pdf.

Bonacchi, M., Perego, P., & Ravagli, R. (2012). *Chapter The Evolution of Corporate Social Responsibility in Gucci: From Risk Management to Stakeholder Engagement*. Routledge.

Boström, M. (2012). A missing pillar? Challenges in theorizing and practicing social sustainability: Introduction to the special issue. Sustainability: *Science Practice and Policy*, 8(1), 3-14.

Bourdieu, P. (1979). La Distinction: Critique sociale du jugement. Les Editions de Minuit.

Broccardo, L., Culasso, F., Dhir, A., & Truant, E. (2023). Corporate social responsibility: Does it really matter in the luxury context? *Corporate Social Responsibility and Environmental Management*, 30(1), 105-118.

Brondoni, S.M. (2014). Global capitalism and sustainable growth. From global products to network globalisation. *Symphonya Emerging Issues in Management*, 1.

Brundtland, G.H. (1987). *Our common future: Report of the World Commission on Environment and Development*. UN Document A/42/427. United Nations.

Buallay, A., Kukreja, G., Aldhaen, E., Al Mubarak, M., & Hamdan, A.M. (2020).

Corporate social responsibility disclosure and firms' performance in Mediterranean countries: A stakeholders' perspective. *EuroMed Journal of Business*, 15(3), 361-375.

Campos Franco, J., Hussain, D., & McColl, R. (2019). Luxury fashion and sustainability: looking good together. *The Journal of Business Strategy*, 41(4), 55-61.
Carroll, A.B. (1991). The pyramid of corporate social responsibility: Toward the moral management of organizational stakeholders. *Business Horizons*, 34(4), 39-48.
Carroll, A.B. (2009). *A history of corporate social responsibility*, Ed. by A. Crane, D. Matten, A. McWilliams, J. Moon, & D.S. Siegel, Oxford University Press.
Carroll, A.B. (2015). Corporate social responsibility. *Organizational Dynamics*, 44(2), 87-96.
Carroll, A.B. (2021). Corporate social responsibility: Perspectives on the CSR construct's development and future. *Business and Society*, 60(6), 1258-1278.
Casalegno, C., & Civera, C. (2016). *Impresa e CSR: La «Non comunicazione» di successo. Regole per una gestione responsabile delle relazioni.*
Castillo-Abdul, B., Ortega Fernandez, E., & Romero-Rodriguez, L.M. (2022). Corporate social responsibility communication of male luxury fashion brands: analysis on Instagram, Facebook and TikTok. *Management Decision*.
Castillo-Abdul, B., Pérez-Escoda, A., & Núñez-Barriopedro, E. (2022b). Promoting social media engagement via branded content communication: A fashion brands study on Instagram. *Media and Communication*, 10(1).
Cerin, P. (2002). Communication in corporate environmental reports. *Corporate Social Responsibility and Environmental Management*, 9(1), 46-65.
Cervellon, M.-C. (2013). Conspicuous conservation: Using semiotics to understand sustainable luxury. *International Journal of Market Research*, 55(5), 695-717.
Cervellon, M.-C., & Shammas, L. (2013). The value of sustainable luxury in mature markets: A customer-based approach. *Journal of Corporate Citizenship*, 2013(52), 90-101.
Cheah, I., Zainol, Z., & Phau, I. (2016). Conceptualizing country-of-ingredient authenticity of luxury brands. *Journal of Business Research*, 69(12), 5819-5826.
Chen, Z., & Xie, G. (2022). ESG disclosure and financial performance: Moderating role of ESG investors. *International Review of Financial Analysis*, 83(C), 102291.
Chevalier, M., & Mazzalovo, G. (2012). *Luxury brand management: A world of privilege* (2nd ed.). John Wiley & Sons.
Chevalier, M., & Mazzalovo, G. (2020). *Luxury brand management in digital and sustainable times* (4th ed.). John Wiley & Sons.
Chia-Jung, C., & Pei-Chun, C. (2014). Preferences and willingness to pay for green hotel attributes in tourist choice behavior: The case of Taiwan. *Journal of Travel & Tourism Marketing*, 31(8), 937-957.
Chomvilailuk, R., & Butcher, K. (2018). The impact of strategic CSR marketing communications on customer engagement. *Marketing Intelligence & Planning*, 36(7), 764-777.

Civera, C., Casalegno, C., Mosca, F., & Maple, P. (2018). Customers' judgments and misjudgments of corporate responsibility communication: A cross-country investigation of the effects on confidence and trust within the banking sector. *Psychology & Marketing*, 35(2), 138-149.

Civera, C., de Colle, S., & Casalegno, C. (2019). Stakeholder engagement through empowerment: The case of coffee farmers: XXXX. *Business Ethics*, 28(2), 156-174.

Confetto, M.G., & Covucci, C. (2021). A taxonomy of sustainability topics: a guide to set the corporate sustainability content on the web. *The TQM Journal*, 33(7), 106-130.

Corbellini, E., & Saviolo, S. (2009). *Managing fashion and luxury companies*. Rizzoli.

Costa Pinto, D., Nique, W.M., Maurer Herter, M., & Borges, A. (2016). Green consumers and their identities: how identities change the motivation for green consumption: Green consumers and their identities. *International Journal of Consumer Studies*, 40(6), 742-753.

Cristini, H., Kauppinen-Räisänen, H., Barthod-Prothade, M., & Woodside, A. (2017). Toward a general theory of luxury: Advancing from workbench definitions and theoretical transformations. *Journal of Business Research*, 70, 101-107.

D'Andrea, A., Grifoni, P., & Ferri, F. (2022). Discussing the role of ICT in sustainable disaster management. *Sustainability*, 14(12), 7182.

D'Anolfo, M., Amatulli, C., De Angelis, M., & Pino, G. (2017). Luxury, sustainability, and corporate social responsibility: Insights from fashion luxury case studies and consumers' perceptions. In M. Gardetti (Eds.). *Sustainable Management of Luxury Environmental Footprints and Eco-design of Products and Processes*. Springer Singapore, 427-448.

D'Arpizio, C., Levato, F., Kavanagh, A., & De Montgolfier, J. (2022). *The Luxury Goods Worldwide Market Study*. https://altagamma.it/media/source/Summary%20Altagamma-Bain%20WW%20Monitor%202022.pdf.

Da Giau, A., Macchion, L., Caniato, F., Caridi, M., Danese, P., Rinaldi, R., & Vinelli, A. (2016). Sustainability practices and web-based communication: An analysis of the Italian fashion industry. *Journal of Fashion Marketing and Management*, 20(1), 72-88.

Dall'Olmo Riley, F., & Lacroix, C. (2003). Luxury branding on the Internet: lost opportunity or impossibility? *Marketing Intelligence & Planning*, 21(2), 96-104.

Davies, I.A., Lee, Z., & Ahonkhai, I. (2012). Do consumers care about ethical luxury? *Journal of Business Ethics*, 106(1), 37-51.

Davis, K. (1976). Social responsibility is inevitable. *California Management Review*, 19(1), 14-20.

De Angelis, M., Adıgüzel, F., & Amatulli, C. (2017). The role of design similarity in consumers' evaluation of new green products: An investigation of luxury fashion brands. *Journal of Cleaner Production*, 141, 1515-1527.

De Vellis, R.F. (2016). *Scale development: Theory and applications* (4th ed.). Sage Publications.

Dekhili, S., Achabou, M.A., & Alharbi, F. (2019). Could sustainability improve the promotion of luxury products? *European Business Review*, 31(4), 488-511.

Deloitte (2022). *Global Powers of Luxury Goods. Deloitte*. https://www.deloitte.com/global/en/Industries/consumer/analysis/gx-cb-global-powers-of-luxury-goods.html.

Di Benedetto, C.A. (2017). Corporate social responsibility as an emerging business model in fashion marketing. *Journal of Global Fashion Marketing*, 8(4), 251-265.

Dubois, B., & Duquesne, P. (1993). The market for luxury goods: Income versus culture. *European Journal of Marketing*, 27(1), 35-44.

Duncan, T., & Moriarty, S.E. (1998). A communication-based marketing model for managing relationships. *Journal of Marketing*, 62(2), 1.

Durgee, J.F., & Colarelli O'Connor, G. (1995). An exploration into renting as consumption behavior. *Psychology & Marketing*, 12(2), 89-104.

Eberle, D., Berens, G., & Li, T. (2013). The impact of interactive corporate social responsibility communication on corporate reputation. *Journal of Business Ethics*, 118(4), 731-746.

Elkington, J. (1998). Accounting for the triple bottom line. *Measuring Business Excellence*, 2(3), 18-22.

Ertekin, Z.O., & Atik, D. (2020). Institutional constituents of change for a sustainable fashion system. *Journal of Macromarketing*, 40(3), 362-379.

Evan, W., & Freeman, E.R. (1988). A stakeholder theory of the modern corporation: Kantian capitalism. In T.L. Beauchamp & N.E. Bowie (Eds.), *Ethical theory and business* (3rd ed.). Prentice Hall, 97-106.

Farooq, R., Zhang, Z., Talwar, S., & Dhir, A. (2022). Do green human resource management and self-efficacy facilitate green creativity? A study of luxury hotels and resorts. *Journal of Sustainable Tourism*, 30(4), 824-845.

Faust, M.-E. (2013). Cashmere: A lux-story supply chain told by retailers to build a competitive sustainable advantage. *International Journal of Retail & Distribution Management*, 41(11/12), 973-985.

Fiandrino, S., Busso, D., & Vrontis, D. (2019). Sustainable responsible conduct beyond the boundaries of compliance. *British Food Journal*, 121(5), 1035-1049.

Fionda, A.M., & Moore, C.M. (2009). The anatomy of the luxury fashion brand. *Journal of Brand Management*, 16(5-6), 347-363.

Fortunati, S., Martiniello, L., & Morea, D. (2020). The strategic role of the corporate social responsibility and circular economy in the cosmetic industry. *Sustainability*, 12(12), 5120.

Francis, T., & Hoefel, F. (2018, November 12). *'True Gen': Generation Z and its implications for companies*. Mckinsey.com; McKinsey & Company. https://www.mckinsey.com/industries/consumer-packaged-goods/our-insights/true-gen-generation-z-and-its-implications-for-companies.

Freeman, E.R., & Gilbert, D.R. (1988). *Corporate strategy and the search for ethics*. Prentice-Hall.

Freeman, R.E. (2010) *Strategic management: A stakeholder approach*. Cambridge University Press.

Freeman, R.E. (2017). The new story of business: Towards a more responsible capitalism. *Business and Society Review*, 122, 449-465.

Freeman, R.E., & Dmytriyev, S. (2017). Corporate social responsibility and stakeholder theory: Learning from each other. *Symphonya Emerging Issues in Management*, 1, 7-15.

Freeman, R.E., & Velamuri, S.R. (2008). A new approach to CSR: Company stakeholder responsibility. *SSRN Electronic Journal.*

Freeman, R.E., Harrison, J.S., Wicks, A.C., Parmar, B.L., & de Colle, S. (2010). *Stakeholder theory: The state of the art.* Cambridge University Press.

Freeman, R.E., Parmar, B.L., & Martin, K. (2020). *The power of and the power of and: Responsible business without trade-offs.* Columbia Business School Publishing.

Friedman, M. (1970). The social responsibility of business is to increase its profits. *New York Times Magazine*, 17.

Gardetti, M.A., & Torres, A.L. (Eds.). (2017). *Sustainable luxury: Managing social and environmental performance in iconic brands.* Routledge.

Garfield, E., & Sher, I.H. (1993). KeyWords PlusTM - algorithmic derivative indexing. Journal of the American Society for Information Science. *American Society for Information Science*, 44(5), 298-299. https://doi.org/10.1002/(sici)1097-4571(199306)44:5<298::aid-asi5>3.0.co;2-a.

Gavel, Y., & Iselid, L. (2008). Web of Science and Scopus: a journal title overlap study. *Online Information Review,* 32(1), 8-21.

Gehringer, T. (2021). Corporate foundations as hybrid organizations: A systematic review of literature. *VOLUNTAS International Journal of Voluntary and Nonprofit Organizations*, 32(2), 257-275.

Gentina, E., Shrum, L.J., & Lowrey, T.M. (2016). Teen attitudes toward luxury fashion brands from a social identity perspective: A cross-cultural study of French and US teenagers. *Journal of Business Research*, 69(12), 5785-5792.

Global Reporting Initiative. (2023). *Universal standards: Setting a new global benchmark for sustainability reporting.* https://www.globalreporting.org/standards/standards-development/universal-standards/.

Godfrey, P.C., Merrill, C.B., & Hansen, J.M. (2009). The relationship between corporate social responsibility and shareholder value: An empirical test of the risk management hypothesis. *Strategic Management Journal*, 30(4), 425-445.

Guillot, J. (2020). *Sustainability Accounting Standards Board: SEC AMAC ESG* subcommittee. https://dsxx4t8pjznor.cloudfront.net/wp-content/uploads/2022/09/12165724/10152020-sasb-sec-amac-esg-subcommittee.pdf.

Han, H., Lee, J.-S., & Koo, B. (2021). Impact of green atmospherics on guest and employee well-being response, place dependence, and behavior in the luxury hotel sector. *Journal of Sustainable Tourism*, 29(10), 1613-1634.

Hang, H., Rodrigo, P., & Ghaffari, M. (2021). Corporate social responsibility in the luxury sector: The role of moral foundations. *Psychology & Marketing*, 38(12), 2227-2239.

Hart, S.L. (1995). A natural-resource-based view of the firm. *Academy of Management Review*, 20(4), 986.

Hawn, O., & Ioannou, I. (2016). Mind the gap: The interplay between external and internal actions in the case of corporate social responsibility. *Strategic Management Journal*, 37(13), 2569-2588.

Hemonnet-Goujot, A., Kessous, A., & Magnoni, F. (2022). The effect of sustainable product innovation on the consumer-luxury brand relationship: The role of past identity salience. *Journal of Business Research*, 139, 1513-1524.

Hepner, J., Chandon, J.-L., & Bakardzhieva, D. (2020). Competitive advantage from marketing the SDGs: a luxury perspective. *Marketing Intelligence & Planning*, 39(2), 284-299.

Herzig, C., & Godemann, J. (2010). Internet-supported sustainability reporting: developments in Germany. *Management Research Review*, 33(11), 1064-1082.

Hillman, A.J., & Keim, G.D. (2001). Shareholder value, stakeholder management, and social issues: What's the bottom line? *Strategic Management Journal*, 22(2), 125-139.

Hodkinson, S.N., Lewis, H., Waite, L., & Dwyer, P. (2021). Fighting or fuelling forced labour? The Modern Slavery Act 2015, irregular migrants and the vulnerabilising role of the UK's hostile environment. *Critical Social Policy*, 41(1), 68-90.

Holmqvist, J., Wirtz, J., & Fritze, M.P. (2020). Luxury in the digital age: A multi-actor service encounter perspective. *Journal of Business Research*, 121, 747-756.

Hoque, N., Rahman, A.R.A., Molla, R.I., Noman, A.H.M., & Bhuiyan, M.Z.H. (2018). Is corporate social responsibility pursuing pristine business goals for sustainable development? *Corporate Social Responsibility and Environmental Management*, 25(6), 1130-1142.

Huff, A.S. (1998). *Writing for Scholarly Publication*. Sage Publications.

Hwang, J., Lee, J.J., Park, S., Chang, H., & Kim, S.S. (2014). The impact of occupational stress on employee's turnover intention in the luxury hotel segment. *International Journal of Hospitality & Tourism Administration*, 15(1), 60-77.

Jaegler, A. (2016). A sustainable supply chain in the leather sector: dilemmas, challenges and learnings. *Supply Chain Forum an International Journal*, 17(3), 136-142.

Jahdi, K.S., & Acikdilli, G. (2009). Marketing communications and corporate social responsibility (CSR): Marriage of convenience or shotgun wedding? *Journal of Business Ethics*, 88(1), 103-113.

Jahn, B., Kunz, W.H., & Meyer, A. (2013). The role of social media for luxury-brands - motives for consumer engagement and opportunities for businesses. *SSRN Electronic Journal*.

Jain, S. (2019). Factors affecting sustainable luxury purchase behavior: A conceptual framework. *Journal of International Consumer Marketing*, 31(2), 130-146.

Janssen, C., Vanhamme, J., & Leblanc, S. (2017). Should luxury brands say it out loud? Brand conspicuousness and consumer perceptions of responsible luxury. *Journal of Business Research*, 77, 167-174.

Jestratijevic, I., Rudd, N.A., & Uanhoro, J. (2020). Transparency of sustainability disclosures among luxury and mass-market fashion brands. *Journal of Global Fashion Marketing*, 11(2), 99-116.

Jin, C.-H., & Lee, J.-Y. (2019). The halo effect of CSR activity: Types of CSR activity and negative information effects. *Sustainability*, 11(7), 2067.

Johnson, H. (1971). *Business in contemporary society: Framework and issues.* Wadsworth Publishing Company.

Johnson, S.D., & Leach, J.A. (2001). Using expert employees to train on the job. *Advances in Developing Human Resources*, 3(4), 425-434.

Jose, A., & Lee, S.-M. (2007). Environmental reporting of global corporations: A content analysis based on website disclosures. *Journal of Business Ethics*, 72(4), 307-321.

Joy, A., Sherry, J.F., Jr, Venkatesh, A., Wang, J., & Chan, R. (2012). Fast fashion, sustainability, and the ethical appeal of luxury brands. *Fashion Theory*, 16(3), 273-295.

Kamleitner, B., Thürridl, C., & Martin, B.A.S. (2019). A Cinderella story: How past identity salience boosts demand for repurposed products. *Journal of Marketing*, 83(6), 76-92.

Kang, E.Y., & Sung, Y.H. (2022). Luxury and sustainability: The role of message appeals and objectivity on luxury brands' green corporate social responsibility. *Journal of Marketing Communications*, 28(3), 291-312.

Kapferer, J.-N. (1997). Managing luxury brands. *Journal of Brand Management*, 4(4), 251-259.

Kapferer, J.-N. (2010). All that glitters is not green: The challenge of sustainable luxury. *European Business Review*, 40-45.

Kapferer, J.-N. (2016). *Kapferer on luxury: How luxury brands can grow yet remain rare.* Kogan Page.

Kapferer, J.-N., & Bastien, V. (2009). The specificity of luxury management: Turning marketing upside down. *Journal of Brand Management*, 16(5-6), 311-322.

Kapferer, J.-N., & Michaut-Denizeau, A. (2014). Is luxury compatible with sustainability? Luxury consumers' viewpoint. *Journal of Brand Management*, 21(1), 1-22.

Kapferer, J.-N., & Michaut-Denizeau, A. (2020). Are millennials really more sensitive to sustainable luxury? A cross-generational international comparison of sustainability consciousness when buying luxury. *Journal of Brand Management*, 27(1), 35-47.

Kapferer, J.-N., & Valette-Florence, P. (2022). Assessing levers of guilt in luxury consumption: an international perspective. *Journal of Product & Brand Management*, 31(3), 351-367.

Kapil, S., & Rawal, V. (2023). Sustainable investment and environmental, social, and governance investing: A bibliometric and systematic literature review. *Business Ethics, the Environment & Responsibility*, 32(4), 1429-1451.

Karaosman, H., Perry, P., Brun, A., & Morales-Alonso, G. (2020). Behind the runway: Extending sustainability in luxury fashion supply chains. *Journal of Business Research*, 117, 652-663.

Karatzas, S., Kapoulas, A., & Priporas, C. V. (2019). Consumers' perceptions on complexity and prospects of ethical luxury: Qualitative insights from Taiwan. *Australasian Marketing Journal (AMJ)*, 27(4), 224-232.

Keller, K.L. (2009a). Building strong brands in a modern marketing communications environment. *Journal of Marketing Communications*, 15(2-3), 139-155.

Keller, K.L. (2009b). Managing the growth tradeoff: Challenges and opportunities in luxury branding. *Journal of Brand Management*, 16(5-6), 290-301.

Kelly, P., Kahlmeier, S., Götschi, T., Orsini, N., Richards, J., Roberts, N., Scarborough, P., & Foster, C. (2014). Systematic review and meta-analysis of reduction in all-cause mortality from walking and cycling and shape of dose response relationship. *The International Journal of Behavioral Nutrition and Physical Activity*, 11(1), 132.

Kim, A.J., & Ko, E. (2010). Impacts of luxury fashion brand's social media marketing on customer relationship and purchase intention. *Journal of Global Fashion Marketing*, 1(3), 164-171.

Kim, J., & Lee, K.H. (2019). Influence of integration on interactivity in social media luxury brand communities. *Journal of Business Research*, 99, 422-429.

Kong, H.M., Witmaier, A., & Ko, E. (2021). Sustainability and social media communication: How consumers respond to marketing efforts of luxury and non-luxury fashion brands. *Journal of Business Research*, 131, 640-651.

Kotler, P., Armstrong, G., Harris, L., & He, H. (2019). *Principles of marketing* (8th ed.). Pearson Education.

Kotler, P., Kartajaya, H., & Setiawan, I. (2021). *Marketing 5.0: Technology for humanity*. John Wiley & Sons.

Kraus, S., Breier, M., & Dasí-Rodríguez, S. (2020). The art of crafting a systematic literature review in entrepreneurship research. *International Entrepreneurship and Management Journal*, 16(3), 1023-1042.

Kunz, J., May, S., & Schmidt, H.J. (2020). Sustainable luxury: current status and perspectives for future research. *BuR - Business Research*, 13(2), 541-601.

Kurz, C., Li, G., & Vine, D.J. (2018). Are Millennials Different? *Finance and Economics Discussion Series*, 2018(080).

Latapí Agudelo, M.A., Jóhannsdóttir, L., & Davídsdóttir, B. (2019). A literature review of the history and evolution of corporate social responsibility. *International Journal of Corporate Social Responsibility*, 4(1).

Laurent, G., & Czellar, S. (2001). *Consumer rapport to luxury: Analyzing complex and ambivalent attitudes*. Groupe HEC.

Liberati, A., Altman, D.G., Tetzlaff, J., Mulrow, C., Gøtzsche, P.C., Ioannidis, J.P.A., Clarke, M., Devereaux, P.J., Kleijnen, J., & Moher, D. (2009). The PRISMA statement for reporting systematic reviews and meta-analyses of studies that evaluate health care interventions: Explanation and elaboration. *PLoS Medicine*, 6(7), e1000100.

Lichtenstein, D.R., Ridgway, N.M., & Netemeyer, R.G. (1993). Price perceptions and consumer shopping behavior: A field study. JMR, Journal of Marketing Research, 30(2), 234.

Lim, D.J. (Jay), Youn, N., & Eom, H.J. (2021). Green advertising for the sustainable luxury market. *Australasian Marketing Journal,* 29(4), 288-296.

Lim, J.S., & Greenwood, C.A. (2017). Communicating corporate social responsibility (CSR): Stakeholder responsiveness and engagement strategy to achieve CSR goals. *Public Relations Review*, 43(4), 768-776.

Lipovetsky, G., & Roux, E. (2003). *Le luxe éternel: de l'âge du sacré au temps des marques*. Editions Gallimard.

Lodhia, S.K. (2006). Corporate perceptions of web-based environmental communication: An exploratory study into companies in the Australian minerals industry. *Journal of Accounting & Organizational Change*, 2(1), 74-88.

Luo, S., Henninger, C.E., Le Normand, A., & Blazquez, M. (2021). Sustainable what…? The role of corporate websites in communicating material innovations in the luxury fashion industry. *Journal of Design Business & Society*, 7(1), 83-103.

Mahoney, L.S, Thorne, L., Cecil, L., & LaGore, W. (2013). A research note on standalone corporate social responsibility reports: Signaling or greenwashing? *Critical Perspectives on Accounting*, 24(4-5), 350-359.

Maman Larraufie, A.-F., & Kourdoughli, A. (2014). The e-semiotics of luxury. *Journal of Global Fashion Marketing*, 5(3), 197-208.

Massaro, M., Dumay, J., & Bagnoli, C. (2015). Where there is a will there is a way: IC, strategic intent, diversification and firm performance. *Journal of Intellectual Capital*, 16(3), 490-517.

Massaro, M., Dumay, J., & Guthrie, J. (2016). On the shoulders of giants: undertaking a structured literature review in accounting. *Accounting Auditing & Accountability*, 29(5), 767-801.

McDonnel, M.-H., & King, B. (2013). Keeping up appearances: Reputational threat and impression management after social movement boycotts. *Administrative Science Quarterly*, 58(3), 387-419.

Medalla, M.E., Yamagishi, K., Tiu, A.M., Tanaid, R.A., Abellana, D.P. M., Caballes, S.A., Jabilles, E.M., Himang, C., Bongo, M., & Ocampo, L. (2020). Modeling the hierarchical structure of secondhand clothing buying behavior antecedents of millennials. *Journal of Modelling in Management*, 15(4), 1679-1708.

Miller, K.W., & Mills, M.K. (2012). Contributing clarity by examining brand luxury in the fashion market. *Journal of Business Research*, 65(10), 1471-1479.

Mishra, S., Jain, S., & Jham, V. (2021). Luxury rental purchase intention among millennials - A cross-national study. *Thunderbird International Business Review*, 63(4), 503-516.

Moher, D., Liberati, A., Tetzlaff, J., & Altman, D.G. (2010). Preferred reporting items for systematic reviews and meta-analyses: The PRISMA statement. *International Journal of Surgery*, 8(5), 336-341.

Morse, J.M., Barrett, M., Mayan, M., Olson, K., & Spiers, J. (2002). Verification strategies for establishing reliability and validity in qualitative research. *International Journal of Qualitative Methods*, 1(2), 13-22.

Mosca, F. (2017). *Strategie nei mercati del lusso. Marketing, digitalizzazione, sostenibilità*. Egea.

Mosca, F., & Chiaudano, V. (2020). Digital channels and distribution in luxury market. Marché et organisations, 37(1), 147-163.

Mosca, F., & Chiaudano, V. (2022). How could well-being-centered business strategies increase competitiveness and innovation among luxury firms? In *The Rise of Positive Luxury*. Routledge.

Mosca, F., & Civera, C. (2017a). *Digital channels and social media management in luxury markets*. Routledge.

Mosca, F., & Civera, C. (2017b). The evolution of CSR: An integrated approach. *Symphonya Emerging Issues in Management*, 1, 16-35.

Mosca, F., Kitchen, P.J., & Chiaudano, V. (2021). *Investigating the Impact of Luxury Brands' Traditional and Digital Contents on Customer-Based Brand Equity*. IGI Global.

Muirhead, S.A. (1999). Corporate Contributions: The View from 50 Years. *Conference Board.*

Mundel, J., Huddleston, P., & Vodermeier, M. (2017). An exploratory study of consumers' perceptions: What are affordable luxuries? *Journal of Retailing and Consumer Services*, 35, 68-75.

Nayak, R., Van Thang, L.N., Nguyen, T., Gaimster, J., Morris, R., & George, M. (2022). Sustainable developments and corporate social responsibility in Vietnamese fashion enterprises. *Journal of Fashion Marketing and Management*, 26(2), 307-327.

Nazir, O., & Islam, J.U. (2020a). Effect of CSR activities on meaningfulness, compassion, and employee engagement: A sense-making theoretical approach. *International Journal of Hospitality Management*, 90(102630), 102630.

Nazir, O., & Islam, J.U. (2020b). Influence of CSR-specific activities on work engagement and employees' innovative work behaviour: an empirical investigation. *Current Issues in Tourism*, 23(24), 3054-3072.

Neerattiparambil, N.N., & Belli, S.M. (2020). Why rent a dress ?: A study on renting intention for fashion clothing products. *Indian Journal of Marketing*, 50(2), 20.

Neuendorf, K.A. (2017). The content analysis guidebook. SAGE Publications, Inc.

Nirino, N., Miglietta, N., & Salvi, A. (2019). The impact of corporate social responsibility on firms' financial performance, evidence from the food and beverage industry. *British Food Journal*, 122(1), 1-13.

Nunnally, J.C., & Bernstein, I. (1993). *Psychometric Theory* (3rd ed.). McGraw Hill Higher Education.

Okonkwo, U. (2010). *Luxury online: Styles, systems, strategies*. Palgrave Macmillan.

Pangarkar, A., Patel, J., & Kumar, S.K. (2023). Drivers of eWOM engagement on social media for luxury consumers: Analysis, implications, and future research directions. *Journal of Retailing and Consumer Services*, 74(103410), 103410.

Pankiw, S.A., Phillips, B.J., & Williams, D.E. (2021). Luxury brands' use of CSR and femvertising: the case of jewelry advertising. *Qualitative Market Research An International Journal*, 24(3), 302-325.

Pantano, E., & Stylos, N. (2020). The Cinderella moment: Exploring consumers' motivations to engage with renting as collaborative luxury consumption mode. *Psychology & Marketing*, 37(5), 740-753.

Pantano, E., Passavanti, R., Priporas, C.-V., & Verteramo, S. (2018). To what extent luxury retailing can be smart? *Journal of Retailing and Consumer Services*, 43, 94-100.

Peng, X., & Lee, S. (2019). Self-discipline or self-interest? The antecedents of hotel employees' pro-environmental behaviours. *Journal of Sustainable Tourism*, 27(9), 1457-1476.

Perez, D., Stockheim, I., Tevet, D., & Matan Rubin, M. (2020). Consumers value manufacturer sincerity: The effect of central eco-friendly attributes on luxury product evaluations. *Journal of Cleaner Production*, 267(122132), 122132.

Petticrew, M., & Roberts, H. (Eds.). (2006). *Systematic reviews in the social sciences*. Blackwell Publishing Ltd.

Porter, M.E., & Kramer, M.R. (2002). The competitive advantage of corporate philanthropy. *Harvard Business Review*, 80(12), 56-68, 133.

Radhakrishnan, S. (2016). Environmental implications of reuse and recycling of packaging. In S. Muthu (Ed). *Environmental Footprints of Packaging*. Springer Singapore, 165-192.

Ramkumar, B., Woo, H., & Kim, N. (lauren). (2021). The cross-cultural effects of brand status and social facilitation on enhancing consumer perception toward circular fashion services. *Corporate Social Responsibility and Environmental Management*, 28(4), 1254-1269.

Rathi, R., Kaswan, M.S., Garza-Reyes, J.A., Antony, J., & Cross, J. (2022). Green Lean Six Sigma for improving manufacturing sustainability: Framework development and validation. *Journal of Cleaner Production*, 345(131130), 131130.

Raza, A., Farrukh, M., Iqbal, M.K., Farhan, M., & Wu, Y. (2021). Corporate social responsibility and employees' voluntary pro-environmental behavior: The role of organizational pride and employee engagement. *Corporate Social Responsibility and Environmental Management*, 28(3), 1104-1116.

Retail X. (2021). *Luxury 2021: Sector Analyst Report*.

Ricciardi, F., & Rossignoli, C. (2016). Research methods in the itAIS community: Building a Classification Framework for Management and Information Systems Studies. In T. Torre, A. M. Braccini, & R. Spinelli (Eds.). *Empowering Organizations*. Springer International Publishing, 297-315.

Roberts, J. (2019). Is contemporary luxury morally acceptable? *Cultural Politics an International Journal*, 15(1), 48-63.

Robinot, É., Corne, A., Peypoch, N., & Trespeuch, L. (2021). Environmental actions and consumer participation: Which impacts on brand relationship? The multiple realities of the hospitality sector. *International Journal of Hospitality Management*, 92(102713), 102713.

Rolling, V., & Sadachar, A. (2018). Are sustainable luxury goods a paradox for millennials? *Social Responsibility Journal*, 14(4), 802-815.

Rolling, V., Seifert, C., Chattaraman, V., & Sadachar, A. (2021). Pro-environmental millennial consumers' responses to the fur conundrum of luxury brands. *International Journal of Consumer Studies*, 45(3), 350-363.

Roper, S., Caruana, R., Medway, D., & Murphy, P. (2013). Constructing luxury brands: exploring the role of consumer discourse. *European Journal of Marketing*, 47(3/4), 375-400.

Rosenbaum, M.S., & Wong, I. A. (2015). Green marketing programs as strategic initiatives in hospitality. *Journal of Services Marketing*, 29(2), 81-92.

Rossi, A., & Tarquinio, L. (2017). An analysis of sustainability report assurance statements: Evidence from Italian listed companies. *Managerial Auditing Journal*, 32(6), 578-602.

Saeidi, S.P., Sofian, S., Saeidi, P., Saeidi, S.P., & Saaeidi, S.A. (2015). How does corporate social responsibility contribute to firm financial performance? The mediating role of competitive advantage, reputation, and customer satisfaction. *Journal of Business Research*, 68(2), 341-350.

Saini, N., Singhania, M., Hasan, M., Yadav, M.P., & Abedin, M. Z. (2022). Non-financial disclosures and sustainable development: A scientometric analysis. *Journal of Cleaner Production*, 381(1), 135173.

Salehi, M., DashtBayaz, M.L., & Khorashadizadeh, S. (2018). Corporate social responsibility and future financial performance. *EuroMed Journal of Business*, 13(3), 351-371.

Schill, M., & Godefroit-Winkel, D. (2022). Consumer responses to environmental corporate social responsibility and luxury. *Journal of Services Marketing*, 36(6), 769-780.

Schons, L., & Steinmeier, M. (2016). Walk the talk? How symbolic and substantive CSR actions affect firm performance depending on stakeholder proximity. *Corporate Social Responsibility and Environmental Management*, 23(6), 358-372.

Secinaro, S., Brescia, V., Calandra, D., & Biancone, P. (2020). Employing bibliometric analysis to identify suitable business models for electric cars. *Journal of Cleaner Production*, 264(121503), 121503.

Secinaro, S., Calandra, D., Secinaro, A., Muthurangu, V., & Biancone, P. (2021). The role of artificial intelligence in healthcare: a structured literature review. *BMC Medical Informatics and Decision Making*, 21(1).

Secundo, G., Del Vecchio, P., & Mele, G. (2021). Social media for entrepreneurship: myth or reality? A structured literature review and a future research agenda. *International Journal of Entrepreneurial Behaviour & Research*, 27(1), 149-177.

Sengabira, C.N., Septianto, F., & Northey, G. (2020). Committed to help: the effects of frequency of corporate donations on luxury brand evaluations. *Asia Pacific Journal of Marketing and Logistics*, 32(3), 681-694.

Seo, Y., & Buchanan-Oliver, M. (2019). Constructing a typology of luxury brand consumption practices. *Journal of Business Research*, 99, 414-421.

Serafeim, G. (2022). *Purpose and profit: How business can lift up the world.* HarperCollins Focus.

Severo, E.A., De Guimarães, J.C.F., & Dellarmelin, M.L. (2021). Impact of the COVID-19 pandemic on environmental awareness, sustainable consumption and social responsibility: Evidence from generations in Brazil and Portugal. *Journal of Cleaner Production*, 286(124947), 124947.

Sharma, A., Soni, M., Borah, S.B., & Haque, T. (2022). From silos to synergies: A systematic review of luxury in marketing research. *Journal of Business Research*, 139, 893-907.

Sharma, S., & Mishra, P. (2018). Impact of corporate social responsibility practices on the corporate performance of luxury chain hotels. *Journal of Services Research*, 18(1), 47-57.

Shashi, Centobelli, P., Cerchione, R., & Mittal, A. (2021). Managing sustainability in luxury industry to pursue circular economy strategies. *Business Strategy and the Environment,* 30(1), 432-462.

Silvestre, W.J., & Fonseca, A. (2020). Integrative Sustainable Intelligence: A holistic model to integrate corporate sustainability strategies. *Corporate Social Responsibility and Environmental Management*, 27(4), 1578-1590.

Smith, A.E., & Humphreys, M.S. (2006). Evaluation of unsupervised semantic mapping of natural language with Leximancer concept mapping. *Behavior Research Methods*, 38(2), 262-279.

Sotomayor, S., Ventes, N., & Gronau, W. (2021). Corporate social responsibility in luxury hotels in Cusco (Peru) to benefit indigenous communities. *Hospitality & Society*, 11(2), 137-157.

Sourvinou, A., & Filimonau, V. (2018). Planning for an environmental management programme in a luxury hotel and its perceived impact on staff: an exploratory case study. *Journal of Sustainable Tourism*, 26(4), 649-667.

Starik, M., & Rands, G.P. (1995). Weaving an integrated web: Multilevel and multisystem perspectives of ecologically sustainable organizations. *Academy of Management Review*, 20(4), 908.

Sthapita, A., Yun-yong, H., & Jo, G.-Y. (2017). Communicating responsible luxury brand: The role of luxury-CSR fit and dispositional consensus on brand evaluation. *Journal of Distribution Science*, 15(2), 7-14.

Tang, Z., Hull, C.E., & Rothenberg, S. (2012). How corporate social responsibility engagement strategy moderates the CSR-financial performance relationship: CSR engagement strategy. *Journal of Management Studies*, 49(7), 1274-1303.

Teah, K., Sung, B., & Phau, I. (2022). CSR motives on situational scepticism towards luxury brands. *Marketing Intelligence & Planning*, 40(1), 1-17.

Thomas, A.K., & James, P.S. (2012). An empirical case study on successful luxury resorts. *Asia Pacific Journal of Management & Entrepreneurship Research*, 1(3), 332-348.

Torelli, C.J., Monga, A.B., & Kaikati, A.M. (2012). Doing poorly by doing good: Corporate social responsibility and brand concepts. *The Journal of Consumer Research*, 38(5), 948-963.

Turunen, L.L.M., Cervellon, M.-C., & Carey, L.D. (2020). Selling second-hand luxury: Empowerment and enactment of social roles. *Journal of Business Research*, 116, 474-481.

Tynan, C., McKechnie, S., & Chhuon, C. (2010). Co-creating value for luxury brands. Journal of Business Research, 63(11), 1156-1163.

Usunier, J.-C. (2006). Relevance in business research: the case of country-of-origin research in marketing. *European Management Review*, 3(1), 60-73.

Vallaster, C., Lindgreen, A., & Maon, F. (2012). Strategically leveraging corporate social responsibility: A corporate branding perspective. *California Management Review*, 54(3), 34-60.

Veblen, T. (1912). *The theory of the leisure class: An economic study of institutions*. BW Huebsch.

Vieira, E.S., & Gomes, J.A.N.F. (2009). A comparison of Scopus and Web of Science for a typical university. *Scientometrics*, 81(2), 587-600.

Vigneron, F., & Johnson, L.W. (2004). Measuring perceptions of brand luxury. *Journal of Brand Management*, 11(6), 484-506.

Vilasanti da Luz, V., Mantovani, D., & Nepomuceno, M.V. (2020). Matching green messages with brand positioning to improve brand evaluation. *Journal of Business Research*, 119, 25-40.

Vincent, R.L., & Gaur, S.S. (2021). Luxury for hire: Motivations to use closet sharing. *Australasian Marketing Journal (AMJ)*, 29(4), 306-319.

Visser, W. (2010). The Age of Responsibility: CSR 2.0 and the new DNA of business. *Journal of Business Systems Governance & Ethics*, 5(3).

Vrontis, D., & Christofi, M. (2021). R&D internationalization and innovation: A systematic review, integrative framework and future research directions. *Journal of Business Research*, 128, 812-823.

Walker, K., & Wan, F. (2012). The harm of symbolic actions and green washing: Corporate actions and communications on environmental performance and their financial implications. *Journal of Business Ethics*, 109(2), 227-242.

Waltman, L. (2016). A review of the literature on citation impact indicators. *Journal of Informetrics*, 10(2), 365-391.

Wang, P., Kuah, A.T.H., Lu, Q., Wong, C., Thirumaran, K., Adegbite, E., & Kendall, W. (2021). The impact of value perceptions on purchase intention of sustainable luxury brands in China and the UK. *Journal of Brand Management*, 28(3), 325-346.

Wang, Y. (2022). A conceptual framework of contemporary luxury consumption. *International Journal of Research in Marketing*, 39(3), 788-803.

Wang, Z., & Sarkis, J. (2017). Corporate social responsibility governance, outcomes, and financial performance. *Journal of Cleaner Production*, 162, 1607-1616.

Wells, V., Athwal, N., Nervino, E., & Carrigan, M. (2021). How legitimate are the environmental sustainability claims of luxury conglomerates? *Journal of Fashion Marketing and Management*, 25(4), 697-722.

Werther, W.B., Jr, & Chandler, D. (2005). Strategic corporate social responsibility as global brand insurance. *Business Horizons*, 48(4), 317-324.

Wiedmann, K.-P., Hennigs, N. and Siebels, A. (2007). Measuring Consumers' Luxury Value Perception: A Cross-Cultural Framework, *Academy of Marketing Science Review*, 7.

Willersdorf, S., Hazan, J., Ricci, G., Prénaud, A., Bianchi, F., Seara, J., & Yang, V. (2020). *A New Era and a new look for luxury*. Bcg.com. https://web-assets.bcg.com/img-src/BCG-A-New-Era-and-a-New-Look-for-Luxury-Jun-2020_tcm9-252101.pdf.

Wong, J.Y. & Dhanesh, G.S. (2016). Luxury Industry: Managing CSR-Luxury Paradox Online Through Acceptance Strategies of Coexistence and Convergence'. *Management Communication Quarterly*, 25.

Wong, J.Y., & Dhanesh, G.S. (2017). Communicating corporate social responsibility (CSR) in the luxury industry: Managing CSR-luxury paradox online through acceptance strategies of coexistence and convergence. *Management Communication Quarterly*, 31(1), 88-112.

Yin, R.K. (2018). *Case study research and applications: Design and methods* (6th ed.). SAGE Publications.

Zetzsche, D.A., & Anker-Sørensen, L. (2022). Regulating sustainable finance in the dark. *European Business Organization Law Review*, 23(1), 47-85.

Zhang, Y., Lee, T.J., & Xiong, Y. (2019). Residents' perception of the influence of luxury chain hotels on ethnic tourism communities. *Journal of Tourism and Cultural Change*, 17(4), 432-448.

Ziek, P. (2009). Making sense of CSR communication. *Corporate Social Responsibility and Environmental Management*, 16(3), 137-145.

Zupic, I., & Čater, T. (2015). Bibliometric methods in management and organization. *Organizational Research Methods*, 18(3), 429-472.

APPENDIX 1
STRUCTURED LITERATURE

A1.1. Introduction

A literature review is the research methodology that aims to analyze and synthesize the extant literature on a specific field. By representing a summary of prior studies published about a particular topic, literature reviews allow scholars to enter the scientific debate with more awareness and effectiveness (Huff, 1998) and advance the general knowledge of the explored topic (Kraus et al., 2020).

The reasons that support the applicability of a further literature review to explore the relationship between luxury and sustainability are different. First, the documents collected from the previous literature reviews do not consider the articles written in recent times when the growing body of studies about sustainability is expected. The pressure exerted by regulations and the pandemic has renewed people's and companies' sensitivity toward ethics and environmental sustainability, by requesting new studies aiming at analyzing and interpreting the ongoing trends (Severo et al., 2021). Second, the extant literature provides just one bibliometric analysis of sustainable luxury that covers exclusively articles related to supply chain and circular economy practices in the fashion luxury market (Shashi et al., 2021). A bibliometric study that looks at the global luxury market must still be developed. We define the global luxury market as the sum of nine markets, in line with the framework proposed by D'Arpizio et al. (2022). Finally, as Zupic & Čater (2015) suggest, using bibliometric analysis in management favors objectivity and mitigates researchers' bias. Thus, we value an additional literature review on the topic as an effective tool to deepen sustainability in the global luxury market.

A1.2. Foundations of corporate social responsibility

Given the above premises, this appendix intends to enrich the current knowledge by performing a bibliometric and content analysis that collects papers published until 2022 related to sustainability in the global luxury market. In this endeavor, a structured review is performed. According to Massaro et al. (2016), a structured review is the research methodology that allows scholars to integrate the literature review with the bibliometric analysis. Some authors agree that a structured review enhances the body of research in compliance with the scientific rigor, reliability and replicability of the steps conducted. Managerial studies suggest five main steps to performing a structured review (Massaro et al., 2015; Secinaro et al., 2021; Secundo et al., 2021):

a) Determine the research questions;
b) Define the protocol of research;
c) Identify the articles to include in the analysis;
d) Write codes to analyze the selected articles, and;
e) Conduct a critical evaluation and discussion to identify future research and directions.

As this chapter follows all the authors' suggested steps, it starts from the definition of the research questions, which in the current study are expressed as follows:

RQ.1 What is the impact of sustainability on luxury brand literature?
RQ.2 What is the focus of the literature on sustainability for luxury brand management?
RQ.3 What are the research implications of sustainability for luxury brand management?

The first research question seeks to determine the "state of the art" of the literature on sustainability and its impact on research topics related to luxury brand management. The second question aims to highlight to what extent the role of sustainability has been studied concerning luxury brand management. The third research question allows researchers to share insights and offers implications in the areas of sustainability for luxury brand management.

As suggested by Kraus et al. (2020) the research questions are formulated by an interdisciplinary team of researchers following the opinion of industry experts, to ensure a deep understanding of the topic to investigate. Afterward, the second phase of the structured review consists of defining the research protocol. In this phase, researchers identify the database used as an information source, the methods, and tools to analyze and synthesize the collected documents (Petticrew & Roberts, 2006). Figure A1.1 summarizes and explains all the steps of the research protocol. Transparent reporting in a structured review is essential to conduct a reproducible and transparent process. Thus, this study uses the PRISMA statement (Figure A1.2) to set and develop the reporting strategy, as it offers guidelines to guarantee the replicability of the findings (Liberati et al., 2009; Moher et al., 2010).

Figure A1.1. Step of the research protocol

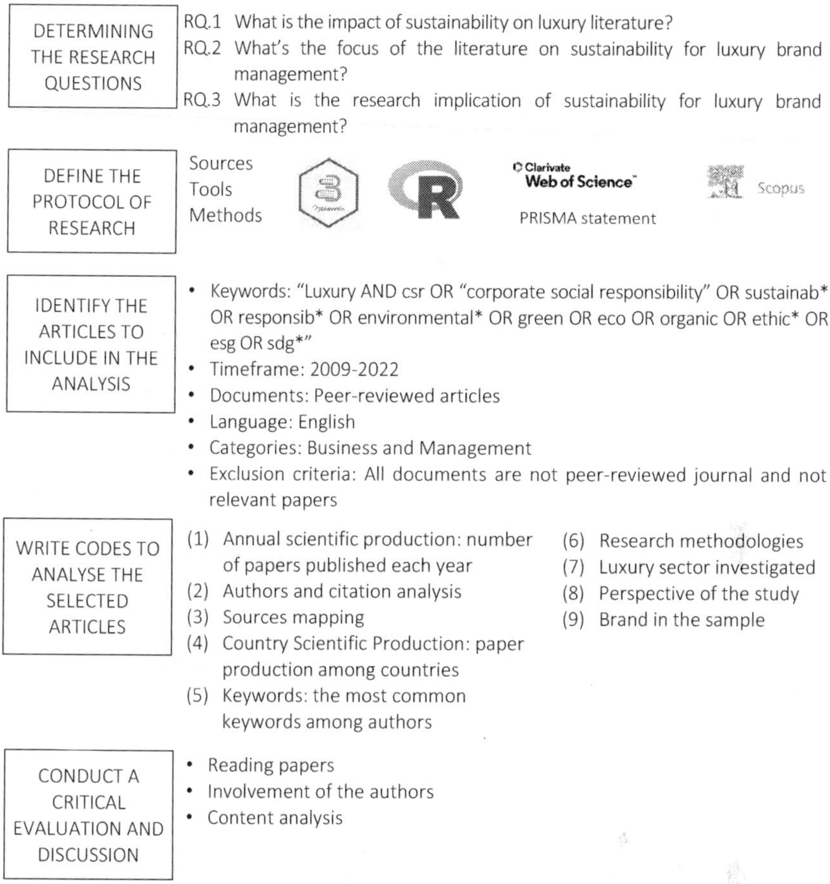

Source: Authors' elaboration.

Next, the third phase of the structured review aims to specify the articles to analyze in the review. This study formulates the following query for extracting the list of candidate articles that include the selected keyword in the title, summary, or keywords: Luxury AND csr OR "corporate social responsibility" OR sustainab* OR responsib* OR environmental* OR green OR eco OR organic OR "circular econom*" OR ethic* OR esg OR sdg*. The asterisk at the end of the keywords allows different suffixes (e.g., responsib* means responsibility or responsible). Following the suggestion of Kraus et al. (2020) the choice of the keywords arises from the help of researchers who are from different disciplines and varying degrees of knowledge about the topic.

Records excluded based on abstract/title: no sustainability issue in the luxury market (n= 196; 145 from Scopus and 51 Web of Science). Moreover, the keywords research pays attention to the holistic view of sustainability (Cervellon & Shammas, 2013) by combining environmental sustainability with social and economic sustainability.

The articles are extracted from two databases: Scopus and Web of Science. While Scopus contains a higher number of papers from more than 20,000 journals, Web of Science is considered the most influential database. It includes papers published exclusively in a selection of prestigious journals that are indexed by the International Scientific Indexing (Vieira & Gomes, 2009). Generally, authors prefer choosing Scopus or Web of Science as their sole citation database due to the overlap among articles extracted (Waltman, 2016). According to Gavel & Iselid (2008) 84% of Web of Science articles are also indexed in Scopus. However, in the case of the current research query, the overlap between Scopus and Web of Science's articles is lower. After comparing the databases extracted by Web of Science and Scopus by using the exact keywords in both databases, we calculate an overlap of 68%. Therefore, we agree that the collection of articles extracted from either database can offer enough papers to cover the field of sustainability in the luxury market.

Following this step, the use of the Boolean Operats on the selected databases results in 3,729 entries. At this point, we refine the research by limiting the results obtained to the specific field of business and management. This filter yields 975 records. Regarding the document type, the current review considers only peer-reviewed journal articles and excludes other document types (i.e. book chapters, peer-reviewed editorials). According to (Kraus et al., 2020) only peer-reviewed journals need to be included in the systematic review to maintain the principles of transparency and objectivity. Similarly, Kelly et al., (2014) agree on analyzing exclusively peer-reviewed articles, to ensure the inclusion of documents that perform a scientific and well-developed methodology. After including peer-reviewed articles as a sole document type, the number of papers to analyze counts 633.

In the third step, articles were filtered once again, specifically, by making sure that all contributions were written in English, considering the language limitations of the authors (Vrontis & Christofi, 2021). At this point, the number of papers reaches the threshold of 624 to become 369 after removing the duplicates. As shown by the PRISMA statement represented in Figure A1.2, the list of extracted papers is filtered again to remove non-relevant documents. Thus, the final papers list includes 177 peer-reviewed articles to analyze. For transparency and replicability, all data were collected on 15 March 2022.

The fourth step of the structured review deals with writing the codes to analyze the selected articles. In this study, codes were settled as follows:

(1) Annual scientific production;
(2) Authors and citation analysis;
(3) Analysis of sources;
(4) Country Scientific production
(5) Luxury sector explored;
(6) Luxury brand involved;
(7) Research methodologies;
(8) Keywords and network analysis.

The last step of the structured review consists of critically analyzing and discussing the findings. Data were processed with the tool R and its package Bibliometrix (Aria & Cuccurullo, 2017) to perform the quantitative analysis. Then, at least two researchers analyze each paper independently in the dataset to find the logical units and enhance the reliability of the findings, as suggested by Massaro et al. (2016) and Secinaro et al. (2020). Finally, the article offers the implications and the future research agenda at this phase.

Figure A1.2. The PRISMA statement

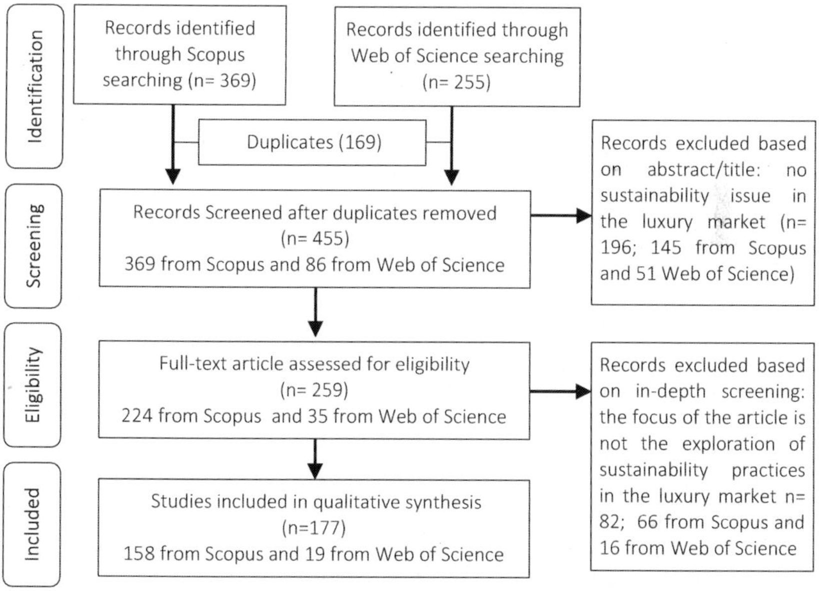

Source: Authors' elaboration.

A1.3. Research findings

Table A1.1 collects critical information on 177 peer-reviewed articles extracted from the Web of Science and Scopus databases and published between January 2009 and March 2022 in 78 different journals.

Table A1.1. General overview of the collected articles

Main information	Description	Results
Period	The publication year of each manuscript	2009-2022
Peer-reviewed articles	The total number of manuscripts	177
Peer-reviewed journals	The frequency distribution of sources	78
Keywords Plus (ID)	The frequency distribution of keywords associated with the manuscript by databases	540
Author's Keywords (DE)	The frequency distribution of authors' keywords	576
Authors	The total number of authors	444
Author Appearances	The authors' frequency distribution	528
Authors of single-authored peer-reviewed articles		11
Authors of multi-authored peer-reviewed articles	The number of authors of multi-authored articles	433
Authors per peer-reviewed articles	The average number of authors in each document	2,51
Co-Authors peer-reviewed articles	The average number of co-authors in each document	2,98
Average citations per peer-review articles	The average number of quotes in each article	18,48

Source: Authors' elaboration.

A1.3.1. The annual scientific production

This research takes the year 2009 as a starting point, when Patagonia and Walmart signed the Sustainable apparel coalition. Then, the research about sustainability in the luxury market registered a peak in 2017, as shown in Figure A1.3 The growth of peer-reviewed publications starting in 2017 is a consequence of two important events: the Modern Slavery Act's approval on 26th March 2015 and the release of "The Sustainable Development Goals" (officially known as 'Transforming our World: The 2030 Agenda for Sustainable Development) by the United Nations organization. Another peak in the publication of articles about luxury and sustainability is registered in 2019 and 2021. This growing trend is the result of many events. First, in 2018, the European Commission published a "Sustainable Finance Action Plan". Then, in December 2019, the 27 member countries of the European Union signed the Green Deal. Finally, the Covid-19 pandemic in 2020 increased the attention on sustainability. After Covid-19, the attention to sustainability increased among businesses and institutions that committed significant resources to transforming their business model (D'Arpizio et al., 2022).

Figure A1.3. The annual scientific production[1]

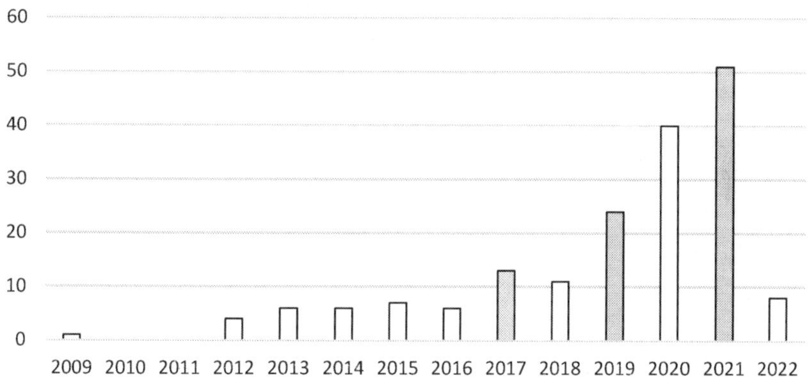

Source: Authors' elaboration.

A1.3.2. Authors and citations analysis

This section related to authors classifies who published the most local cited papers, to reveal the authors whose contribution is considered relevant by the other researchers (Table A1.2). Local citations measure the impact of documents in the dataset, in contrast with the global citations that analyze the effect of records in the bibliographic database. Aria & Cuccurullo (2017) suggest leveraging local sources, instead of global ones, because many global citations could come from other disciplines for many documents and, consequently, they could be misleading. Achabou & Dekhili (2013) published the most locally cited articles in the Journal of Business Research. The authors demonstrate that incorporating recycled materials in luxury goods affects consumer preferences negatively and reveals a specific incompatibility between recycling and luxury. Then, with 35 local citations, we find the article published in the Journal of Brand Management by Kapferer & Michaut-Denizeau (2014). The peer-reviewed paper reveals that luxury consumers still have ambivalent attitudes. They consider luxury and sustainability somewhat contradictory, especially concerning sustainable development's social and economic harmony. Another relevant article that received 27 local citations is the one published by De Angelis et al. (2017) in the Journal of Cleaner Production. The article states that luxury companies need to launch sustainable products that are more like traditional luxury products than models made by green companies. Then Torelli et al. (2012), in the Journal of Consumer Research, stated that the perceived compatibility of luxury brand values with CSR communication is critical in how consumers respond to CSR activities. When consumers perceive that something is wrong or that there is a mismatch between actions and luxury brand value, they respond with lower evaluations than if the brand provides no CSR information. Table A1.3 offers an in-depth overview of the 20 most cited articles related to sustainability in the luxury market.

A1.3.3. Sources

Table A1.4 shows the top 20 academic journals published peer-reviewed papers about sustainability and luxury.

The *Journal of Business Research* and the *Journal of Cleaner Production* are the most relevant sources, publishing thirteen articles each. Considering the other journals included in our list, the number of publications about luxury and sustainability ranges from three to seven. They are journals that focus more on a specific sector, from fashion to luxury hospitality. For example, with seven peer-reviewed articles published each, we find the *Journal of Global Fashion Marketing* (JGFM) and the *Journal of Sustainable Tourism.* Moreover, Table A1.4 reveals that most journals from five to three publications are marketing-oriented. For example, we find the *Journal of Fashion Marketing and Management*, *Journal of Product and Brand Management, Psychology and Marketing*, and *Journal of Brand Management.* This reflects again to what extent sustainability represents a relevant challenge for marketing luxury brands and satisfying current customer expectations.

Table A1.2. The most local cited papers

Document	Year	Local Citations	Global Citations	LC/GC Ratio (%)	Normalized Local Citations	Normalized Global Citations
Achabou Ma., 2013, J Bus Res	2013	53	143	37,06	3,42	2,96
Kapferer Jn., 2014, J Brand Manage	2014	35	89	39,33	5,12	1,43
De Angelis M., 2017, J Clean Prod	2017	27	59	45,76	3,73	2,17
Torelli Cj., 2012, J Consum Res	2012	26	190	13,68	2,74	1,14
Athwal N., 2019, Int J Manage Rev	2019	24	48	50,00	7,56	3,25
Steinhart Y., 2013, J Clean Prod	2013	21	45	46,67	1,35	0,93
Amatulli C., 2018, J Clean Prod	2018	17	50	34,00	4,07	2,57
Han J., 2017, J Bus Res	2017	16	62	25,81	2,21	2,28
Janssen C., 2017, J Bus Res	2017	15	53	28,30	2,07	1,95
Moraes C., 2017, J Bus Ethics	2017	12	43	27,91	1,66	1,58
Dekhili S., 2019, Eur Bus Rev	2019	8	17	47,06	2,52	1,15
Carrigan M., 2013, J Mark Manage	2013	8	42	19,05	0,52	0,87
Kang Kh., 2012, Int J Hosp Manage	2012	8	349	2,29	0,84	2,10
Kapferer Jn., 2020, J Brand Manage	2020	7	30	23,33	6,22	2,96

continued

Document	Year	Local Citations	Global Citations	LC/GC Ratio (%)	Normalized Local Citations	Normalized Global Citations
Arrigo E., 2018, J Retail Consum Serv	2018	7	21	33,33	1,67	1,08
Cervellon Mc., 2013, Int J Mark Res	2013	7	31	22,58	0,45	0,64
Kunz J., 2020, Bus Res	2020	6	9	66,67	5,33	0,89
Chang Dr., 2019, Psychol Mark	2019	6	17	35,29	1,89	1,15
Line Nd., 2016, J Sustainable Tour	2016	6	65	9,23	2,40	1,69
Costa Pinto D., 2019, J Clean Prod	2019	5	11	45,45	1,58	0,74

Source: Authors' elaboration.

Table A1.3. An in depth-analysis of the 20 most cited papers related to sustainability in the luxury market

Articles	Main topics	Author/s	Journal and Doi	ABS Ranking Journal	Research design	Sector	Key findings	Date
Luxury and sustainable development: is there a match?	conjoint analysis, consumer preference, luxury products, recycling, sustainable development, textile	Achabou Ma, Dekhili S	Journal Of Business Research 10.1016/j.jbusres.2013.02.011	3	Survey	Personal Luxury goods and luxury cars	Incorporating recycled materials in such goods affects consumer preferences negatively and reveals a certain incompatibility between recycling and the category of luxury products. Sustainability remains the second criterion for choosing luxury brands.	2013
Is luxury compatible with sustainability luxury consumers' viewpoint	csr, ecology, ethics, luxury, sustainable development	Kapferer Jn, Michaut-Denizeau A	Journal Of Brand Management 10.1057/bm.2013.19	2	Survey	General	Luxury buyers have ambivalent attitudes, such that they consider luxury and sustainability somewhat contradictory, especially about the social and economic harmony facet of sustainable development.	2014
The role of design similarity in consumers evaluation of new green products: an investigation of luxury fashion brands	design similarity, environmental sustainability, luxury fashion brand, new green product, sustainable consumption, sustainable design	De Angelis M, Adgzel F, Amatulli C	Journal Of Cleaner Production 10.1016/j.jclepro.2016.09.230	2	Experiments	Personal luxury goods	The design of the new green luxury products may crucially affect consumers' evaluation of the brand that introduces it. When launching a new green product, luxury brand companies need to create a new green luxury product like the luxury company's previous models rather than models made by green companies. Especially for consumers who are knowledgeable about the brand and for products that are durable rather than ephemeral.	2017
Doing poorly by doing good: corporate social responsibility and brand concepts	corporate social responsibility, brand concept,	Torelli Cj, Monga Ab, Kaikati Am	Journal Of Consumer Research 10.1086/660851	4*	Experiments	Personal Luxury goods, Luxury Cars	The brand concept is a key factor in how consumers respond to CSR activities.	2012

continued

Articles	Main topics	Author/s	Journal and Doi	ABS Ranking Journal	Research design	Sector	Key findings	Date
Sustainable luxury marketing: a synthesis and research agenda	luxury, review, sustainability, luxury marketing	Athwal N, Wells Vk, Carrigan M, Henninger Ce	International Journal of Management Reviews 10.1111/ijmr.12195	3	Literature review	Global luxury market	Sustainable luxury marketing: a synthesis and research agenda.	2019
The effect of an environmental claim on consumers' perceptions about luxury and utilitarian products	eco-labels, environmental claim, luxury product, utilitarian product	Steinhart Y, Ayalon O, Puterman H	Journal Of Cleaner Production 10.1016/j.jclepro.2013.04.024	2	Experiments	Design and luxury furniture	Environmental claims improve consumers' evaluations of utilitarian products, especially when the content of the claims stresses global-environmental benefits. Moreover, the environmental claim enhances evaluations of luxury products by providing available justification to indulge and use luxuries.	2013
Consumer's perceptions of luxury brands csr initiatives: an investigation of the role of status and conspicuous consumption	conspicuous consumption, corporate social responsibility (csr), luxury marketing, status consumption, sustainability	Amatulli C, De Angelis M, Korschun D, Romani S	Journal Of Cleaner Production 10.1016/j.jclepro.2018.05.111	2	Experiments	Personal Luxury goods	In the luxury market, external csr initiatives increase consumers' willingness to buy more than internal csr initiatives.	2018
Staging luxury experiences for understanding sustainable fashion consumption: a balance theory application	balance theory, eco- fashion, luxury experiences, sustainable fashion	Han J, Seo Y, Ko E	Journal Of Business Research 10.1016/j.jbusres.2016.10.029	3	Action Research	Personal luxury goods	Developing and staging memorable consumer-centered experiences that orient consumers toward sustainable fashion consumption behaviors encourages the consumers to achieve balance states between concerns and actual consumption decisions and behaviors.	2017

continued

Articles	Main topics	Author/s	Journal and Doi	ABS Ranking Journal	Research design	Sector	Key findings	Date
Should luxury brands say it out loud? brand conspicuousness and consumer perceptions of responsible luxury	brand conspicuousness, consumer perceptions, corporate social responsibility, luxury, self-identity	Janssen C, Vanhamme J, Leblanc S	Journal Of Business Research 10.1016/j.jbusres.2016.12.009	3	Experiments	Personal luxury goods	Luxury brand managers must assess how luxury consumers perceive luxury brands when promoting responsible luxury. The research underlines that a specific luxury branding strategy and CSR shapes consumers' CSR beliefs and attitudes.	2017
Understanding ethical luxury consumption through practice theories: a study of fine Jewellery purchases	consumer ethics; luxury consumption; marketing ethics; practice theory; qualitative research	Moraes C; Carrigan M;Bosangit C;Ferreira C;Mcgrath M	Journal Of Business Ethics 10.1007/S10551-015-2893-9	3	Theory building	Personal Luxury goods	our findings and discussion provide an analysis of intentional and less intentional ethical consumer performances within the interconnected nexus of activities of consumers' fine Jewellery consumption practice, where meanings, understandings and intelligibility of social phenomena are worked through the various activities that shape such a practice.	2017
Could sustainability improve the promotion of luxury products?	Csr, developed countries, developing countries, luxury, perceived quality, sustainable consumption	Dekhili S, Achabou Ma, Alharbi F	European Business Review 10.1108/EBR-04-2018-0083	2	Experiments	General	Sustainability information negatively impacts the perceived quality of luxury products. This result varies regarding the consumers' country of origin. While no significant effect was observed in the case of French respondents, Saudi consumers lower the evaluation of quality when social information is provided. In addition, the negative effect of sustainability information is moderated by the consumers' degree of liking luxury and by the brand's corporate social responsibility image.	2019
From conspicuous to considered fashion: a harm-chain approach to the responsibilities of luxury-fashion	corporate social responsibility, harm chain, institutional theory, luxury fash-	Carrigan M, Moraes C, Mceachern M	Journal of Marketing Management 10.1080/0267257X.2013.79	2	Conceptual	Personal Luxury goods and luxury cars	The paper urges luxury fashion businesses to embed social and environmental responsibilities within their core business, adopting a transformational approach to CSR that transcends self-interest and 'business as usual'.	2013

continued

Articles	Main topics	Author/s	Journal and Doi	ABS Ranking Journal	Research design	Sector	Key findings	Date
businesses	ion, value co-creation		8675					
Consumers' willingness to pay for green initiatives of the hotel industry	environmental concern, green practice, hotel, hotel type, new ecological paradigm scale, willingness to pay	Kang Kh, Stein L, Heo Cy, Lee S	International Journal of Hospitality Management 10.1016/j.ijhm.2011.08.001	3	Survey	Luxury Hospitality	The level of environmental concern, measured by the New Ecological Paradigm, (NEP) impacts positively on willingness to pay a premium for green practices.	2012
Are millennials more sensitive to sustainable luxury? a cross-generational international comparison of sustainability consciousness when buying luxury	csr, ethics, luxury, millennials, social responsibility, sustainability	Kapferer Jn, Michaut-Denizeau A	Journal of Brand Management 10.1057/s41262-019-00165-7	2	Survey	General	Millennials' sensitivity to the sustainability of luxury brands when purchasing luxuries is not different from older generations. Millennials are those who consider the most that luxury and sustainability are contradictory.	2020
The flagship stores as sustainability communication channels for luxury fashion retailers	flagship store, in-store communication, luxury fashion brands, luxury sustainability, sustainable retailing	Arrigo E	Journal of Retailing and Consumer Services 10.1016/j.jretconser.2018.06.011	2	Theory building	Personal Luxury goods	Flagship stores can be an effective environmental and social sustainability communication channel.	2018
Conspicuous conservation: using semiotics to understand sustainable luxury	conspicuous conservation, semiotics, sustainable luxury	Cervellon Mc	International Journal of Market Research 10.2501/ijmr-2013-030	2	Conceptual	Personal Luxury goods and luxury cars	Sustainable and philanthropic programs should not alter the authenticity of luxury brands.	2013

continued

Articles	Main topics	Author/s	Journal and Doi	ABS Ranking Journal	Research design	Sector	Key findings	Date
Sustainable luxury: status and perspectives for future research	csr, luxury, sustainability, sustainable luxury, systematic literature review	Kunz J, May S, Schmidt Hj	Business Research 10.1007/s40685-020-00111-3	x	Literature review	Global luxury market	State of the art of sustainable luxury at international level and relevant paths for future research.	2020
The effects of power on consumers evaluation of a luxury brand's corporate social responsibility	csr, fluency, luxury brands, psychological power	Chang Dr, Jang J, Lee H, Nam M	Psychology And Marketing 10.1002/mar.21158	3	Experiments	Personal Luxury goods	High-power individuals evaluated a luxury brand's csr campaign more positively than low-power individuals. high-power individuals viewed csr activities as being more fluent than low-power individuals.	2019
The effects of environmental and luxury beliefs on intention to patronize green hotels: the moderating effect of destination image	consumer behavior, destination image, green hotels, nature-based tourism, urban tourism	Line Nd, Hanks L	Journal of Sustainable Tourism 10.1080/09669582.2015.1091467	3	Survey	Luxury hospitality	The match between green management and luxury is influenced by the image of the destination. consumers are more willing to accept luxury-based trade-offs when the destination is perceived as nature-based than when it is perceived as urban.	2016
Can luxury brands be ethical? reducing the sophistication liability of luxury brands	brand ethicality, brand personality, consumer identity goals, corporate social responsibility, luxury brands	Costa Pinto D, Herter Mm, Gonalves D, Sayin E	Journal of Cleaner Production 10.1016/j.jclepro.2019.06.094	2	Experiments	Personal Luxury goods	Across our studies, we demonstrate that sophisticated brands (e.g., luxury brands) are perceived to be less ethical than sincere brands (i.e., sophistication liability; pilot study).	2019

Source: Authors' elaboration.

Table A1.4. The top 20 academic journals published peer-reviewed papers about sustainability and luxury

Sources	Frequency
Journal of Business Research	13
Journal of Cleaner Production	13
Journal of Global Fashion Marketing	7
Journal of Sustainable Tourism	7
International Journal of Retail and Distribution Management	6
Journal of Fashion Marketing and Management	6
Journal of Consumer Marketing	5
Journal of Product and Brand Management	5
Psychology and Marketing	5
Australasian Marketing Journal	4
Business Strategy and The Environment	4
Cornell Hospitality Quarterly	4
Corporate Social Responsibility and Environmental Management	4
Journal Of Brand Management	4
Journal Of Retailing and Consumer Services	4
Asia Pacific Journal of Marketing and Logistics	3
International Journal of Contemporary Hospitality Management	3
International Journal of Hospitality Management	3
Journal of Services Marketing	3
Marketing Intelligence and Planning	3

Source: Authors' elaboration.

A1.3.4. Countries' scientific production

This section aims to offer an overview of the countries, to highlight the geographies of the sustainable luxury research topic. It explores all published articles per country, the total number of citations of the top 20 countries, and the collaboration networks. We start this subsection by analyzing the total number of published articles.

Table A1.5 shows the countries that most contribute to exploring sustainability in the luxury market. With 71 peer-reviewed articles published, the US has produced more publications.

Other countries with a relevant number of publications are Italy (42), the UK (41), France (38), India (23), South Korea (20) and China (10). These countries are the most relevant when looking at the luxury brand market as they are the country of origin of most luxury brands. In contrast, India, South Korea, and China are the new economies where luxury consumption has enormously increased in recent years (Mosca, 2017; D'Arpizio et al., 2022). Moreover, the figure surprisingly displays that Russia, whose population counts a relevant number of luxury consumers, still does not work on sustainability for luxury. On the contrary, Australia, traditionally a non-luxury-oriented country, has contributed to the issue with ten publications.

Table A1.5. Sample geographic distribution frequency

Country	Frequency
USA	71
Italy	42
Uk	41
France	38
India	23
South Korea	20
China	18
Australia	10
Canada	9
Israel	8
Spain	8
Germany	7
Czech Republic	5
New Zealand	5
Greece	4
Monaco	4
Pakistan	4
Singapore	4
Denmark	3
Egypt	3

Source: Authors' elaboration.

A1.3.5. Luxury market involved

D'Arpizio et al. (2022) explain the global luxury market as a sum of different markets. This subsection aims to discover which luxury market is explored in the paper focused on luxury and sustainability.

Figure A1.4 shows that 57% of the papers in the dataset investigated the personal luxury goods market by focusing on luxury apparel, watches, accessories, eyewear, and jewelry. Then 20% of publications conduct research in the context of luxury hospitality. Another interesting insight reveals that new luxury markets never investigated before, have attracted the attention of researchers. Figure A1.4 shows the growth in research about emerging sectors such as high-quality design furniture and homeware, luxury cars, gourmet food and fine dining. Then, the following subsections enrich the sustainability topic for luxury brand management by analyzing the methodologies, and brands used to test the hypothesis or conduct interviews and the keywords.

Figure A1.4. Luxury market segments analyzed

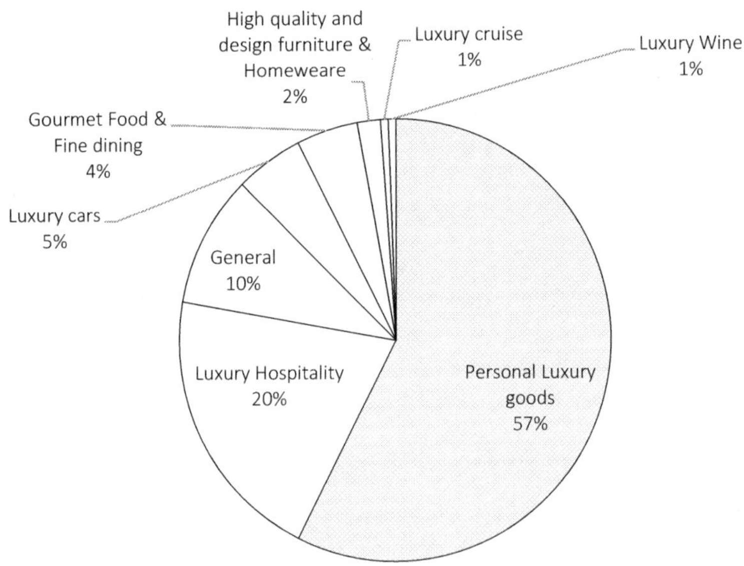

Source: Authors' elaboration.

A1.3.6. Research methodologies

In the endeavor to define the research methodologies used to investigate the topic of sustainability in the luxury market, we applied the framework proposed by Ricciardi & Rossignoli, (2016). They classify methodologies according to the research design that considers how authors combine the research contribution and epistemology with data gathering and elaboration techniques.

Table A1.6 displays the distribution of papers' research design methodology. Survey prevails over other methodologies, as it is performed by 30% of the articles examined. Moreover, we find a consistent number of articles performing experiments. This methodology is well suited, as it allows to control for extraneous variables (any variable, not of interest for the research, which could have an impact on the dependent and independent variables).

Table A1.6. Research methodologies for sustainability in the luxury market

Research design	Number	%
Survey	56	30%
Experiment	49	27%
Case Study	23	13%
Theory Building	13	7%
Conceptual	10	5%
Secondary Data analysis	9	5%
Grounded Theory	8	4%
Action Research	4	2%
Literature review	3	2%
Ethnography	3	2%
Construct development	3	2%
Text analysis	2	1%
QCA	1	1%

Source: Authors' elaboration.

A1.3.7. Luxury brand involved

Concerning the luxury brands involved in the study, Table A1.7 collects all luxury brands found in the papers. Researchers employ these brands mainly when conducting experiments or surveys to explore consumers' responses. In experiments, researchers use well-known luxury brands vis-à-vis other less familiar brands or set up with a sustainable ethos, to investigate consumers' reactions to sustainable practices. In the case of surveys, brands are included in the questionnaires delivered to test consumers' preferences for sustainable products.

Table A1.7. Luxury brands cited in the study

Brand	Number
Gucci	10
Louis Vuitton	9
Rolex	8
Prada	7
Hermès	7
Burberry	6
Chanel	6
Armani	6
Stella McCartney	4
Dior	4

Source: Authors' elaboration.

A1.3.8. Keywords analysis

Table A1.8 highlights the total number of keywords plus in the top 20 positions. The keywords plus are automatically generated by an algorithm leveraging words or phrases frequently appearing in the titles of an article's references. Even if they do not necessarily coincide with the authors' chosen keywords to represent the article's content, Garfield & Sher (1993) agree that the keyword plus can capture content better than the authors' keywords, considering their greater depth and variety. Moreover, as stated by Zhang et al. (2019) keywords plus are useful for investigating the knowledge structure of the scientific field. The top 20 keywords plus collected and summarized in Table A1.8, confirm that the research field about sustainability in the luxury market deals with the following topics: green, consumption, corporate social responsibility, behavior, fashion, and perception. Thus, it emerges how studies focused on customer consumption and behavior have a central role in sustainable luxury research. Then the keyword analysis shows the relations of words in the publication set by performing the topic dendrogram (Figure A1.5), which applies the correspondence analysis to identify research subfields, which are analyzed in paragraph 2.5 (Chapter II, p. 28).

Table A1.8. Twenty most cited keywords plus

Terms	Frequency
green	23
consumption	21
corporate social responsibility	19
behavior	17
fashion	17
perceptions	16
consumers	15
impact	15
sustainability	13
sustainable development	12
values	11
brand	10
attitudes	9
management	8
products	8
attitude	7
brands	7
csr	7
conspicuous consumption	6
materialism	6

Source: Authors' elaboration.

Figure A1.5. The topic dendrogram

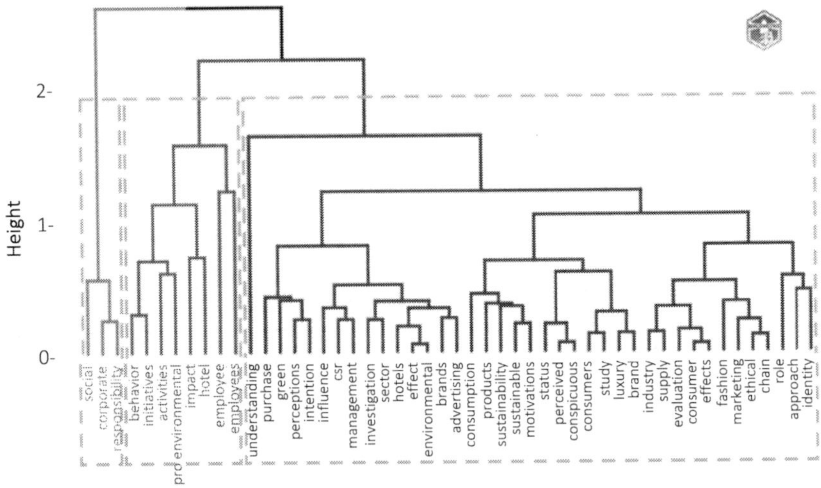

Source: Authors' elaboration.

APPENDIX 2

FROM THE INTEGRATED CSR FRAMEWORK TO A CHECKLIST FOR ASSESSING CSR INITIATIVES

A2.1. Introduction

This appendix explains how the authors applied the checklist (Table 2, p. 45) to evaluate how luxury brands have embraced sustainability within their business model (Table 9, p. 76).

A2.2. Sample

Our study collected a sample of luxury companies from the "Deloitte Global Powers of Luxury Goods 2022" list. This report grouped the 100 leading luxury companies by revenue and growth. However, our final sample did not comprise the entire list of luxury companies in the Deloitte report. On the contrary, we chose the top 22 companies based on revenue but then excluded four of them. Chanel, Rolex, and Lao Feng Xiang Co. Ltd were omitted because they didn't provide non financial disclosures, and Pandora was excluded because it's classified as a premium company. We replaced the companies excluded with Moncler, Salvatore Ferragamo Tod's and Cuccinelli. These are Italian firms that have distinguished themselves for their commitment to sustainability. Moreover, we decided to add Cucinelli to the list, considering that sustainability is a core practice for the company defined by its founder "Humanistic Enterprise". In this way, our final sample included 22 companies that represent an adequate approximation of the target industry.

As stated by Deloitte (2022), the market concentration in the luxury industry has grown in recent years, resulting in an increasing number of big conglomerates. For this reason, when analyzing the first 23 luxury companies in revenue according to Deloitte, we considered the largest conglomerates in the luxury market (e.g., LVMH, Kering, and Richmont), and consequently, an extensive sample that includes all firms owned by the luxury conglomerate. For example, LVMH owns more than 60 luxury companies, representing the leading brands in the luxury market.

Table A2.1. The 25 luxury brand companies selected

Company name	Country	Sector	Sustainability report
LVMH Moet Hennessy-Louis Vuitton SE	France	Leather Goods	✓
Kering SA	France	Leather Goods	✓
The Estée Lauder Companies Inc.	the United States	Parfume & Cosmetics	✓
Chanel Limited	France	Fashion	X
L'Orèal Luxe	France	Parfume & Cosmetics	✓
Compagnie Financièr Rich-mont	Switzerland	Watches and Jewelry	✓
Hermès International SCA	France	Leather Goods	✓
Chow Tai Fook Jewellery Group Limited	China/HKSAR	Watches and Jewelry	✓
Rolex SA	Switzerland	Watches and Jewelry	X
China National Group Gold	China/HKSAR	Watches and Jewelry	✓
The Swatch Group Ltd.	Switzerland	Watches and Jewelry	✓
Lao Feng Xiang Co. Ltd.	China/HKSAR	Watches and Jewelry	X
PVH Corp.	the United States	Fashion	✓
Tapestry, Inc	the United States	Fashion	✓
Shiseido Prestige & Fragrance	Japan	Parfume & Cosmetics	✓
Ralph Lauren Corporation	the United States	Fashion	✓
Capri Holding Limited	the United Kingdom	Fashion	✓
Prada Group	Italy	Leather Group	✓
Amore Pacific Corporation	China/HKSAR	Parfume & Cosmetics	✓
Pandora	the United States	Watches and Jewelry	X
Hugo Boss	the United	Fashion	✓

continued

Company name	Country	Sector	Sustainability report
	States		
Burberry Group plc	the United Kingdom	Fashion	✓
Moncler S.p.A.	Italy	Fashion	✓
Salvatore Ferragamo	Italy	Leather Goods	✓
Tod's	Italy	Leather Goods	✓
Cucinelli	Italy	Fashion	✓

Source: Authors' elaboration from from"Deloitte Global Powers of Luxury Goods 2022".

A2.3. Content analysis

Once selecting the companies to analyze, we conduct a content analysis to evaluate how companies integrated CSR practices in the luxury market. The analysis was performed in the period between September 2022 and December 2022 and followed the steps suggested by Neuendorf (2002):

a) Coding scheme: After developing a checklist based on the integrated CSR framework (Casalegno & Civera, 2016; Mosca & Civera, 2017b) we conducted a pilot study of five brands to check the applicability of the checklist to the luxury market. Some factors of the initial checklist were confirmed, while others were deleted or revised. Finally, to confirm the effectiveness of the given dimensions, we consulted a group of 40 luxury brand management experts. They evaluated each question using a 7-point Likert scale, ranging from 1 = "strongly disagree" to 7 = "strongly agree". This process was done by publishing the proposed checklist online via Google Moduli and contacting experts mainly through LinkedIn, the most internationally well-known social network to contact business experts. Researchers use Cronbach's alpha and the Corrected Item–Total Correlation (CITC) to test the internal consistency. For all 17 factors, Cronbach's alpha scored 0.967, indicating high internal consistency, following DeVellis (2016), who suggests 0.7 as the cut-off value for internal consistency. Regarding CITC, which defines the degree of correlation of internal consistency within the scale factors, ranges from 0.664 and 0.861. Thus, we did not exclude elements by Nunnally & Bernstein, (1993), who suggest deleting only factors whose CITC scored below the cut-off value of 0.4. All factors included in the checklist are summarized in Table A2.2.
b) Coders' training: Two coders participated in a training session to im-

prove reliability. Each coder performs a pilot analysis of five luxury brands. Then they discuss the differences between their results.

c) Coding process: Coders check the evidence on the checklist elements indicating 1 (presence) or 0 (absence). They perform the analysis independently according to the factors on the checklist. Then, the two coders conduct the second coding round together to achieve greater agreement. We chose Excel as the primary tool to perform the analysis.
d) Descriptive analysis: We perform a descriptive analysis and calculated scores and averages for each factor.

Table A2.2. The Integrated CSR checklist

Dimensions	Factors
1. Standards	Environmental sustainability standards
	Quality standards
	People standards
	Economic and social reporting
2. Strategic philanthropy	Sponsorship of artistic or cultural initiatives
	Donations
	Cause related marketing
	Community project
	Creating and managing foundations
	Employee volunteering time donations
3. Integrated outputs	The use of new or recycled raw materials
	Traceability of the supply chain
	Capacity to reduce the use of materials, energy or water, and to find more eco-efficient solutions
	Reducing environmental emission
	Employees' training and development policy
	Welfare policies to benefit employees
	Code of ethics

Source: Adapted from (Mosca & Civera, 2017b).

APPENDIX 3
METHODS TO ANALYZE SUSTAINABILITY COMMUNICATION

A3.1. Methods to analyze sustainability communication on corporate website

In line with the study conducted by Confetto & Covucci (2021), the company website is the primary tool for communicating CSR practices. The authors argue that the website remains the most comprehensive and informative source of information for any audience. The selection of luxury brands for analysis was drawn from the Brand Finance list 2022, encompassing a diverse array of 50 brands spanning fashion, leather goods, automotive, cosmetics, and hospitality sectors. Brand Finance utilizes the Royalty Relief approach, a brand valuation methodology conforming to ISO 10668 industry standards, ensuring a consistent and standardized evaluation methodology that bolsters the credibility and reliability of the study's outcomes. The examination of luxury brand websites is executed through the application of the CSR integration checklist developed in Chapter 3 (Table 1; p. 45). Drawing on the conceptual framework of residual and integrated CSR delineated by Freeman et al. (2010), this checklist aids in discerning which activities exemplify effective CSR integration and which do not.

The checklist structures the integration of CSR into three dimensions: standards and norms, strategic philanthropy, and integrated output.

To assess the degree of integration of each CSR factor in the website communication, it was decided to assign a dummy variable for each of the 17 factors that compose the framework, specifically:

- 1, when the company's website includes information related to the factor;
- 0, when the company's website does not include information related to the factor.

A3.2. Methods to analyze sustainability communication on social media

The analysis of social media follows 3 steps:

1. **PILOT TEST.** A pilot test was conducted to refine the data collection methods (Morse et al., 2002). The primary objective of this pilot test was to ascertain the most appropriate social media platform for gathering posts pertaining to sustainability-related content.
   The findings of the pilot test revealed that Instagram and Facebook predominantly focus on product and heritage communication, whereas LinkedIn emerged as the most utilized social platform for showcasing sustainability efforts.
2. **DATA COLLECTION AND EVALUATION.** For each brand two independent researchers collected all contents related to CSR posted on selected luxury brand profile from September 2022 to March 2023. Then, after calculating the number of posts published by each brand, the researchers assigned a score from 0 to 5 considering the consistency and frequency of publishing content related to social, ethical, and environmental issues. The brand with the most CSR content published was given the highest score, i.e., 5; instead, the brand that never shared CSR content in the time horizon considered was given the lowest score, i.e., 0. Based on this score, the ranking position of each brand in terms of CSR communication on LinkedIn was defined.
3. **DATA ANALYSIS.** After collecting all contents related to CSR issues posted by luxury brands on LinkedIn, the content analysis was conducted by using a specific tool called Leximancer. It is a software that analyzes the content of textual documents and subsequently visualized the extracted information through a conceptual map (Smith & Humphreys, 2006). The conceptual map represents the main themes contained in the text and how the interrelation among them (Arici et al., 2023).

INDEX

Kolibri 360 GmbH
Ferdinand-Jühlke-Straße 7
99095 Erfurt, Deutschland
produktsicherheit@kolibri360.de